JUNKIE
MEETS
JESUS

C O L I N G A R N E T T

BALBOA.
PRESS
A DIVISION OF HAY HOUSE

Balboa Press books may be ordered through booksellers or by contacting:

Balboa Press
A Division of Hay House
1663 Liberty Drive
Bloomington, IN 47403
www.balboapress.com.au
1-(877) 407-4847

Because of the dynamic nature of the Internet, any web addresses or links contained in this book may have changed since publication and may no longer be valid. The views expressed in this work are solely those of the author and do not necessarily reflect the views of the publisher, and the publisher hereby disclaims any responsibility for them.

The author of this book does not dispense medical advice or prescribe the use of any technique as a form of treatment for physical, emotional, or medical problems without the advice of a physician, either directly or indirectly. The intent of the author is only to offer information of a general nature to help you in your quest for emotional and spiritual well-being. In the event you use any of the information in this book for yourself, which is your constitutional right, the author and the publisher assume no responsibility for your actions.

Printed in the United States of America

ISBN: 978-1-4525-3837-2 (sc)
ISBN: 978-1-4525-3838-9 (hc)
ISBN: 978-1-4525-3836-5 (e)

Library of Congress Control Number: 2011914400

Balboa Press rev. date: 12/15/2011

Matthew 24:4-13

[4] And Jesus answered them, "See that no one leads you astray. [5] For many will come in my name, saying, 'I am the Christ,' and they will lead many astray. [6] And you will hear of wars and rumors of wars. See that you are not alarmed, for this must take place, but the end is not yet. [7] For nation will rise against nation, and kingdom against kingdom, and there will be famines and earthquakes in various places. [8] All these are but the beginning of the birth pains. [9] "Then they will deliver you up to tribulation and put you to death, and you will be hated by all nations for my name's sake. [10] And then many will fall away and betray one another and hate one another. [11] And many false prophets will arise and lead many astray. [12] And because lawlessness will be increased, the love of many will grow cold. [13] But the one who endures to the end will be saved. [14] And this gospel of the kingdom will be proclaimed throughout the whole world as a testimony to all nations, and then the end will come. [1]

With fond memories of the vagrant we loved
who died in enemy territory

---

1   THE HOLY BIBLE: ENGLISH STANDARD VERSION

Trapped By an Imaginary Reputation

I came to South Africa as a missionary to gangsters in 2001 with a view to becoming head of Hope Now International Prison Ministry[2]; primarily because of my 'rags to royalty' type of storyline. I had been transformed by a wonderful conversion experience in an English prison rubbish bin, where I had been changed from an academic drop out heroin addict who had spent years in and out of prisons, hospitals and rehabs, to having a living free from addiction playing an active role in missionary work in some of the world's hardest prisons and loneliest orphanages. Then, at the age of 37, I was offered an opportunity to undertake a Bachelor of Theology re-educational program at Moorlands Bible College[3] from which I successfully graduated in 2001. I was then Ordained under Rev. Vic Jackopson M.B.E. as an evangelistic missionary before setting out on a pilgrimage into the mission field of South Africa's gang and drug culture.

My past life experiences of darkness and the new life as an evangelistic convert to Christ—supplemented by a wonderful marriage to Deanna, an attorney—gave us a wonderful balance for what I was told would be the 'rigours of Christian ministry'. My secret reaction to the 'threat' of 'Christian ministry' was one of cynicism as I quietly thought to myself, 'how bad can it get'? I had no idea how unprepared I was for the shocks and the attacks to which we would be exposed as we stepped into the battlefield of ministry.

I started to suspect that my story actually qualified me for very little when one particular guy sat and quietly told me of his life, after he had been assured that what he was telling me would remain confidential. Once he felt safe enough with me, he then coldly spoke of being raped as a boy by a member of the clergy, of beatings and rapes of prostitutes, of sibling rape, of beating his own mother half to death and of his brutal wife beating while prostituting her for money to buy heroin.

---

[2]   WWW.HOPENOW.ORG.UK

[3]   WWW.MOORLANDS.AC.UK

In the space of 15 minutes it felt as if this guy had told me his deepest darkest secrets, and I suddenly started feeling that I was way out of my depth. I somehow managed to compose myself though, and actually began to feel that it must soon start getting better until the window of silence between us broke when he started telling me of his drug dealing days in the then infamous Hillbrow district of Johannesburg. Over quite a short process of time I started to see that my criminal past was actually working against me. I became a hostage to some of the vilest secrets and it seemed to be assumed that I would not be affected by them because I was an ex-con. I had an increasing sense of concern that I was becoming a cultural prisoner deep within a people of intense abuse and suppressed rage; and I was right, I did.

I did not feel any type of *physical* threat from any of these people but I had the strangest feeling that that would only be the case as long as I agreed with them. My suspicions proved accurate, as soon I (a) disagreed with them (b) started saying 'no' to them and/or (c) threatened their many hidden agendas, another story started to unfold. A progression of poison would start to seep from behind the veneers of these relationships as soon they perceived any form of threat to their hypocrisy.

Initially the decline was slow but definite as these guys first started to undermine my position between them, making their minds up that I needed to be taught a lesson, and from there I was verbally abused, publicly ridiculed and physically attacked. One particularly damaged individual went from being my best friend to being my arch-enemy, bent on destroying what he saw as 'my reputation', a slur campaign was launched where I was accused of sexual harassment, of interactions with internet pornography, and of having sexual fantasies and adulterous relationships with women from within the congregations where I regularly preached; this was followed by how I was a gay prostitute selling Jesus for cash at our rehabilitation facility, where I was willing to perform lewd sex acts for financial gain. Plans were also hatched to have me kidnapped and 'done away with once and for all' and it was publicly announced that I was responsible for causing miscarriages in people who worked for me. We were stolen from and received blackmail threats and were the target of an extortion attempt for hundreds of thousands of Rand.

You would be forgiven for thinking: 'well this is why these guys are in prison, these are the low-life of society and no one really believes them anyway; so what's the problem? And to some degree you would be right, but let me explain what the problem is—none of these attacks came from behind a prison cell door or from within the gang culture; they came from individuals who had worked their way into a Christian congregation where they remained hidden and therefore unchallenged, claiming to be born again, spirit filled Christians. And that was my welcome to the spiritual battlefield of Christian ministry.

Titus 1:15
'To the pure in heart, all things are pure, but to the defiled and corrupt and unbelieving, nothing is pure; their very minds and consciences are defiled and polluted'
Amplified Version

If you quietly meditated on this verse I believe you may catch a glimpse of what spiritual warfare holds. Although it means that while we the redeemed are called to get up close and personal with the most damaged and the most deceptive of people, we must see beyond any contempt that we might feel for their sin and manifest compassion for the dying sinner. We must however remain vigilant with an urgency to settle for nothing less than authentic 'fruit that will last' as the only milestone by which we should assess the authenticity of the professing 'converts' within our ministry.

For the true converts, the purity of their heart will be seen by how they view and bless everyone around them. For the false converts— those who profess piety yet remain defiled in heart—their poison will eventually erupt and be seen by the way they hate and curse anyone whom they perceive to be a threat to their distortions. The individual flavour of defilement by which each false convert is polluted will eventually be identifiable by the contents of that which comes out of their mouths when war breaks out:

"Keep your heart with all vigilance for from
it flow the springs of life"
Proverbs 4:23

I knew this was going to be dangerous, but I suddenly started feeling a deep sense of gratitude for who I am and for where I am from. I started to see that in God's incomprehensibly gracious providence, I had actually been a very fortunate child. Although my path had included a self designed chaos of heroin addiction, prisons and rehabs, it was actually preceded by a loving family life. I had no real idea what family alcoholism, parental abuse, incest or abandonment felt like. I had no real comprehension of what it meant to see my mum being beaten or left to look after the kids on her own by my dad, so if I was ever going to be used within the brutal context where I suddenly found myself, it would have to be a miracle and it would have to be in spite of me. And that's exactly how it worked out—welcome to my story.

I was never rejected or abused as a child; I never went to bed hungry, I was cared for and loved by a family whom I loved. I knew what it felt like to wake up on a snowy Christmas morning to find the bicycle of my dreams sitting waiting for me under the Christmas tree. I knew what it felt like to have a dad who really was the strongest dad in the whole wide world and I knew what it felt like to have a mum who intimately groomed me and tucked my shirt in for me, that special someone who would get up on dark winter mornings so that we could have warm porridge in our tummies before the day began. I knew the love and joy of becoming an uncle and I knew how precious it was to be seen as responsible enough to look after my nephews and nieces when they were babies, and I knew, that they knew, that I would put my life on the line for them. So from within our culture I think it could be said that we were probably one of the more fortunate families, a lot of other families had it a lot worse than we did and a lot of other kids from my era died in, or are still trapped in, their poverty. So I do not complain or blame when I tell you how in spite of all the comfort and the safety of my childhood and the evidences of stability, for some reason, there was always a niggling sense within me that I did not belong and that I was actually somehow *in the way*.

Our parents came from lower working class England and met during the Second World War. In my mind's eye, they represent a lovely picture: dad, handsome and always well dressed; standing well over 6ft he towered over mum's tiny but stunningly attractive frame. These guys not only really loved each other—they knew exactly how to show their children and the world around us exactly how much they loved each other.

Alan was the first born and the story goes that mum actually struggled with the pregnancy and birth, then Linda came a few years later and that same struggle was quite intense for mum's tiny frame. Following Lin's birth, it was suggested by her doctors that to have a third child could very possibly prove fatal for one or both mum and child. Seven years on, feeling strong, mum fell pregnant with me. These guys came from a generation where openness and honesty about feelings was simply never considered or practiced. One could safely therefore hazard a guess that as her third pregnancy progressed, there would very possibly have been a resurrection of fears and doubts about the sanity of going against medical advice. I'm pretty sure she would had to have developed an emotional and psychological coping program for the fears within her about the impending birth and potential deaths. At the very least one would expect some form of subconscious disconnection from the vulnerable tiny existence within her, even if only to overcome her own fears of its death. Guidance and counselling were not an option in those days. People simply had to use what they had and get on with it; and so, from the cultural backdrop of economic poverty, emotional suppression and personal struggle, Blossom—our mum, Nanna—took on and totally defied the odds.

Intimacy and honest expression of emotions were virtually unheard of for all of us of that era which now sheds some light on why, right from the start, my formative years felt like a fight for acceptance. I had no means of figuring out that I was not actually responsible for any relational disconnection between me and the people around me, and at some level I therefore felt at fault. It was never explained to me that my mum did the very best she could with what she had or that I was not the cause of any emotional coldness on her part. I was never able to develop or nurture any protective internal emotional boundaries that would in turn allow me a sense of stability within my individuality. I lacked the ability to protect myself from what to me felt like the irrational feelings of everyone around me. Consequently, if ever there was a bad mood in the home, I would somehow feel responsible, not only for causing it, but also for repairing it. I had no way of setting limits around myself, and it is from that beautiful yet dysfunctional platform that I set out on the journey that follows.

Foundational Deception

I went to a Catholic school and my foundational belief was that Catholics went to heaven and Protestants went to hell and while this confused me, in the cold light of day I seized a distant but definite sense of security from the thought of being on God's side. Most of my friends however, attended Protestant schools and I used to force the thought out of my mind that, because they were not Catholic, they would go to hell when they died. I never questioned this belief because it was God's way and not to be questioned.

Nuns, who I found to be very intimidating, ran our school and I actually believed that these women were God's secretaries and in direct contact with Him each night. They seemed to float around school when we all had to walk. I had a twisted fear of these nuns, but regularly cheated under their noses by copying during lessons despite my belief that they knew everything; the fear of capture was there, but never any fear of consequence.

In my first year at primary school, at the age of five and having apparently failed to work out or manage my eating and digestive system appropriately, I found myself sitting in class, with an approaching emergency. I can still recall asking, even begging, for permission to go to the toilet but was refused. I quietly obeyed the authority over me, even to the extent of trying to resist the very forces of nature. Eventually, my young body reached its optimum ability to resist a bowel movement, and despite my pleas, I was just coldly told that 'you should have gone earlier" (when I had no need!) I subsequently failed to hold anything in and made one almighty mess of myself.

In a futile last gasp state of hopeful denial I clung on to an invisible hope that no one would notice. However, the whole classroom slowly became aware, and people started pointing at me, turning away from me, and laughing at me.

Something died in me that day and my belief that I did not really fit in was set in concrete.

I received no help, compassion or apology. The teacher ushered me out of her classroom at arm's length, with a look of disgust on her face, to be cleaned up. I'm not sure how true this is, but in my mind—from that moment—I started becoming the butt of everyone's jokes. I felt a traumatic amount of shame over spoiling myself in public, and an electrifying sense of rejection at what felt like everyone talking about me. It felt as though all the other children in my class were mocking me and I had no way of freeing myself from what was developing into a terribly destructive emotional state. I could only internalise everything, and very soon I was having graphic anger fantasies about anyone who, in my eyes, and in any way, was against me. I started picking on people smaller than myself. My self-confidence was extremely low so those whom I saw as weaker people around me unfortunately bore the brunt of my simmering and potentially explosive turmoil. I internalised a deep hatred for my teachers and I felt absolutely no respect for them at all.

A few years later at the same school, I was kept behind after class because I had failed to answer any questions in a mathematics test. I daydreamed all the way through the test, about violence and football, because it all felt very intimidating to me. The only equation I believed told me how authority + obedience = trauma. I hit a mental block every time I tried to do the maths, none of the numbers would make any sense to me. I was kept behind after school and my teacher, another nun, set about trying to teach me how to solve long multiplication. I was totally disinterested and looking out of the window to make sure my mates were waiting for me out in the playground. She caught me looking out of the window and totally blew a fuse; she lost her cool with me and struck me on the head with the point of her pencil several times, almost spitting out "why can't you get this into your thick head?"

She hit a nerve in me and I just thought to myself 'Oh screw this' and I blew a fuse. I could clearly see that she had no idea of the amount of rage in me as my response sent her into a shocked silence; she went deathly pale as I exploded. I snatched the pencil from her hand and snapped it in half right in front of her face and through gritted teeth and tear-filled eyes I quietly growled, "Just piss off", and with that I turned and ran out of class. I was only nine or ten years old, but I know in my heart that if that lady had tried stopping me I would have attacked her.

God Thrown into the Trash Can

Once I was outside the classroom I knew that I had crossed some sort of invisible line. In my heart I felt that I had just told one of God's secretaries where to go and the enormity of the situation started to hit me as I ran from that classroom, so much so that I stopped on the stairs in disbelief. I sat for a moment with my head in my hands, partially wanting to return to class and apologise for disrespecting her in that way, but then my true feelings rose from within me, and it was right there and then on those stairs that I took a good long look at this God of mine. I looked at this impersonal God who sent 'never to be mentioned' shock waves through my young heart because He was sending my friends to hell because they went to the wrong school. I looked at His secretaries who to me were nothing more than intolerant thugs and unfeeling bullies, and in my heart I looked towards this God and prayed, "if she belongs to you, you can piss off as well; I don't want to know, I would rather go to hell with friends than to heaven with bullying hypocrites". And at that moment I threw my concept of God into the trash can where I felt it belonged and in my heart I flashed a middle finger to the system and ran out of school.

I started playing truant and practicing forgery and deception by writing counterfeit letters of excuse 'from my parents' to the school about my absenteeism. I quickly worked out what to do and managed to forge my mum's signature.

Dad was a disciplinarian yet quite approachable with an amazing sense of humour. He rarely held back from displaying his love for mum, whom he affectionately called Blossom, a perfect name for her. Mum was small, kind and as I soon worked out, very easy to manipulate. I got my way with her most of the time yet I always felt like I was in her way. As I started to grow, Alan became more and more aloof in my eyes. I don't think he knew this but I idolised him. He was an individual in every sense of the word. He set his sights on what he wanted to do in life and went for it; he was focused, studious and stabilised. Linda, on the other hand was a little less studious, a little less focused and a little less stable, but she was always approachable and caring. I somehow felt like the world owed me a favour and I would always have difficulty concentrating on anything which did not stimulate me. It was once suggested by one of my teachers that I was academically challenged and extremely cocky. My interpretation of my behaviour and attitude would be summed up this way: I was continuously disinterested and very insecure.

I always felt very protective around Linda, but she was a girl in every sense of the word, and I was the little brother always in the way. While it would be fair to say that we had many a fight between the three of us, we were also conditioned never to go to sleep without making friends and bidding each other good night.

My role models outside the home were the back-end of the sixties trendsetter type. Mods and Rockers were the rival gangs in England at that time, and our district—known as China Town—was predominantly Mod. The local Mod leader, as we kids saw him, unknowingly turned out to have a huge impact on my life. The Mods would often gather on our streets on their scooters, and ride off in twos, looking fantastic to us younger, wannabe Mods. In my eyes, Marko, their leader, was my hero. He had long hair, a Scooter full of mirrors, a loud and carefree attitude, and one hand covered in tattoos. When it came to 'the man', Marko was it, and this was the character type I secretly emulated. My brother Alan was certainly an idol for me, but nothing like Marko, if that makes sense. Alan was focused, studious, funny, good looking, and in my eyes a wonderfully talented footballer. It was easier for me to emulate Marko though because he was a rebel and a dropout. Alan was always going to do well, and that threatened me. I was convinced Alan would play for Manchester United one day. So much so that I actually wrote to Sir Matt Busby about Alan, inviting United to watch Alan play in our local Sunday league. Marko's footsteps were easy to follow—all I had to do was drop-out.

Our home was a Manchester United home and for every home game we would pile into my dad's work van and shoot off to Old Trafford. For the first few years my friend Carl and I would get right behind the goal at the Scoreboard End to watch the likes of George Best and Denis Law. I would often imagine myself at the opposite end, in the Stretford End, where, in my dad's opinion, 'all the idiots went'. That was where all the very loud singing came from, including some very abusive songs toward the opposition. I always felt a pull toward the Stretford End, and wanted to be in with the skinheads and boot boys as they were known. My early fantasy life was always of being in with the thugs and troublemakers. It was at an early stage of life that I started to see the police as an enemy—they were always getting abuse from the crowds and I would inwardly idolise those who went too far and were thrown out of the stadium by two or three police officers.

My twisted allegiance to the thuggish element of the human race gave birth to an inner, unfounded dislike of the police. This resentment even stretched to the extent of even hating the children of police officers. Near to where we lived was a newly built area called Park Drive where several police houses had been built, and from time to time a crowd of us would run through this new estate looking for 'coppers kids', and on finding any we would ensure they went home in tears. I grew to feel a deep stirring of contempt within me if a police officer simply entered a room or a bar that I might be in. In later years this was going to backfire on me.

By 1973 Tommy Docherty had taken the manager's slot at Old Trafford and the following legions of United fans, with me very often in the middle of them, were becoming known as the 'United Tartan Army'. My parents had given me permission to go to the united games with friends from school, but they had no idea of the metamorphosis that took place in me once I was out of the home. We used to leave at 9:30 in the morning and get to Old Trafford three or four hours early, in order to get in at the front of the queue and ultimately a central position with 'the idiots' of the Stretford End. The 2 hour train ride to Old Trafford from Stockport involved systematic destruction of the train, and hurling things like light bulbs out of the windows. From that time on, that was the way it went, there was trouble everywhere we went and I was always right in the thick of it. I would wear what I saw as my 'United outfit': a red and white skullcap, red-united-baggies, a red sweatshirt and red Doc Martin boots. The trousers would be halfway up my leg and the boots polished. I was fourteen, trying to be twenty-one. I was loud, abusive and by all outward appearances 'one of the boys'.

But mum and dad had the rule that I be in by 9 p.m. at the latest, and in bed by 10 p.m.—so the world saw one person while the home life thought it was creating another.

1974 was a particularly bad season as a Manchester United fan. At the end of that season, our 1st Division status was about to end; not only that but Manchester City were involved. Manchester United needed other relegation candidates to lose if we stood any chance of avoiding relegation, and on the last day of the season, our fate was in the hands of others, who subsequently lost and Manchester United were relegated. As if that wasn't bad enough, the sting really came because Manchester United were playing Manchester City that day, and Denis Law—who had served and loved Manchester United for years—was not only now finishing his career playing for 'the enemy', but it was Denis himself who scored, giving them a 1-0 victory over us.

At the visitors' end the Manchester City fans were dancing with glee, trying to claim sending Manchester United down. Smoke billowed out from the Stretford End for some reason and the whole atmosphere just got more and more intense as the match drew nearer to a close. From the various sections of the ground people ran on to the pitch in what looked like an attempt to delay the inevitable by getting the match abandoned. I made my way down to the touchline, and got into a position where I could get on the pitch if anything did happen. The police normally stood around the parameter of the pitch to prevent pitch invasions, but on this particular day it was a lost cause for them. Just before the end of the official 90 minutes, the police were overrun and thousands of very fired up Manchester United fans poured out of the Stretford End, and then from all around the ground and onto the pitch. The referee abandoned the match and both teams ran for the dressing rooms to avoid the hysterical mob and the whole atmosphere completely seduced me, I loved it and I just joined in the chanting and the shouting and I got totally lost in it all.

The police did an amazing job of keeping the two sets of fans apart, and so the attentions of the stampeding mass turned to the players' entrance and the television cameras, where under normal circumstances, on the last game of the season, we would gather to express our support (and to try and get on television). Until this season I had personally witnessed police officers helping youngsters onto the pitch for this occasion because it was just the accepted thing to do. But this was the year that everything changed.

There was the customary line of police officers linking arms in order to secure the entrance to the changing rooms, but it was definitely different his time; it was very intense because of the context, and there was a hostile atmosphere of aggression, spitting and shouting. I dug up a chunk of the pitch and threw it towards the line of police, but was horrified to see that it hit one of the officers on the helmet, causing his chinstrap to get stuck under his nose. Instantly I knew I was in trouble and a deep sense of panic started to well up from the pit of my belly. I saw that he had seen me and I was acutely aware that he was fully focused on me as manoeuvred his way towards me before breaking rank to arrest me. I knew that I had no choice but to run, but as I turned to escape, I was suddenly blocked by thousands of inconsiderate Manchester United fans. It was like sea of red and white hooligans but not even Moses could have parted this lot, and I slowly started to feel really insignificant.

This actual scene is perfectly captured in a photograph in Jim White's book:

'Manchester United
The Biography'

On page 311 there is a black and white photo of the pitch invasion with the caption:

'Foot soldiers of Doc's Red Army occupy the Old Trafford pitch but fail to stop their team sinking in to Division Two[4]'

That was the very scene where the right arm of the law came up from behind me, round my neck, under my chin, and I was hoisted up off the ground, and carried off towards the players' tunnel.

---

[4]   MANCHESTER UNITED THE BIOGRAPHY, SPHERE PUBLISHING, 2008/09 ©
     JIM WHITE

It was at that moment of arrest that I transformed from being a hooligan to suddenly becoming a 15 year old school boy! I was babbling all kinds of apologies and excuses as this irate police officer effortlessly carried me away, simultaneously slapping me in the face with the palm of his free hand. He said something into my ear as he carried me off, but I only heard menace in his tone and it released that inner panic in me. I took about eight good slaps to the face, but felt nothing because of the fear. In between slaps I could hear myself yelling my apologies and kicking like hell to try and break free. I heard myself saying the most stupid things in those few minutes of volcanic panic. I told him my dad was an ex-paratrooper, I told him I was still at school, I told him I had asthma (lie), I told him I was Catholic, I mentioned wanting to be an alter boy (lie) and I really tried to reassure him that I'd never ever do anything like this again, and how I'd learned my lesson. It was in that 30 second window of terror that I saw how lurking deep within me—at root level—there was a coward. I was not the person in the hooligan as seen on TV.

The Coward Within

Somewhere along the line I had heard of a 'custody room' at Old Trafford, where troublemakers were taken and beaten up by the police. I had heard that the police would roll thugs up in a mattress, and kick and beat them without bruising them, and because the copper was slapping me with palm of his hand, in the midst of all the panic and excuses, I took a mental note of him not wanting to bruise me, he must therefore be taking me for a beating. I remember seeing a door looming and I really believed that this door was the doorway to the beating of my young life. Somehow I managed to get one foot either side of the doorframe, and I went as stiff as a board, exerting every ounce of adrenalin induced strength I could muster and yelling "You're not getting me in there" over and over. I was writhing and twisting and tearfully growling "I am not going in there". It is amazing what absolute fear can do in a coward. I had brief thoughts that the police officer was actually fighting a losing battle with me, until a colleague of his got involved. My legs were removed from the doorframe and I was thrown into this room, still yelling. By then I had reached a point of exhaustion and extreme tension and I expected an onslaught by police 'hit-men'.

Sweat was pouring out of me as I was thrown feet first into what I believed to be a dungeon. I was suddenly aware of a very pretty policewoman staring at me as if I had just fallen out of a space ship and I then noticed a couple of other police officers, and a few secretaries and a very calm looking police sergeant peeping over his spectacles at me. It was a charge office. I was so glad to see them. I stood there panting and sweating with my ego and my image in tatters but I didn't really care, I was just happy and wanting to thank everyone for not being the hit squad. When they started asking for my details I was more than happy to tell them everything. They asked me my name, I gladly told them, and I added what class I was in at school. When they asked my age I told them, plus what position I played in the school soccer team and how Everton once expressed an interest in me but how I was only interested in United. I was babbling with relief because I thought they were going to hurt me. Some skinhead boot boy I was. I actually wanted to hug these guys for not wanting to beat me up. What a sad state for such a young boy to be in.

It took something like 2 hours to process and press charges against me, by which time I was like a kitten in their hands. However, the instant they let me go, within three meters from the police station door, the 'thug' re-surfaced and the games resumed.

I got home from the ground two hours later than normal that day and, when confronted by my dad, I spontaneously and very convincingly lied to him. I said I had been in Manchester with 'the boys', because I would not see them, 'my many imaginary friends' again until next season, and somehow he believed me. In truth I had travelled home in silence, feeling very low and very lonely and extremely disappointed in myself. I resolved within myself to sort my life out and to make something of myself. It was only when I reached home that the terrifying ordeal of the day started to subside and I knew it was because I had my family around me. I looked at my family in a new light that night, and really appreciated them; but, I was also secretly enjoying knowing what I had been through that day.

News at Ten was on and just coming to the halfway point. It was my bedtime after the news. The close of part one always gave the headlines of the events coming up in part two, and on this night, the up and coming news item was "Riot at Old Trafford". I felt a surge of excitement that I had actually been involved in a 'Riot'. I could not wait for school on Monday, and the stories I could tell. "I was fighting with the police"; "I gave one of them a good hiding"; the possibilities were limitless and I felt like the man of the match that day. Fame at last. I was sitting on the arm of the settee. Alan and Linda were on the settee to my right, with mum sitting between dad's legs off to their right. The television was just in front of me to the left. We all waited for the news to come back on. When it did, I felt like my young life was about to come to an end. The trauma I felt when that police officer started to break ranks to come and get me, and the panic I felt wrestling with him outside the room of death, suddenly felt like kid's stuff. As I sat there, still wearing my red skullcap, red sweatshirt, red baggies and red boots, I suddenly appeared on television, getting lifted off the pitch in a headlock, by an irate bobby and away up the players' tunnel. My life fell into one of those deafening silences. I could feel my dad looking at me, and my blood running down to my toes. The roof of my mouth suddenly held on to my tongue and would not let go and I really think my bowels started to loosen. I started to cringe inwardly and I think one side of my face started to twitch for some reason. I started to feel as if I was getting smaller and smaller as the news broadcast continued to talk about 'arrests' and 'charges being brought'. I became very aware of my skullcap, and my boots, and that I really needed to pee. Dad broke the silence by sending everyone but me upstairs and turning the TV off. Even mum, my one ally, was sent out of the room. Mum's final words before I was left alone were "Don't hit him Fred". As the door closed behind my mum, I stared at the door for what felt like a lifetime. Dad simply sat staring at me. All I could do was sit there on the brink of an emotional explosion and wait. Then it came. What struck me more than his words was the shaking head of disapproval. During the tirade of rebuke from my dad, I remember thinking, 'can't you just belt me and have done'. He went on and on at me: "You lied to me, you looked me in the eye and you lied to me, and to your mum. We believed you. You lied to us". He was devastated. I was sobbing as he expressed his hurt over how I had lied to him. This big tough boot-boy caught a glimpse of his true colours twice that day. Once when the bobby was doing his thing, and then again when my dad was giving me the roasting of my young life. I was a fake thug, full of bravado, and very much the home-boy sensitive to the feelings of those around me.

However, by the following Monday at school, I was once again behind my mask trying to be 'the man'. I believed the younger kids at school to be looking at me in much the same way that I had always looked at Marko. In my mind I became some sort of folk-hero to these guys. I sensed they were looking up to me in some way, but felt that if they had seen the real me, wanting to donate information not even asked for by the police, and the sobbing wreck trying to apologise to his daddy two nights earlier, I just know they would have had a very different opinion of me.

In my world, the message I was picking up from what seemed like everyone around me was that I was something that I really wasn't. I was actually very confused, but said nothing to put the record straight. Overnight I was becoming trapped behind a reputation, enhanced tenfold by my imagination, and life turned inside out for me. In reality, when no one was watching, I would cry when watching The Waltons, yet out in the world I thought nothing of inflicting quite vicious assaults with weapons on people. I started tattooing myself. You have to understand how strict a disciplinarian our dad was to fully grasp how insane the idea of tattooing myself at that age was. Dad never once raised a hand to hit any of us because he never had to. Right up to and including the day he died in March 2002, what dad said, went. In his frail and dying frame, although he was only just about able to talk, he instructed Alan to 'help me up'. Alan said to dad, 'just lay still dad, you'll be alright', but in our conversations afterwards Alan said he still almost jumped to attention when dad resorted to his 'authoritative tone' and demanded, 'sit me up'. Alan sat him up. He just carried authority in his voice, he said what he meant and meant what he said, so if he said it was Tuesday, believe me, it was Tuesday.

I first of all tattooed a solitary 'gang dot' on my leg. It was easily hidden, and I inwardly enjoyed having this secret from everyone in our home. I then tried to tattoo what had become a very popular symbol on my other leg. It was 'The Saint', a TV programme of that time. It should have been a matchstick man with a halo above his head. Because of my artistic inadequacy, it came out as an odd-footed devilish looking figure, holding a fork twice the size of itself! It resulted in being no more than a very childish drawing. I was left with a deeply embarrassing tattoo, and the hope no one would ask me what it was supposed to be. I had no concept of it being there for life. I never saw past the moment. Determined to press on, I asked Marko if he would tattoo 'Col' on my right arm and he agreed. Just as he started, Marko's cousin said, "Have you any idea what his dad will say if he finds out you did that?" With that, Marko abandoned the tattoo half done. I was left with a very tidy 'C', not quite central of my right forearm. I told myself I could finish it, not for one moment considering the recent disaster on my leg, which was done with my *good* hand. I now proceeded to try and finish the tattoo myself with my left hand, because no one was willing to put himself in my dad's firing line. I ended up with COL and it looked like a child's writing.

I found the secrecy of hiding my tattoos in the house a source of excitement to begin with. What became very typical of me, though, was the more I got away with, the further I would push something and eventually I tattooed MUFC, in bold capital letters across the back of my left hand, and my attitude had slid to that of 'screw the consequences'. Such is the phenomenon of an imaginary reputation: it will drive you to where you need to get until you feel that you have proved a point. Pretty soon I had the whole back of my left hand covered in tattoos. I never actually entertained any thought of Marko, but all of a sudden I become aware of people looking at me in much the same way as I thought they would look at Marko—I thought it was with some sort of respect; now I see that, for the biggest part, it was with confusion, contempt and oftentimes even pity.

From time to time I would catch a glimpse of myself in a mirror or a shop window, and I would inwardly think to myself, 'what have I done to myself'? The reputation actually ruined any opportunity there may have been for me to make it as a professional footballer. In sober judgement of myself today, I would have to say I could have made it with any of the big clubs of my day. I did things with a ball during football matches that people would believe to have been accidental, but deep down in me I knew they were not. For instance, in a gym one afternoon a few years later I was trapped in a corner with the ball at my feet, and I knew the goalkeeper at the other end would be standing on the edge of the D-shaped goal area. This guy was goal-keeping because he was undoubtedly the tallest guy in the jail. In fact it was his height that attracted me to the idea of 'chipping' him. So I made myself just enough room to turn and as I did so I hit the ball upwards and towards his goal. No one expected it. The face of the guy in goal went from disinterested to freaky-shock when it dawned on him what I had done. He tried to react but was just a split second too late. He actually had to jump in order to try and touch the ball as it dropped over his head just behind him and in to the goal. The ball bounced once and went up into the roof of net, followed by what felt like a magnificent silence in the gym. It was one of those moments that will always be mine. I lay awake in my cell that night with tears in my eyes and a huge lump of resentment in my chest and I can clearly remember that my closing thoughts were: 'I could have made it'. However, for the 'insecure people pleaser' trying to uphold an imaginary reputation, the ability to be natural gets lost on stage and the prison system knows no sympathy.

Soccer was my form of expression, but it is a poor substitute for self-honesty. Dancing was another form of expression, and it got me noticed, but it did nothing for the guy who cried at The Waltons. The football and the dancing were fuelled by bravado and ego;

the crying when no one could see was fuelled by fear, shame and loneliness, the former simply being a denial of the latter. We are not created to function from behind oppression or suppression because they cause loss of identity, damage the personality and—by the time I was supposedly mature enough to be considered by professional talent scouts—was emotionally trapped and suppressed by what I thought I had to be. The reputation I had would not allow me to lose in the game I truly loved and defeat for me was always personal and it stirred up horrible feelings in me. I would take any and every defeat deeply personally, and I was actually afraid of this venomous passion to win within me.

At one point, I heard of a scout from Everton Football Club asking for my parents' permission to watch me play, with a view to inviting me along for trials. When I found out, it actually proved too much for me to handle emotionally and I started to panic because there could be a possibility of someone seeing through me, and telling me that I was not actually good enough. I told my dad that I was not interested when really I was and that I just wanted to play for a local team with my mates, when really I didn't. The real Colin, the naturally talented footballer, was slowly drifting further and further out to sea on a piece of driftwood, and no one could hear his cries of insecurity and for understanding.

Shame was the primary governing block for me. At one point I was offered trials for Stockport Boys, but my parents could not afford new boots for me so I had to go in a tatty old pair, one size too big, and wearing two pairs of socks. All the other kids had sports bags, track suits and sparkling new kit. I had a China Town standard sized hole in the arse of my pants and attitude to match. The shame was immense, and my reputation just took on fuel when I got into a fight at that trial and was asked to leave. I was fourteen, fed up with being poor and fast running out of hope.

In my mind I had a lot of friends in China Town and I saw myself as 'one of the crowd'. However, unknown to me, the majority of my peers had grown to dislike me because I was always portraying myself to be better than them, and when our family moved from China Town in 1975 for the refurbishment of our area, on the eve of our leaving I was attacked by one of them from behind for 'no apparent reason'. Three or four guys, whom I thought to be friends, surrounded me with the intention of all joining in if I retaliated. The punch was nothing compared to the hurt of rejection that I felt inside and I went home with one of those emotional lumps in my throat feeling disliked by the kids I'd grown up with.

As we left 31 Branksome Road the next day in the back of a furniture truck, I sat broken hearted, peeping out through the back doors of the truck and as that chapter of my life closed, it did so with a sense of hurt and rejection. In my imagination I expected a going away party. In reality I got a smack in the mouth.

Call it a coincidence if you will, but since the day I had rejected God, it seemed to be that rejection had become my closest companion.

At our new home I soon experienced my first encounter with a chemically induced high and also felt as if I had found a friend, in the form of a bottle of cider shared with my best friend Langy; I did not start drinking or thinking alcoholically at that point. I cannot lay claim to any sense of euphoria at my initial exposure to alcohol but I do clearly remember a deep sense of release and relief as the chemical took effect on me. It was this 'release reaction' which became my default desire whenever my emotional state became confusing and whenever I believed that life was too much to handle. I do not believe an alcoholic was triggered in me at my first drink, I think it would be more reasonable of me to identify myself more as a recipient of 'social and psychological rewards' spoken of by Dr. William L White in his 'Travel Guide for Addiction Professionals'.[5]

"What occurs during this initial exposure that dictates a pathway into controlled or non-use versus a pathway into addiction? The initial exposure may be different for susceptible versus

---

5   PATHWAYS FROM THE CULTURE OF ADDICTION TO THE CULTURE OF RECOVERY, WILLIAM L WHITE, HAZLEDEN 1996, (PAGE 128F).

non-susceptible populations. The susceptible population is very special; it is composed of people for whom the initial drug experience has tremendous meaning and power. The factor that distinguishes the susceptible from non-susceptible is the existence and intensity of rewards experienced from initial drug use."

However, Dr. White also adds:

'Later events and decisions can lead the non-susceptible population into an addictive pathway by actually altering and increasing their susceptibility'

I believe my story adds credence to Dr. White's observation.

Cider, and now cigarettes, did not actually give me a good feeling, but they did seem to take away the bad feelings that I carried within myself, and straight away—from the age of fourteen or fifteen—I was drinking for effect. The smell and the taste of alcohol actually repulsed me, but, in accordance with my reputation, I would do the things I did not want to, because the feeling of 'drunk' was far more exciting than anything being 'sober' was offering me at that time.

The Mods of that era had hit the local headlines more than once for things like gang fights and drug possession. The thought of 'drug possession' appealed to me far more than the gang fights. I would love the terminology used by the older guys around me like 'getting busted' for 'drug possession' and 'over-dosing on smack', and in some twisted way, I wanted in.

I would entertain this new language in my mind, and picture myself 'getting busted'. I was heavily tattooed, smoking and drinking, and had thrown my virginity away, all in the call of reputation. My hard working parents had actually instilled a healthy regard for the one-man-one-woman picture of marriage within our home. Dad often boasted about not even kissing mum until they were engaged, and only then on the cheek. He treated mum like a rose, and actually called her Blossom and deep within me I wanted to follow that example. My virginity disappeared on a wave of cider and bravado two years before I left school. I can actually remember not wanting to throw this virtue away, but that truth was easily suppressed under the fear of 'what people might think'.

I felt a deep sense of dread and intimidation as my schooling was coming to an end and it was time for exams. I did absolutely no revision for any subject. A reputation is hard enough to maintain without having to stay in and study. While an atmosphere of seriousness descended over most of the school, I ridiculed the whole system and showed them all my middle finger. I failed everything they put in front of me. I was more interested in becoming a what William White describes in his 'Pathways' book as a 'pseudo-junky': "Pseudo junkies are individuals who, for whatever reason, have been unable to find any social niche in life, but who have discovered a certain identity and acceptance within the culture of addiction that is more satisfying than their alternative life experiences offer".

Although I had not yet interacted with the culture of addiction long enough to establish an identity, the dissatisfaction of normality had set in, so addiction was more of a probability for me than a possibility. Already fluent with the gift of persuasion, and for the sake of appearances and expectations, I managed to get a decent job straight after leaving school.

I talked my way into an apprentiship in Mechanical Engineering, specialising in replacement, reconditioning and/or repair of Automatic Transmissions. I was dead chuffed with myself for talking my way in to that job and I actually enjoyed working with my hands and the opportunity to explore my own initiative from time to time. Once again the signs were good, but with the weekly pay packet came an added opportunity to meet the increasing attraction within me toward the drug scene. I soon started to flirt with amphetamines and right at my very first point of contact with the influence of the stimulant, I suddenly discovered that I had found a way to meet my every need. They gave me an immense sense of well-being, a twisted sense of social belonging, and enough energy to do whatever I wanted to do for as long as was possible. The influence of the chemical took me to a place I believed everyone should be: euphoria. I was suddenly brave, friendly, funny and I actually felt as if people liked me, so much so that I talked to them whether they wanted me to or not. On amphetamines my life took on a sense of significance and I felt a sense of 'arrival'.

I have to be honest though, despite the strength of the chemicals that we used to use, the sad reality of my condition never actually left me and I was ever aware of feeling very lonely.

My hair had grown very long, and my attitude was loud and carefree and yet inwardly, I knew that something was drastically wrong about my life. While I was aware of feeling satiated from my inner 'uncomfortableness' while I was on the drugs, in all honesty I could not pinpoint any specific feelings within me. My inner discontent was never really ever removed—I just stopped feeling it.

As the influence of the drugs and the drug culture increased, my desires and abilities to relate to people as their equal diminished. I started to feel a deep sense of inferiority and failure, and my thought-life through the week revolved around more and more amphetamines.

They became my motivating influence because they offered me:

A (temporary) sense of (counterfeit) confidence
A (temporary) sense of (counterfeit) significance
A (temporary) sense of (counterfeit) belonging

While it was these three key spiritual principles which generated my desire for the drugs, it never occurred to me that it was actually a fear of their opposites which had always dictated my life. Every week I promised myself that 'next weekend' I would not consume any drugs, but that 'drug free' weekend never arrived. I was full of ambition yet empty of honesty or awareness. I had no way of knowing that it was actually the physical and psychological withdrawal from the chemicals to which I had exposed myself at the weekend, which created the haunting sense of social insecurity within me and the deep sense of shame loneliness.

I felt naked and vulnerable without the chemical.

I was seventeen, and life was already sliding downhill.

Alan and Linda were married by this time and I was pretending to myself that I was happy at home having both my mum and dad to myself, but I wasn't. I was at the age where I believed I should be out there conquering the world but in reality I was afraid of life, depressed most of the time, physically untidy, hygienically below par and haunted by a sense if inferiority.

My apprentice status called for me to revisit the classroom once a week at Stockport College and it soon became apparent to me that nothing had changed; I was completely disinterested in anything the lecturer had to say and fully preoccupied with my developing drug-affair. As a child I would daydream about football during class, as a teenager, it was chemicals. The lecturer may just as well have been talking another language as far as I was concerned as he waffled on about various percentages and ratios of the internal combustion engine. I would sit there thinking something along the lines of 'frankly sir, I don't give a damn'.

I was soon falling behind in studies and once again I would suffer embarrassment from the sketches that I was expected to draw because they were like those of a three or four year old child. I was deeply ashamed of my childlike efforts. I was internally screwed up because of these inadequacies and my obvious inability to absorb information because at another level, I knew that I was by no means stupid. The problem was I was forever looking at those around me as a means of assessing myself and it really bothered me that everyone else appeared to be confident and getting on with it; I felt like I was the only one struggling.

Losing Control

I inwardly knew that I was taking too many drugs and drinking too heavily, but the idea of cutting down never really entered the theatre of thought because it was all taking place in the name of fun and there were no obvious consequences to speak of. What I have since learned though is, while a chemical dependency might not be in place at the recreational era of life, unforeseen circumstances in a person's life can very easily push a person beyond the point of no return. It would be unfair to categorize myself as an addict or an alcoholic at this early stage, but a quick succession of traumatic events plunged me into an abyss of chemical chaos. I went through some really heavy rejection from my 'first love', Tina. Tina told me that she wanted to have a baby with me, but with all my other confusions I simply could not find it within me to agree to it. I was a self-centred kid of 17 with years of adventures ahead of me; I couldn't cope with the idea of taking on parental responsibility.

I did feel as if this relationship was a match made in heaven, and I really did believe that we were made for each other, and I also believed that Tina felt the same way. But I was quite wrong. The novelty of going out with me wore off for Tina as soon as I said 'no' to her and I was quite quickly dumped for someone else. For several months that followed I remained painfully and totally preoccupied with what she had done to me, and was deeply heartbroken. I chose to forget how selfish I was in that relationship and of how my ego was far too big for me to ever seriously considering someone else's needs. Yet despite that, my 17 year old heart had found its 'first love' and contained daydreams of us always being together.

I was totally devastated when it became apparent that it all suddenly meant nothing to her. I went into a personal deterioration period of not washing, even after a day working in a garage and I would have oil ingrained into my skin and hair; I just did not care. I went through the motions of work and college, but my preoccupations were with Tina and whoever the other guy was and of what I would like to do to them for hurting me.

My mum had been very poorly at this time, but I was too wrapped up in my own teenage world to fully appreciate the extent of her illness. Then one day, while I was at the lowest emotional period of my life, Dad, Alan and Linda arrived at College in our car. I'm not sure how, but somehow, as soon as I saw the car, I instantly knew that my mum was going to die.

Mum had been suffering from cancer for many months, and I was right, that was the day she died. As I sat holding her hand on one side of her hospital bed, Dad, Alan and Linda stood hopelessly around the bed, and I think it would be fair to say that we all silently hoped for some sort of a miracle from the God that we had never acknowledged. It didn't arrive. Mum simply faded away in front of us. As I watched her final breath leave her and as she stopped breathing I stopped feeling. I did not feel angry or confused or even sad. I did not feel any more pain about Tina or about her new boyfriend and I did not feel any more stress about my failing college course. I simply did not feel anything, I emotionally just switched off.

As that week progressed, with every one of our family and friends freely crying about mum's passing, and as the enormity of it all starting to sink in, I grew further and further away from my feelings as I hid behind a 'brave face'. I did a lot of caretaking in those first few mum-less weeks, making sure every one else was alright. The only feelings I had were of a self-pitying nature. My thoughts would regularly drift back to Tina, and how I could maybe win her back by means of pity. I hated my thought life and the fact that I did not feel like everyone else looked. I felt no loss, no remorse and shed no authentic tears.

Then as I tried to bluff my way through the grief of mum and deny any hurt of losing Tina, I heard that she was pregnant from her new boyfriend.

They say when it rains it pours. It did for me.

My shattered teenage heart got harder and harder as I went into the eye of this emotional hurricane where the eye was 'how could she'? I did not wash for the days leading up to mum's funeral; my hair was long and very greasy and my skin was dark from ingrained oil and the lack of soap. On the day of the funeral, as I stood at the graveside, looking into this hole containing a box with my mum in it, I felt as if I was having one of those 'out of body' experiences that some people talk about. Emotionally I felt nothing, but in a very weird spiritual way, I saw the scene around me. I was very aware of family and friends around me, and enviously aware of how many of them were weeping, but in truth, my focus fell upon on the pathetic figure that used to be me and I can clearly remember knowing: "I'm losing it".

I could not focus on my mum dying for any longer than a second or two. I could see it all at an intellectual level, but as soon as any corresponding feelings began to stir, I ran off in my mind, and invariably yet uncontrollably ended up in thoughts of a self-centred nature.

I went to work the day after mum died and then the following week I went to College. I can be honest now and say that there was a side of me that actually enjoyed the fact that I would now be at the centre of attention with a justified sympathy story. The lecturer at College made a very silly but innocent mistake. He asked me, "What happened to you last week"? I was aware of making sure everyone in the class heard me, loving the attention, I said, "My mum died". Everyone was shocked and quite naturally my lecturer placed an arm around me and said, "Oh I'm sorry, I know exactly how you feel". I inwardly exploded. I wanted to attack him, but I walked out of College, went to work and resigned.

As I walked away from college, the world around me felt totally empty, worthless and meaningless. I did not want anything from anyone. Life meant nothing and carried no direction. "I know how you feel?" That was the worst thing anyone could have said to me at that point. I was in personal turmoil because of my academic disability and the inner sense of impending failure, I knew at an intellectual level that my drinking and drugging was getting out of hand but could do nothing to stop it. I inwardly wanted blood to revenge Tina hurting me with rejection and betrayal, and to top it all off one week ago, my mum had died practically in my arms. No one knew how I felt. I did not know how I felt.

I spent the next 9 months or so just bumming around, sinking lower and lower into my own well of denial, self-pity and loss, not knowing how to release my inner turmoil. Home life started to disintegrate as Dad and I started to fall out more and more. He was drinking every night and sobbing in my lap about the one whom I was seeing as being 'my mum', but who in reality was, for him, his darling bride, Blossom. At first I used his grief to avoid my own having learned how—if I could be there for my dad—then I would achieve some sense of purpose and avoid my own hurts. Unfortunately, though, I heard the same stories night after night and I actually began to hate these times. I dreaded him coming in at night because the crying would start. I was frozen in my emotions and he was drowning me with his. All I could feel was anger toward these alcohol inspired weeping sessions.

I coldly used those situations to my addictive advantage. I was so far disconnected from any sense of compassion that I would dip his pockets whilst he wept. I would emotionally manipulate him in his vulnerability to get 5 or 10 pounds for my next day's drinks and drugs. I was injecting amphetamines by this stage (1975/76) and nothing else really mattered. Despite the fact that I got as high as I could as often as I could, nothing could detract me from inwardly knowing that my whole life was falling apart around me.

Then one day I walked into a hairdresser in Manchester, and instructed him to shave my head. The guy was stunned into silence because my hair was very long and very naturally curly and, apparently, 'people would pay to have hair like mine'; and there I was, having it all shaved off.

I had seen something, though, and I had made a decision to join the British Army. I had walked passed an Army Careers Information office, and seen a guy in uniform on a poster in the window. This soldier was young, healthy and good-looking. All the things I was missing. I remember thinking, 'that is how I should look'. The promo spoke to me of joining the best team in the world and there I was struggling to involve myself in any form of relationship with anyone. I felt totally alone in life and isolated from anything warm or healthy. The only relationship I was involved in was with the chemicals that I was increasingly taking into my bloodstream. I had to take some initiative, so I took the step, passed the IQ test and signed the line.

I was on a train leaving Stockport within two months, and I once again saw a glimmer of joy in my dad's eyes as he and Linda saw me off. I could not see anything of Linda's eyes, because she was hopelessly sobbing because her 'baby brother was going off to war'. I was only going to Aldershot. It kind of went without saying that I would join the Parachute Regiment because that was dad's regiment and this was all I had ever heard about, and it was his approval that meant the most to me. However, I sat and watched a selection film on the different regiments, and when I saw the Parachute Regiment, with these guys falling out aircrafts, I started to wonder what the point of that would be for my long term future. I felt a strong pull towards The Royal Corps of Transport. The trucks were huge, and it all looked very intimidating, but at least I would not have to jump out of them from over 2000 feet to find approval!

Dad sounded disappointed when I told him over the phone that I had not joined his beloved 'Paras'. But for the first time in my young life, I was taking the initiative and as I picked up on what I believed to be his disappointment I can clearly remember thinking, 'you'll just have to get over it, because this is my life, and I have to do this my way, for me', and a wonderfully crazy new chapter was just about to start.

Military Service

I was accepted into The Royal Corps of Transport, and became 24457602 Driver Garnett. C. It was a fantastic adventure, meeting up with guys from all over Britain of the same age (18) who were also embarking on the same journey. Friendships were formed instantly and were of a quality quite unique to the military. I found myself feeling like this was exactly what I had been lacking. However, within two weeks of joining 65 Training Regiment RCT, I was in serious trouble and in line for Court Martial. The first set of lectures we got on our induction was orientated around 'Team Building'. "The guys around you," was the continual message, "are your buddies; with them you fight and die if need be". It was all around the importance of teamwork and sticking together. It worked. Our first weekend out on the town saw 14 of us drinking in Aldershot, all trying to drink an impression on the other.

At the end of the night, a fight broke out, and I saw a guy to whom I had grown particularly close, Ecky Mitchell from Scotland, running towards a skirmish where a guy was being held up against a fence and being punched mercilessly by a guy twice his size. I was 50 or 60 meters away and I just heard, "The Para's have got Titch", another one of our lads. I took off toward the fight and was travelling flat-out by the time I got to the scene. As I arrived, the guy who had just been doing all the punching had been hit by Ecky and was just getting up off the floor. I did not break my stride. I just booted him across the side of his head, instantly knocking him out. I knew I had gone too far, and that I may well have killed him.

I became aware of everyone stopping when this happened and so I continued my pace and disappeared into the town. I had to pass the scene to get back to camp and as I later walked by, the place was full of police and ambulances. The guy I had kicked was being loaded into an ambulance, still unconscious. I knew it was serious.

By the time I got to camp, the police were everywhere. I managed to sneak in through the back door, just as the Military Police were storming through the front door of the same billet. I shot up two flights of stairs and just dived straight into bed, turned to the wall and pretended to be sleeping. I could hear several sets of studded boots coming down the corridor towards my room and they were getting louder and louder. It sounded as if there was a battalion of them, and they were all coming my way. My room door opened, and four or five really heavy-duty Military Police officers stormed in and came right up to my bed. I just lay there, hoping beyond hope that they would go away. I could feel the pulse behind my ears and wondered if they could heart it. An eternity passed, until one of them placed the brass tip of his pace stick under the blanket near my chin and in one foul swoop, he hurled my bedding to the other side of my room. The three other guys with whom I shared the room were all lying in the exact same state, deadly silent, too scared to move, hoping it was all a dream. It wasn't a dream. With my cover removed, I lay there wearing a red sweatshirt, blue baggy jeans and red Doc Martin boots. There was a sound of their boots backing away from my bed, and then the building shook under an ear piercing military bark of "on your feet". I jumped up onto my bed, and tried to scale the wall behind me with the palms of my hands and soles of my boots.

It was sheer and utter panic. The sight of a high-ranking officer had a twofold effect on me; initially I was relieved that a beating was out of the question, and then my world sank because of the obvious seriousness of the charge. They said nothing more, they simply marched me off to the Military Police Station, and not a word was said. I was made to stand to attention in a little room near a charge desk at 11:55 p.m. All these years later, you might ask, how can he be so sure of the time? But trust me, it was 11:55!

I could see only a clock although the door was left open. A lot of action was taking place just around the corner from where I stood, but no one said a word to me. After approximately an hour, a Military Corporal came and stood right in front of me and said "The Lance Corporal you kicked has lost his eye and his career with The Parachute Regiment is over". I was left alone again, and nothing further was said to me. At 4:45 a.m. (trust me) I leaned forward to ask if I could use the toilet. From nowhere, and in the blink of an eye, two of them seemed to climb out from behind the wall paint and were standing and screaming right in my face: "Who said you could move, you will stand stock still until you are instructed to move and if you move before then you will be beaten beyond anything you could ever imagine, because if you think you can blind a British military man and get away with it you are sadly sadly mistaken and when we get you to MCTC[6] prison we will have our fun with you boy before we send you home in disgrace and if you pee on my floor I will make you clean it up through a straw is everything I just said understood?" To which I then heard a very scared voice reply: "Yes Corporal".

I write these events down, decades after the event, but every detail of that arrest and the verbal onslaught remains forever etched in my memory. I can almost still feel his breath on my face.

If my suspicions were right, these guys were fed up with me.

The rest of that weekend was spent in closed custody. I was put in a cell and given a script to read so that whenever anyone entered my cell, I had to be stood to attention by the time he got there, and before he asked me anything, I had to tell them, at the top of my voice: "24457602 Driver Garnett sir, charged under section 33a of the Army act 1955, sentenced to closed custody by the commanding officer of 65 Training Regiment Royal Corps of Transport, I have no requests or complaints sir".

On the Monday morning I was marched before the Colonel. He read the charge to himself, looking up at me several times as he did so, before sitting back and breathing a long deep sigh. I had two 'escorts' stood right in front me, burning their eyes into me and breathing on me.

The Colonel asked me: "What happened?"

In a very calm voice I simply said, "Sir, I've been here two weeks. All I have heard since I got here is 'stick by your buddies through thick or thin; never leave your buddy'. Well, Sir, that's exactly how it happened—my friend was getting beaten up—I put a stop to it the only way I know how".

---

[6]   THE INFAMOUS COLCHESTER 'MILITARY CORRECTIVE TRAINING CENTRE'

He tapped his teeth with his pen and there was an almost tangible change in the atmosphere. It felt as if everyone suddenly changed towards me, so much so that I started feeling that I was becoming a bit of a cult figure. I felt as if I'd gone from zero to hero in that one statement. They kept me in open arrest because the civilian police were involved, but the Regimental Police Staff definitely eased off and their tone towards me changed. I became the flavour of the month, for a few hours anyway. I was being allowed back into regular training while on bail for 'Wounding with Intent to Cause Grievous Bodily Harm'. I was awaiting trial at Winchester Crown court. Because it took place in the town, the civilian police decided to prosecute me which was not good. It probably meant a prison sentence and dishonourable discharge back into civilian life. For the moment, though, I was 'the man', and I suddenly found that I was once again developing a reputation.

A reputation for being tough is not the wisest thing to have in any Army. The reality is, there are some truly tough guys in there—guys way out of my league.

By the time the court case came up, the Army were pleased with my efforts, my personal discipline and my progress and they decided to defend me as best they could. The guy I had kicked, as it turned out, was suspended from duty at the time of the fight for repeatedly bullying new recruits which worked well for my mitigation. I made a plea of guilty at Crown Court and the Army representative sang my praises for the best part of 20 minutes, requesting that I walked out of court with the only punishment possible for me to keep my uniform, a fine.

I got a fine and was told to soldier on.

Within a few months of the court case I was shipped across to Germany where I slotted right in. It was a drinking culture, with some of the most amusing madcap behaviour being the norm.

My time in Germany was spent mostly on camp because every time I went in to town, I somehow managed to get into trouble. I started becoming known by guys from different regiments, and with that came an anxiety that I would inevitability have to fight these guys at some point. No one really knew the truth about me, that my nerves were shattered by all the recent years of hype and the vast amounts of nightly alcohol consumption. I was still emotionally constipated from my teenage traumas and this frequently caused eruptions of unprovoked and unnecessary violence from me. For these reasons I hated the drink, but it gave me a false sense of calm.

I failed to see that it was the high intake of alcohol at the root of all my trouble, and it was the withdrawal from the alcohol at the root of all the fear that I was feeling on a daily basis.

I did two years in Germany before going to Belfast for a 6-month tour of duty.

I was a kid of nineteen going on twenty, inwardly very insecure and thrust right into the heart of an explosively volatile atmosphere with no margin for any error.

In Belfast, because of the dangers of the job, alcohol was supposedly rationed to where we were allowed a maximum of two cans per night. Some of us, however, regularly managed to 'find' anything between twelve and fourteen cans each night.

While the majority of the Regiment would sit chatting in a respectable manner during time off, enjoying a few beers, I would be right in the thick of another crowd, falling around drunk, stripping off, dancing on tables, singing England songs and breaking things.

As midnight neared on New Year's Eve 1978 in Belfast City centre, I decided to ring home to pass on seasonal greetings to my sister. Linda, also a few sheets to the wind, had her standard big sister cry down the phone because 'her baby brother was at war'. That was enough for me, I instantly hatched a plan. I decided that I was going to stow myself away on a ship from Belfast to Liverpool and make it home by lunchtime the next day and with that I started to walk out of camp towards the very busy, very drunk streets of Belfast. The guard at the gate came out to stop me staggering out into the city and I pulled my (unloaded) Browning 9mm pistol on him and attempted to shove it under his chin. My night ended right at that moment; I woke up on my bed the next morning, with a pounding headache, and several aches and pains all over my body. To this day I do not know if it was the guy on guard duty who took me out or if his mates joined in and if so where they came from! All I do know is I only got the kicking I deserved, and that night those lads saved my life.

During that tour of duty I was selected from 300 men by the elite Bomb Disposal team to train for, and to operate, their new 17-ton armoured water cannon. This vehicle had never been used before, so I was the first RCT Driver to occupy this role. I was trained for the position and was regularly told how prestigious a privilege it was to work with this team and I could easily see that I was among a very special body of men and women on that team. I heard things like, 'this is the first step towards promotion for you' and 'this could turn into a full time posting for you'. I've no idea how much the pressure of that job got to me but I do know this much, the incident on New Year's Eve cost me this position. I was up before the governor the next day and he gave me a choice to make: I either accepted his punishment or I be transferred off the team. I opted for transfer, claiming that 'I'd blown it and would need a new start somewhere else'. They voiced a disappointment in my choice but reluctantly agreed to ship me out.

Everyone around me held me in high regard on that team and they pointed how I was a unique and very important cog in a mind-blowing system of military excellence, but it always felt like they were seeing something in me that I could not see. No one knew of how I used to lay awake in the early hours of the mornings in a state of anxiety and stress about the size of the job before me, so I was deeply relieved to be out. I thought they were being fooled by a reputation because to these guys it seemed to go without saying that I would be dependable in a crisis, but the truth was, I was very intimidated by it all. I would have relished the chance of voicing my insecurities to someone, but that was unheard of then. Had I been given the right counselling, I believe I could have been dependable in a crisis, but the backlog of suppression, frustrations, fears and shame, ruined my stability and I was always in a state of inner anxiety. I lived in fear of a life threatening crisis, believing I would blow it at the moment of truth, never connecting my irrational fears to the amounts of alcohol from which I was either under the influence of or withdrawing from, on a daily basis. What I failed to see was that, at crisis point, I actually did do OK.

During a vehicle breakdown recovery on the outskirts of the Ardoyne, an IRA stronghold, I took point watch, meaning I was to cover our front. I stood in the back of an open topped Landrover with my SLR, scanning the houses and streets in front of us in an arc of between 10 and 2 o'clock. I noticed a car with two guys in the front driving very slowly past our operation. I caught the eye of the passenger and we almost acknowledged each other. It crossed my mind that they were either impressed by the size of the operation because of all the lights and the size of the vehicles involved, or they were up to something. We were hooking up a 15-ton military vehicle, to a 15-ton military vehicle, with troops scattered in various positions for cover. I naively assumed that they were slightly in awe of us because I thought I saw the guy smile at me as he looked me straight in the eye. What then took my notice was that they kept travelling very slowly, until at approximately 150 yards, they stopped. Smiley got out of the passenger side and crouched down next to a street lamp, with cover from his car door, and brought a pistol up to the aim position. In a frozen moment of time, I realised that he was aiming at me. I visited the thought of what my drill should be: to yell something really silly like "gunman dead ahead" to alert team members, and then I was required to give the following warning to the gunman of: "halt hands up, halt hands up, halt hands up I am ready to fire". However, while I was being confronted by a gunman, in what could possibly very quickly turn into a 'contact' (gunfire), I felt a quiet confidence that this guy was never going to threaten us from that distance. There was no panic but a hint of excitement that I might just get a crack at killing a terrorist, and I just decided to zero in on their vehicle. I knew that if he fired at us from that distance that he could not possibly do anyone any harm, and I would then have carte blanche on firing back. I knew that I would have enough time to blow the driver's head off even before the gunman was back in his seat.

Although I had decided to go against my training by not warning everyone and causing a furore, I felt that this was a defining moment for me because following that incident, I started to doubt my doubts about myself. I made a calculated decision, in the heart of a crisis and I started to believe that I was actually up to it.

On our return to Germany the whole regiment hit the town. Most of us made it back to camp that night in one piece. We had done a tour of Belfast with only one casualty; a guy lost an eye when some sort of missile hit him, but apart from that, the feeling was good.

On my way back to camp on that first night back, just for the hell of it, I leapt from a speeding taxi in an attempt to avoid paying, as one does. I tore almost every ligament and tendon in my ankle and lower leg. My right leg was blue and completely swollen. I actually woke up, in several inches of snow, just inside our camp gate, directly opposite the Guard Room. It took me a few minutes to work out that I was looking at it from the outside, and then the pain started to seep through the now fast fading alcohol. Somehow I managed to crawl the kilometre or so to my billet, and slip into bed. Less than 20 minutes later, I was being carried to the medical officer by a couple of buddies. The medic had no choice but to launch an enquiry and I went up before the Colonel again, on crutches this time, for questioning. I just kept saying, "I do not know sir". He thought I was protecting someone and soon got fed up with me. He said to me, 'Well, this blows your home leave; soldiers are not allowed to go on leave on crutches, it would not look good'. While on the one hand I felt like crying. I had nothing to lose now though, so I placed my crutches against the wall in his office and nervously told him; 'With respect sir, I'm going on leave', and I managed to very slowly walk out his office without limping. The pain very nearly caused me to throw up and I believe I was close to passing out because of it. Staying conscious became the focus of my attention because of the burning pain all down my right side. I was given back my crutches and I made my way across the ice-covered parade ground.

I felt terribly afraid and lonely hobbling across that parade ground that morning, and the memory blackout was very disturbing, I really could not remember large parts of what had happened. I stood on the ice on that freezing morning, watching my breath, trembling with cold and feeling very lost. I started to sense that my superiors were getting fed up with me. I went home for a month's leave.

I could not find a girlfriend at this time of my life because I was always in some sort of fracas and I was extremely lonely. I would lie on my bed most nights and silently envy the guys who had pictures of girlfriends by their beds. I had never really known intimacy. Love songs would come on the radio and I would imagine myself singing them to an imaginary girlfriend. On my return to Germany, I soon got into a fight on camp with a guy who punched me from the side without warning or apparent reason. These things often seemed to happen to or near me. The two of us decided to go behind closed doors and punch it out. I battered him for 10 or 15 minutes before getting arrested by the Regimental Police. There I was again, up before the Colonel for fighting. Colonel McDonald offered me an alternative to a prison sentence—an opportunity to fight him; I chose prison. I was given 28 days' detention, which included extreme beatings and daily humiliations around the camp. The rest of the lads from the regiment went on manoeuvres to Canada while I was serving that sentence; I heard them leaving in convoy from my cell. Some blew horns to me, and I knew I was missing out. On my release interview I asked the Colonel to return me to England. I felt like I had let everyone down and I needed a fresh start at a new regiment. I was on a plane within a week, leaving the much coveted 'C Troop of 19 Squadron, 4 Div RCT', without the opportunity of saying goodbye to the lads. I left in sadness and shame, with my tail between my legs because I lacked the courage to admit that I was in need of help for my insecurities and the heavy drinking.

I was transferred to 53 (Five-three) Squadron RCT, Marchwood Military Port and placed in a small troop of men responsible for much of the UK's inland movement of stores and ammunition. This simply meant we did a lot of trucking all over UK, having a laugh; and another adventure began.

Military Prison

The military still held me in high regard and offered me every opportunity of resurrecting what felt like a fast fading career. I was even appointed Colonel's driver to an International shooting competition to be held in Aldershot. I was back where the fun had started, but with an opportunity of somehow making amends this time. I was on my best behaviour, until my first night off. I went for a drink in that same town centre. I drank alone for three hours, until on my way home, I snapped and ran into a packed taxi rank kicking and punching at three guys who (I thought) said something to me as I staggered by. I ended up getting chased back to camp before being arrested by the military police again. I was sent back to my regiment in shame. I was given another prison sentence for assault and bringing my Squadron into disrepute. During these terms of detention, for some reason, probably because I was sober, I would actually shine as a soldier and I got along well with most people.

I had actually met a girl from Manchester around this time and unfortunately ploughed all my emotions into this woman. I had been starved of love and of loving and I almost emotionally devoured her. I rang her every night from the Detention Office, and served my sentence without her knowing. She had no idea of the kind of deceptive idiot she was involved with; she just thought she had met a soldier.

There was one particular Sergeant-major who every one hated and feared, and in return, he appeared to hate everyone but feared no one. He was the ugliest thing I had ever seen. He was a prisoner's nightmare. No matter what your cell was like for inspections, he would come in and destroy it for his own pleasure. The same song had to be sung every time he or any officer walked into my cell: '24457602 Driver Garnett, charged under section 33a of the Army act 1955, sentenced to 21 days detention by the Commanding Officer of 53 Port Support Squadron, Royal Corps of Transport, I have no requests and no complaints sir".

Every time this guy was on duty he did two things. He would throw my kit all over the cell, and he would verbally abuse my regiment. The throwing of the kit did nothing to bother me, but the remarks about my regiment really got to me. He was on duty toward the end of my sentence, and came in to my cell for the standard abuse session. I had stewed on this guy's bullying tactics, every night, for weeks; I hated him and everything that he stood for. I am being perfectly honest when I say that I was actually unable to keep my mouth shut when I discovered that he was duty officer a few nights before I was due to be released. Knowing exactly what I was going to say, I sang the song for him, but this time it was with a difference: "24457602 Driver Garnett, charged under section 33a of the Army act of1955, sentenced to 21 days detention by the commanding officer of 53 Port Support Squadron RCT, I have no requests but one complaint sir".

The silence was deafening. The whole guard staff sat up to listen. No one had ever complained, especially to this guy. One simply did not complain. He walked right up to me and got his nose touching my nose and he said, "What is your problem?" I was stood to attention, looking straight ahead. I had learned never to actually make eye-to-eye contact with an officer, but to simply stare into space somewhere in the area of their forehead. Tonight though something was different, and to voice my complaint, I shifted my eyes down ever so slightly in order to look him directly in the eyes and I smiled and quietly said to him: "You are sir; in my opinion, you are an arsehole". No one but God and him heard me. I was past worrying. He went ballistic. He was gesturing me to fight him in my cell, calling me all the names his filthy vocabulary contained. I simply stood there. At one point I looked at him and started smiling at him, this was like throwing petrol on a fire. He was going crazy. But I knew two things: he should not have been in my cell on his own, and he was not allowed to slander my regiment. Every other officer who came into my cell did so under the accompaniment of a regimental police officer, and none of them ever got personal about another man's cap badge. He came in to my space alone each time he was on duty because he held the RP staff in contempt, he hated everyone. When the duty RP made his report out about my complaint, he could only quote the Sergeant-major, and even then it was all abuse and threats. Up in front of my Colonel the next day, I lied through my teeth—in the midst of the truth—about him criticising my Regiment. I made him look like the instigator, which was supported by the police report, and once again I went from zero to hero.

Following that sentence I was appointed driver to the Royal Marines. These guys were unbelievably switched on, and in my opinion, they must be the best in the world. So to be appointed their driver was a real honour and a pleasure. They were stationed in Portland and doing manoeuvres from the belly of a ship docked there. My job was to drive them wherever was requested. I slept on board their ship, and I just enjoyed watching the cream of the British Military at work. One night we had a late hour drinking session, not unlike Marines versus Army. We were all out to impress the other. Once again, I drank like a pig, but somehow managed to find my bunk. Just before it got light the next morning I woke up on the brink of peeing. I had no time at all to waste on things like remembering where the bathroom was, I was still drunk. I shot up the nearest stairs and just about made it out onto the deck and to the side of the ship. There I stood, in my shorts, like a fountain figure, urinated over the side of the ship. I got goose pimples from the sense of relief, and as I started to relax I broke wind, as one does. Never satisfied with half a job, or by just making a tiny mess of things, I noisily cleared my nasal passages and 'gobbed' over the side of the ship into the sea below. Then it came, it was like a sixth sense, I just kind of knew they were there without looking round and a nightmare just grew from deep within me. I fell into a pit of internal horror as I turned round to go back below decks. The Royal Marines were all on parade, in their best uniform, being inspected by their top brass, right behind where I stood. My life flashed before my eyes. It could have been taken right out of one of those old 'Carry On' films. I actually tiptoed back to the stairs, maybe, hoping they had not seen or heard me. That day, I was once again sent back to my regiment in shame.

As 1980 arrived, my military service was coming to an end, and I could not wait to get away. My SSM called me into his office and took his beret and belt off. This meant it was all off record. He asked me to sit down, and he asked me to seriously consider what he was about to tell me. He said, "Colin, you are not cut out for civilian life. You are a squaddy through and through. If you get out now, it could prove to be the worst mistake of your life. If you extend your service for another 6 years, I will send you home for a month and then send you anywhere in the world for 6 months with a guarantee of promotion when you come back." I sat there speechless. Not so much about the suggestion, but because of the genuine concern in this hard man's voice and he called me Colin! I just said, 'Sir, I'll sign'. We filled in the forms together, still on first name terms, him calling me Colin and me calling him Sir. When we reached the point where all I had to do was sign my name, I picked all the forms up and said, 'I need to phone my girlfriend'. He sat back shaking his head and threw his hands in the air.

In the phone booth, I tore the forms up when I heard my girlfriend crying. I left that phone booth, forcing thoughts out of my mind that I had made a mistake by telling Julie, and I did not sign. I actually refused to believe that all she truly thought about was herself and not what was best for me. I went back to his office, but by that time he had his whole uniform on and when I told him of my decision, he called me a rude name and dismissed me.

The Civilian Nightmare

By the end of June 1980, I was back in Stockport where I could immediately see that nothing had changed. In every pub I went in to, it dawned on me that the same people were sitting in the same seats talking about the same superficial things and repeating the same jokes to each other, as they had been over three years before. I had managed to reach a Class One standard of driving so I was never out of work for long, but SSM Ron Walters was right, civilian life is for civilians. I had experienced things like marching in a body of men to a military band. I had experienced the bitter and painful struggles of, and the victorious pride of, completing basic training with a team of friends. I had tasted the sweetness of a passing-out parade where our training was recognised by family and ranks alike. I saw the tears of pride in the eyes of my dad. I had gone through hell and high water with guys just like myself. I had seen active service on the bomb disposal team in Belfast, jumped out of aircraft over Germany on a free-fall course, and a whole catalogue of wonderful experiences with the Army and made amazing friends. I had in fact become the young soldier I had seen in the Army Careers Information Office window three years earlier, and more. However, in truth, even in the midst of everything I had going for me, I still felt inwardly dissatisfied and constantly angry.

In Civvie Street, what the average civilian saw as entertaining, I now thought to be utterly boring and dangerously superficial. What the average civilian saw as friendship, I saw as fickle, untrustworthy and unhealthy.

My drinking soon became extreme, as did the violence, and work starting to get in the way. Julie and I decided we would get married. I promised her that I would go the romantic route and ask her father's blessing on our marriage. I had to build up the courage to ask him for over two weeks. I knew that he was not at all impressed with me because of my first encounter with him where my first two words to him had been very aggressive, the second one of which was 'off'. I was drunk and sound asleep in his house before he arrived home and he shook me to wake me up. I did not know where I was or what the shaking was about. I apparently sat up, wide eyed, looked him straight in the eye and growled my obscenity at him. He staggered backwards and although I slid back into the chair I could not quite escape the tension of them moment and I could not quite make it back into my slumber. The silence was deafening. I was in 'no-man's land' somewhere between sleep and nowhere else, and as I gradually started to wake up I was dreading that it was Julie's dad on the receiving end of my verbal trash. I was just starting to hope that I had dreamed it when I heard his voice in the background, "I won't be talked to like that in my own home by anyone". I knew I was in trouble. I stirred and tried to pretend I had no idea, but the damage was done. So when the time came, I nervously approached the subject about Julie and I getting married and he started to shake his head before I even got the question out. He simply said "No". I shrugged and thought, "Screw you mister, I was only trying to be polite, who needs your say so?" He went on to say "I know our Julie and I know she will never marry".

After long persuasion from Julie's mum, he agreed; Julie and I did get engaged and a party was thrown where I got ridiculously pissed, wondering why everyone else was being so reserved. I treated it like a NAAFI session and was staggering around drunk being explicitly rude to everyone I met.

No one enjoyed my sense of humour more than I did and I regularly heard myself howling at my own jokes.

The Relief of Prison

Dad had met another woman by this time, and when I walked in one night and saw her for the first time, I knew there was going to be trouble. She was a drinking buddy for my dad. I came in one night and she was sprawled out on the floor with her skirt undone and a bottle of vodka next to her. I looked at my dad and simply said, 'get this fat cow out of this house'. They broke up quite soon afterwards, and dad resorted back to coming in drunk and sobbing in my lap about mum. I was right back to where I was when I had joined up. In the end I took hold of him and yelled at him, "Dad will you please shut up, she is dead man, stop digging her up every night". It visibly shocked him and I sadly gained a sense of having just been heard but I also knew that he was unable to break free from his torment. By 1982 I was drinking too heavily, smoking too much weed, back on amphetamines and flirting with heroin.

Active Addiction

By the start of 1983 I was injecting two or three times a day. I was stealing from dad and from my girlfriend, and from her parents, her sister and my employers. I lost my driving license and my job in 1983, at which time Julie made a secret decision to get pregnant before ending our relationship, telling me never to come near her or the baby.

I visited her in the hospital as soon as I found out that she had had a boy, and as soon as I walked into the ward I knew she did not want me there. I asked her if my suspicions were right and she said they were, asking me to leave. I stared at her for a few moments, but she had changed. She looked like a person who had gotten what she wanted and now there was no more need of me. I was devastated. That same weekend I went out and picked up a woman from one of the town's notoriously underprivileged neighborhoods in one of the town's notoriously seediest nightclubs and woke up next to her the following morning. As I lay there in the quiet hours of the morning, I felt as if my whole life, and my character, were about to plunge into a deep dark hole. I was living life in a way that laughed in the face of every one of my personal and family beliefs, morals and ethics. I was on the brink of quietly slipping out of bed and running back to my dad when I saw that three children had joined us and stood staring at me in the room. All of a sudden, I had a family. I started to see Sue more and more and to sleep over at weekends actually using her place as a break from witnessing my dad as a sobbing wreck each night.

I used my dad's pain and suffering as an excuse to leave home and because I left my family home under a cloud of sadness and unresolved pain, that was exactly what I took with me, sadness and pain. While it actually was the right time for me to leave home, I did so for the wrong reasons and in the wrong ways.

My visits to Sue and the kids soon increased to midweek, and it wasn't long before I started to go out from her house in the middle of the night with another heroin user, Alex, to commit burglaries throughout the night and to buy drugs. By the end of 1982 I was committing a burglary a day for funding the heroin addiction, while imitating what I believed to be a 'father figure' to the kids. I wanted to stay off the drugs, and I told myself day after day that I had to stop this lifestyle, but it was quite simply impossible. One or two days without drugs would cause an emotional storm in me, with intense anxiety that I just did not know how to handle. I took the drugs to stop myself from feeling bad, but to buy the drugs I had to do things that I hated and which made me feel bad; and for that I needed more drugs.

Life was a swamp of pain and frustration, but in the midst of it all I did find that I had one area of comfort, Sue's children. Joseph was 2, Matthew was 4 and Sherane was 7 and with these guys I found that I could just be myself. I felt very safe with them. I felt very protective around them, and I actually desired to be a father for them. Joseph (Jo-Jo) called me dad and I loved it. Matthew tried to call me dad but he had experienced quite a lot of his real dad and it was a half-hearted attempt. Sherane saw me as Colin and that was really nice. I was living life as a single man with a pseudo-family to meet my relational needs, until I arrived 'home' one afternoon to find Sue crying in the kitchen. She looked at me and said, "I'm pregnant". I tried to make it sound as if this was the best news ever. I made all the right noises about never leaving her, and stopping the drugs and getting a job and settling down etc. etc. To celebrate, I went out and injected heroin.

I decided to move in full-time with Sue and the children with the silent hope that it might help me find direction and get me off the heroin; but by the time the baby was born in the December of 1984, I was serving my first prison sentence for 10 burglaries. The build-up to that sentence saw me fall to 15 kilogram's underweight and into a severe state of threefold deterioration: physical, emotional and spiritual. My family members often looked at me with shock in their expressions whenever I saw any of them, and I would see from their reaction to me the extent of my decay. I had not been in prison at this point and in a really distorted way I knew that I would have to in order to belong in the tribe that I was trying to fit in with because everyone had done time but me.

During that first prison sentence, the psychological and physical withdrawal I experienced from the heroin was like nothing else on earth. I went without sleep for 17 days and 16 nights. Not one minute's sleep. For the first two weeks I went through a physical nightmare of sweats and intense backache, but the sleeplessness was a killer. I was doing two sentences: days and nights. It was on the 17th day that I lay down on my bed after my lunch, and all of a sudden I was waking up. I sat on my bed and could not believe that I had slept. I needed to know what time it was to confirm that I had dropped off and for how long. I started sleeping from that point, getting a little bit more each passing night. It was two months before I was getting a full night's sleep. Alan came to visit me at the start of that sentence in Manchester and as he looked across the visiting table at me I could see that he was going to start crying over what he saw. Everything within me wanted to say 'please do not cry, because what will people think of me if they see you crying?' I was totally self-absorbed.

Hayley-Mary

I met my daughter Hayley, for the first time over a prison visiting table, and the simple sight of her stirred all my innermost desires and longings for normality, and yet, prison actually offered me a sense of relief from the frightening and counterfeit relationships of my civilian life. I was heroin-free only by incarceration, but my promises and determinations to stay off heroin when I got out, were very real to me. My letters to Sue began to fill with plans of staying drug free when I got out and getting a job and settling down. From within the darkness of my soul, there came sounds of empty promises and false hope. I made Hayley out to be my reason to live and wrote of how she was my missing piece and I convinced everyone that I had turned a corner, but I still knew, deep down inside, that I was addicted to heroin. I wrote all these promises in every letter to each of my family even in a celebratory tone because I was now drug free and going to the prison gym five times a week. I believed my dreams, and I felt an inner resolve, strength and determination: I truly believed that I would stay clean now. Hayley was the final piece to my picture and the seasoning to my motives and determinations. I came out of prison in the march of 1985 and within three days I was back to using heroin and amphetamine by needle.

It hit me like a runaway train. When the euphoria of release wore off, I started to forget the power of heroin's addictive qualities and started to imagine 'one hit'. I set out to see my old drug dealer with every intention of limiting my intake to a minimal amount of five pounds worth of heroin, 'just the once'. I made that first hit into a kind of farewell ceremony, the goodbye that I did not have the opportunity to say when I got arrested; I would just have one more hit for old time's sake, one for the road kind of thing, and I made it sound like a reasonable act. Before I knew it I was once again totally swept away by it all. I stole the clothes Sue had bought to look nice for my homecoming and sold them for a hit of speed. I stole Sue's gold chain from around her neck, as I drove her to the shop. Whilst she thought I was being affectionate by tickling her neck, I was actually unfastening her necklace. Within one week, I was very much back to robbing a house a day and spending up to 250 pounds a day for heroin and amphetamine. I had truly believed the prison sentence had changed me. I really believed that Hayley's arrival had changed me. I deeply believed that my love for her was strong enough to keep me clean.

I then started to believe that getting my driving licence back would be the change of me. "I am at a loss without my driving licence; once I can work, everything else will work out". Then when I eventually got my licence back and found work I started to resent the world because no one trusted me, so I turned to 'so what's the point of trying"; I reasoned that because I was working and earning, I should be allowed to govern the amount of drugs I used. Every morning though, fearful of going into the day without a hit, I would drain diesel from the truck I was driving and sell it for 25 pounds. I would then park the truck on the side of the road and I would mix the heroin with vinegar and water in a spoon, burn it for 10 seconds or so and then inject it. The smell of the mix would cause severe wrenching, but nothing was going to stop me having this hit. Once I had injected, I would aim the vehicle in the general direction of wherever it was I was going, and somehow get on with a day's work.

Seeing the dangers of driving on heroin, amphetamines started to play a very prominent role during those trucking days, but heroin was my first love. Inevitably my employees would eventually work out that the diesel was not going as far as it used to and I would be confronted. On more than one occasion I simply shrugged and said, "I've been selling it to buy drugs" and I would then just walk away and start committing burglaries again. Every firm I worked for I robbed in this way. My desire for heroin and amphetamines really was insatiable. I was never satisfied. I actually started wanting to go back to prison.

On one driving job, where the company was very keen on diesel receipts, I stopped the truck in the middle of the afternoon in a busy built up area. I could see from the height of the truck that a house was empty of occupants. This day I got out of the truck and walked up the garden path of a house. On my way, I picked up a white ornamental rock from the front garden onto my shoulder, and without concern for there being anyone in, I simply hurled this huge rock through the front window. I sliced my wrist on the glass and blood pumped out of me, but I had seen a video recorder, and it had 150 pounds worth of heroin and amphetamine written on it, so I carried on with blood going everywhere, until I got my goal. During one of these raids, I noticed something about myself, but could not tell how long it had been happening. I got back into the truck on this, or some similar raid, and I realised I was having to fight to stop myself from crying. I was thoroughly sick of it and hated every minute of this life I was trapped in, but could see no other way. I often saw deep sadness in my family's eyes every time I met with them, but the madness continued.

I was in and out of court for drunk and disorderly and criminal damage and things like that. Sitting in the waiting rooms of the Magistrate's Court at Stockport on one of these silly charges, I saw a lady put in a code to unlock an office and enter. I saw that she had pressed one number from the top and two from the bottom. When the lady came out of the office, I walked up to the door, pressed what I thought she had pressed and I unlocked the door. Once inside I ransacked all the drawers in the office looking for drug money for after my case was dealt with until I heard the combination lock being tapped and dived behind the door. Another woman walked in, but did not see me behind the door. I stepped out from the behind the door, got myself behind her as she entered the office and pushed her to the other end of the office and ran for it, down through two flights of stairs and several stunned and half-startled police officers and court officials. They knew something was wrong, but did not to stop me until, when I got to the bottom of the stairs, I heard the woman screaming: 'stop him, stop him'; but it was too late, I was out into the town and gone.

I had previously experienced life on the run from the law, and despite sounding very exciting to me at first, the thought of it did not take long to diminish the fear of prison for me; I would rather get back to jail and get everything sorted out and start again than try to exist in the twilight zone of a crook. So after a swift change of clothing I returned to the court a few hours later, ready to face any consequences, but no one recognized me.

The headlines of the next day's Manchester Evening News read:

'THIEF BRINGS COURT TO STANDSTILL'

I sat staring at the headline with an inner sense of celebration. So much so that I told everyone in the pub that it was me who "froze the system".

I then spent a year of petty crimes, unemployment, relationship deterioration and an increase in the intensity of my addiction. Then exactly one year later, in the same courtrooms at Stockport, while waiting to answer to charges of criminal damage, I noticed a solicitor hanging his long and very trendy overcoat in the changing rooms next to the interview rooms. I knew I could sell a coat like that so as soon as the solicitor left the changing rooms, I walked in, put the overcoat on, checked myself out in the mirror, and walked out again.

The headlines in the Manchester Evening News the next day read:

'THIEF BRINGS COURT TO STANDSTILL'

This was how life went, flitting from one opportunist crime to another, just getting enough money to buy enough heroin and amphetamines to see me through each miserable day.

I was soon back in prison, and my letters to Sue sounded just like the ones on the previous sentence: "I am off the heroin and amphetamines now, and I can see that it was the drugs that were destroying me." I wrote pretty much the same to all my family, "I have learned my lesson now, I have a daughter, and a woman who loves me; I can get work and I really do not want heroin again". I was very aware of the repetition, but I actually believed that everything I was saying was going to be true 'this time'. Every letter I wrote, and every promise I made, I believed. I would lay awake at night and inwardly celebrate the fact that I was off the powders.

I still felt ripped off by the girl who had given birth to my son, and even more so now because I kept hearing via secondhand means that he had some problems with his growth and that there was something wrong in his development. But in all honesty I also still secretly yearned to contact Tina for reasons of unresolved hurt. But all these frustrations could easily be denied now because I had a little girl to whom I could direct all my love.

Hayley had brown eyes like my mum and I, and no one knew the joy that this little girl gave me and with every ounce of determination within me I resolved that I was going to be her all-in-all 'as soon as I sort myself out'.

Overdose for Christmas

I went back to prison for 10 burglaries and once again my letters contained all the same promises with 'humble acknowledgements' of 'now realizing that I made the mistake of going back for just one more hit'. Once again I found myself writing 'this time, when I get out, I'm not going anywhere near the stuff'.

I think I was so convincing because I actually believed my own idealism and I never actually set out to tell a lie in all of my confessed failures and expressions of hope. This time I saw Hayley once a month and had to settle for watching her run around a prison visiting room, and my resolve to get it right for this little lady grew stronger by the week. I impressed the parole boards and probation officers alike with my sincerity to go straight this time. My family was once again sucked in by my ability to talk the talk, and Sue and I once again looked forward to a future free from drug addiction.

I got out on parole on the 22nd December 1986. All my promises to stay off heroin stood strong for two days. On the afternoon of Christmas Eve I woke up in intensive care wired to a heart monitor, surrounded by several medical people and painfully aware of a drip in my arm and another in my hand.

I had overdosed injecting another form of drug that had been stolen from a chemist the previous night. An old friend of mine, Gary Ball, actually kept me alive by heart massage and injecting my lifeless body with cocaine each time he revived me until the ambulance arrived. I had taken in quite a lot of alcohol in the few days that I had been out and I had gone to the pub over the Christmas Eve lunch time was enjoying a couple of bottles. I then heard about the chemist being robbed and the wheels started to turn in my head. I had a sneaky suspicion that if anyone would know who had stung the chemist, Gary would. When I got to his place he had somehow got his hands on a lot of the stolen drugs. Adrenalin took over. I assured him I had not had any booze, and we set about sharing a hit of palfium in his kitchen. My twisted logic told me that I could have a couple of these pills known as 'Palf', and get away with it because they would not affect me like heroin did. I had heard of the dangers of mixing this particular drug with alcohol but dismissed them, not believing that those rules would apply to me.

I woke up wired to a heart monitor, with a 'peep, peep' sound echoing into my soul.

I somehow knew that the sound was that of my life on its approach to flat lining. In panic I sat up and removed the drips myself and started to fight my way out of the hospital. I somehow managed to get home and up the stairs and into bed before Sue had heard anything, but as I lay there I had to admit that this incident had really scared me; I lay in bed in excruciating pain with what I concluded must be a blood clot on my brain, so intense was my headache. I had the most horrendous, pounding headache for hours. When I felt strong enough to stand up it was dark, and all I could think about was my little girl in the next room. I went into Hayley's room and took my sleeping daughter in my arms, and with eyes welled up with tears of torment I quietly just watched her chest rise and fall with her precious life breath, and wondered why the hell I was willing to flirt with death without consideration for anything or anyone.

Hayley was the one bright spot in my terribly sad and lonely life.

During the darkness of my prison sentences, I always managed to get a picture of her next to my pillow, and her picture became my sustenance in the darkness. I would smoke a weed or take powders and pills with other prisoners, and then at night I would silently touch her face and inwardly vow to get clean for her.

I worked pretty much the whole of 1987 and really put on a good show of intent, I was working and keeping out of trouble; but life seemed to get heavier and heavier as the year wore on. The overdose had really scared me, but as the year passed, I started to believe that I could stay clean now. That belief then grew into a very destructive message in my mind: I could actually have a hit of heroin 'from time to time' now. So on Christmas Eve, exactly twelve months on from my last overdose, I went to the house of a guy who I knew had some Diamorphine Hydrochloride, white heroin from a chemist burglary. The guy was reluctant to deal with me due to my close dance with death the year before and he really tried to warn me. I eventually convinced him to give me a hit though and he put a little bit of heroin in the spoon. When I saw the small amount that he was offering me I laughed at him and arrogantly boasted: 'Kevin, turn me on man, don't insult me'.

I woke up again in intensive care wired to a very similar sounding heart monitor, surrounded by very similar looking medical staff, with a drip in my arm and my hand. It was like an eruption of panic. I sat up and tried to remove the drips myself once again, but this time I became very groggy and a nurse had to quickly remove them for me because I was starting to want a fight with them. I clearly remember her saying, "Oh, another know-it-all", and I was instantly reminded of the previous year's episode; it even crossed my mind that she was remembering and referring to that. I sat with head in hands after my 'escape', with a terrible sense of not only was life never going to change, it was not going to last very long either.

By April '88, I was back inside for a burglary where I had had a confrontation with an occupant in the middle of the night. I had entered his house without noise, but got over confident as I removed furniture and fittings to sell the next day. Gary Fitzpatrick and I were scheduled to visit Fitzy's lifelong friend Johnny Hester the next day in Lancaster Prison. John was a good friend to both of us, but Fitz and John went back years. As I came to the end of this particular burglary, I went back in with the thought of, 'I'll get the small TV and whatever I get for it I will buy a parcel for John'. As I was leaving the house with the TV on my shoulder, the owner was suddenly standing at the bottom of the stairs. There was a lull as we stood less than a meter apart, until he nervously asked me what I was doing. I picked up on his fear and capitalized on it. I said, 'I'm robbing you, go back to bed'. He hesitated for a second, until I walked toward him threateningly and he gave in to my intimidation and turned and went back upstairs. He had already phoned the police though and before I could hide the TV, the street was surrounded. I tried to hide in a garden, and once again I found I was crying, feeling a real deep sense of sadness. My feelings were overwhelming. I felt a deep sense of shame about how the guy had just had his domain heartlessly raided by me and how I had probably just trashed his self-esteem. As I lay there waiting for another arrest, I really started to hate what I had become and was painfully aware of how all my insanity was back in full glory.

I lay under some very uncomfortable bushes, in the dark, staring into nowhere, with tears on my cheeks. I saw a policeman peering over the fence into my garden of seclusion and suffering and I knew that he had seen me, but I really did not care. Even when I heard him calling for the dog-handler and I knew that he was going to send the dogs in, all I could think about was the state of my life, and in comparison, a dog attack did not worry me in the slightest. I just lay there.

The dog let into the garden soon found me, but for some strange reason it did not pay much attention to me. The officer was trying to excite the dog against me but it ignored him and explored the rest of the garden. I eventually stood up and held my hands where everyone could see them. I noticed people in the bedroom windows watching this middle of the night police hunt, and I remember feeling jealous of their 'normality'.

I was eventually bundled into the back of a police van by a police officer that I had come to know who climbed into the van with me. As we drove away he quietly said, "Colin, what are you playing at"? I simply sat there and said with my hands cuffed behind my back and I heard myself say, "Mr. Buxton, I need help". He actually voiced a disappointment in me and hinted that he believed that he could see other potential in me. Deep inside of me though, I was haunted by my failures and the damages that I had caused within my family and within society.

While this burglary had contributed to my self-hatred, it was just another one on top of many, but I'd also robbed my dad's house in recent months and he had very aggressively disowned me.

I tried the 'poor me, everybody blames me' routine with him again, but it had lost all value. He looked me right in the eye and said with a heartbroken tremble, "you are not the boy that we gave birth to; I can no longer consider you to be my son" and he walked out and slammed the door behind him. That door echoed in my empty heart for years. There I was again, 25 years on, looking him in the eye and lying, but this time he was washing his hands of me because his heart was as broken as he could ever allow it to get. As he had walked away from the house, Sue sat down trembling and simply said "Oh Colin". She was in a deep state of despair over me. I responded with an offensive, stormed out and robbed another house and bought heroin and amphetamine. I thought about suicide at that point.

So I just looked at Mr. Buxton and shrugged. I felt inwardly hopeless, and started looking forward to the jail and the gym, etc. I made a guilty plea the next day and was remanded in to custody. During the ride from Stockport Magistrates court to Strangeways prison, I knew I had to go for rehab. Once I'd settled on remand I wrote to Sue once or twice just to tell her that I was going for rehabilitation after this sentence. I got no response. She and everyone else were in shock because of my rapid fall back into using, overdosing and crime.

It was at that time and once again in Strangeways, that I found the address of, and decided to limit my letter writing to, a Christian rehabilitation centre in the South of England. The idea of 'doing rehab' held an intriguing form of interest for me, just like going to prison had. I almost felt like I would have to 'do rehab' in order to reach higher levels of recognition within the addiction culture; but I must also say that there was a deep desire for help too. I was sick of making promises I could not keep and so just decided to keep my mouth shut and do something about my problem because going to jail was relief for everyone, me included.

Some of the Christians I wrote to visited me in Strangeways and then invited me to go and stay with them. When I went to Crown Court, I put it to the Judge that I needed help, and was going regardless of his decision, either instead of prison or after it. He decided a prison sentence was unavoidable due to my record and I got fifteen months which to me at that time was like water off a duck's back. I was safe in jail. I always managed to get a smoke of weed for the night times and used the gym every day; I had three meals a day guaranteed and a bed to sleep in, so prison was not a problem. And I knew even then that as long as prison is not a problem, prison is also not a solution.

I did ten months out of the fifteen and I remained deeply serious about getting help to get clean.

Working the kitchen in HMP Risley gave me open access to prison-brew booze, but such was my seriousness about getting clean that I felt no attraction to the stuff.

I wrote every week to the rehab, giving any and all details of my week and my dope usage. I was dead straight with them.

Fitzy was also locked up at this time and we interacted with inter-jail mail throughout our sentences. I was due out six days before him and was forever reminding him that he had longer than me to go. That was until I got a visit from Marko. He brought me a chunk of weed and the screw spotted him handing it to me. I got dragged off the visit for 'suspicion of smuggling drugs in Her Majesty's Prison'. I'd actually swallowed the chunk so the charge only stayed at suspicion; however, I lost seven days, putting my release date a day after Fitz. Needless to say he reveled in this. Fitz got out on the Thursday, I got out on the Friday, and that night he and I committed a very strange burglary, we actually broke *into* a prison and dropped off four big bags of very attractive booty for the guys inside. I knew, and everyone else knew, that the madness was never going to end until I put some footwork in.

My heart was breaking over the separation from Hayley and the fact that I was going to rehab, but I had to concede that my love for her was simply not enough to get me clean. The power of my addiction was stronger than the love I had for my child. This was confirmed to me when earlier that day, having just been released from prison, I went straight from the prison gate to Marko's house for a bag of amphetamines. I injected the whole bag in two hits, and only then did I go to see Hayley, by which time my affections were actually false because of the speed. The best way that I could describe my state at this time is as one of high depression. The speed took me up, and the heroin satiated my downs; but the immense sense of loss and failure never left me.

During the first edition of this book (2004), Marko 'The Pied Piper of China Town' died, all alone in his little flat from, I'm told, severe crack abuse and, I would guess, a deep sense of disappointment. By nature, I do not believe Marko was a drug addict; yes he was a (loveable) outlaw, but I believe his addiction was born of a naive belief that he could flirt with crack cocaine once or twice—and like so many others, it swept him away like tsunami.

Let me share one more memory of Steven Markland. As kids from China Town, we would regularly visit the fairground. On one particular visit, one of us got a clip around the ear from one of the fairground workers. When we got back to China Town, Marko caught wind of what had happened. We were aged between eight and twelve; Marko would have been eighteen or nineteen and as soon as he heard that one of us had been hit, he changed into scruffs, and walked the three miles or so to the fair to fight the traveller. As Marko strode out to the fair, he had something like thirty kids behind him. I now believe there was a two way relationship between us and Marko: (1) he was like the big brother that everyone wanted, and (2) we were the kid brothers he never had. Needless to say Marko kicked that traveller's backside.

In the March of 1989, less than a week after my release, I somehow managed to break away from Stockport and made my way to St. Vincent's rehab in Andover. On my arrival at St. Vincent's I felt a sense of relief because it was off the main road, and surrounded by trees. I spent 7months at the rehab, but in all honesty it was just a hiding place. I was training on weights 6 days a week, eating good food, and growing physically. I manipulated my way back into the life of the mother of my son from that rehab. I was writing to her and Sue, getting both of them to send me tobacco and money, etc. However, when I suggested seeing my son, the door was once again slammed firmly in my face. I swallowed the resentment and the rejection once more and just carried on with Sue as if everything was normal. Deep within me, though, there burned a desire for some sort of revenge for all this pain. The rehab did not push the Christianity issue on us and I was allowed to go to the Catholic services. Everyone else went to a nearby 'happy-clappy' Church and they used to try and get me to come with them, telling me that the music was excellent and the women were plentiful.

I just declined and got on with the Catholic thing. These guys were Protestant and going to hell, if my memory served me correctly. Then one morning, the staff called us all together and told us that a guy called Billy Graham was visiting UK, and was inviting St. Vincent's to his crusade. I was not in the slightest bit interested, until they said, "It is at Wembley Stadium". I instantly knew what I was going to do. In a flash I said 'I'll go'. I spoke to no one, but I had a plan. On the 8th July 1989 we all went on the same bus to Wembley, but no one knew that I had a tennis ball in my pocket. In my heart I vowed 'I'm not missing this opportunity'. The St. Vincent's guys all sat next to each other in the stadium, and for some weird reason we were in the Royal enclosure. I was sat ten or so seats in from the aisle. The songs of praise being sung captivated me, but I felt very self-conscious about joining in.

The stadium filled with approximately 55,000 Christians. Eventually this American guy came onto the stage, and in my opinion, waffled on for what seemed like an eternity. All I was interested in was trying to work out how to execute my plan. Toward the end of Billy's sermon, a bolt of lightning exploded right behind him. 55,000 people gasped, but Billy did not blink, he just preached on. At the end there was an altar call for Salvation. I sat on the edge of my seat. One of the St. Vincent's staff looked at me and I just stood up and said very convincingly, "If I do not answer this call tonight, I might spend the rest of my life regretting it", and with that I stood up to go forward. Everyone stood to let me out and I made my way to the hallowed turf. I got more and more excited as I got closer to the pitch. Just as I got to the bottom of the steps, I looked back to see if the guys were watching me. There was an eruption of excitement building up in me because of what I was about to do, and it had nothing at all to do with Billy Graham or the God he had waffled on about. As I looked back, I was frozen in amazed horror to see everyone else from the rehab coming forward. I was deeply distressed, but I had made it this far, I was not backing out now. As I reached the turf, I took my tennis ball out of my pocket and dropped it to the grass and it was then, on the 8th July 1989, that I, Colin Garnett, kicked a ball on Wembley. I was actually kicking a ball on Wembley. As I looked up, Alison, the girly who managed St. Vincent's, was looking at me with a deep look of disappointment in her eyes, but I just shrugged and thought 'hey who cares man, I'm kicking a ball on Wembley'.

Everything then suddenly went very quiet as Billy Graham prayed for people and led them in the Salvation prayer. I picked my ball up, my heart pounding in my chest from exhilarated pleasure, and then bowed my head in prayer with everyone else. At that point, my heart was pumping with adrenalin as I repeated the sinner's prayer and sort of asked Jesus into my life. At the end of the service we were given a little booklet to take away and fill in every day. I threw mine away as soon as we got back to St. Vincent's. I still refused to go to Church with the happy-clappies, and just went back to my weight training routine.

Three months later, in the October of '89, after seven months of hiding, I walked out of the rehab. I was bored with hiding. I had developed for myself a comfortable situation out of an uncomfortable context. Within 4 hours of returning to Stockport I was injecting amphetamine, smoking weed and drinking very heavily. I got arrested that very same day for possession of a stolen credit card. I was stopped in the street and searched, and ended up in the police cells by lunchtime. I was fingerprinted, charged and bailed within a matter of three hours. I was going to use the credit card to get kitted out, because I was much bigger physically than I had ever been. I had been eating very well and pumping iron six days out every seven. On that first night back a local lad who had been on the beer all day insisted on being sarcastic with me, trying to pick a fight. I tried to warn him off, three times, but he persisted so I punched him with every ounce of anger within me and the same feeling of dread that I'd had when I'd kicked the guy in Aldershot came over me—I truly believed I had killed him. As I punched him the bar we were in fell silent, and I just heard a lady behind me, with a sound of utter shock quietly say, 'Oh good Jesus'.

The guy fell and whacked his head on the pool table on the way down. He was out like a light for ten minutes with a split face which needed nineteen stitches. I had to flip him over onto his face because the blood was pouring into his mouth. I felt I was always going to be in the heart of trouble, and a sense of despair started to grow within me. The next day I injected amphetamine.

This next season of using actually took almost two years to gather momentum, and it was November 1991 before I got nicked again. I was trying to hold down a job, be a husband to a lady for whom I had no feelings, a father for three children who were not mine and be something Hayley could look up to for guidance while also wrestling to keep an amphetamine and heroin habit alive by committing at least one burglary a day. I tried trucking again, and often found myself with the prospect of going off on long distance runs which would take me away for three or four weekdays. I would break out in a sweat at the thought of the withdrawals from heroin and the thought of having to go away would haunt me, until eventually it reached such a state of desperation that I parked the trailer of the truck on a nearby industrial estate, and went cruising the streets in the cab section in the middle of the afternoon looking for somewhere to rob. I noticed a lady leaving her house, locking the door behind her. Making my mind up that it must therefore be empty, I gave her five minutes and set about the burglary. I was aching within my bones for a hit and I was saturated with sweat. At the back of the house I found a spade and simply used it as a bat to smash the window in. It was 1 p.m. I heard the TV on in the front room but thought nothing of it because people regularly left their TV on for effect. I just walked in and went for the video under the TV. As I picked it up, a guy jumped up from behind the door and challenged me. I raised the video above my head and very quietly said, "Sit down and shut up". He sat down and I walked away with his video.

By the time I got to the truck, I was actually crying, sweating and bleeding from a head wound from the window. I got 75 pounds worth of heroin for the video, injecting half of it at the drug dealer's house and the other half just before I left the industrial area where the trailer was. I was then meant to go away for three days without drugs. I went back to the depot and resigned without excuse. The thought of leaving the drugs for three days was on a par with the dread of going to the hospital to see my mum die. I could not bring myself to leave the area where the powder was.

Welcome to the life of a drug addict.

Cultural Reject

At the start of 1991, while committing an afternoon burglary, I made a decision to press the palm of my hand against a window at my point of entry. My reasoning was, 'I had only been out of prison for a few months and already I was right back where I had left off. I knew that it was only going to be a matter of time before I would be going back inside for a much needed jailbreak'.

On the 7th November 1991, at approximately 5:30 am, several police officers burst into our home and arrested me for 'suspicion of burglary' and they gave an address of the house in question. I said, 'yeah that's mine, I did it'. I was admitting to anything, but as it turned out, it was the house with the palm print. It took them almost twelve months to trace that palm print to me, and I was right, I was in need of a break. I was actually relieved that I did not have to go into another day of fighting for where the next hit was going to come from. The mind works extremely fast at times of crisis, and on this particular morning, I heard the police coming through the front door and I knew I could escape through the window if I chose to. However, I summed up my options, and had to concede that going to prison was my best option. During the questioning one of the detectives asked me, "What is an experienced burglar like you doing leaving palm prints"? I told him how I knew back then 'I was going to need a lie-down[7] by the end of the year', and there I was, at the end of the year, being remanded in to custody once again.

I had started robbing from drug dealer's houses, sneakily stealing from the houses of some of them and violently taking drugs off some of the others. I stole from Fitzy's flat when the truth was—in the midst of all my cultural rejection—he was the one guy who stood by me even though he knew that where I was concerned, nothing was sacred.

Eventually one of the main suppliers blacklisted me and told all the other junkies that if they so much as spoke to me, they would be blacklisted too. I was ignored by the ignorant and cast out from the outcasts. I became nocturnal, and many nights I would sit on a local railway embankment and cry from the loneliness and the hopelessness of it all. All my intentions had once been healthy, but

---

[7]   *A SPELL IN POLICE OR PRISON CUSTODY*

I could not live them through, and now I was resigned to unhealthy intentions. So when the police barged in that morning, they were actually welcome.

My solicitor came to me in the cells and shook his head about the prospect of me getting released on bail. I said, 'I don't want bail'. He just stared at me with a confused yet relieved look in his eye and he then walked away. I was remanded to Strangeways yet again. I had graduated to William White's accurately described 'Cultural Reject': 'those addicts who, for a variety of reasons, are no longer in good standing with the culture. This category includes police informers, child molesters, or other addicts whose behaviour has become so outlandish that it poses a threat to the rest of the tribe'[8]. 'Having lived outside society at large and having now been rejected by the culture of addiction, rejects become homeless and helpless, meandering in their isolation from institution to institution.'

Jail was not only a relief; compared to the trauma of the addiction, it was a breeze.

It was November 1991, eight months after the riot which saw prisoners destroy the bulk of that Manchester jail. I'd spent somewhere in the region of three years in Strangeways before this time and talk of a riot was always an undercurrent within the prison population. It was never a case of if; it was just a case of when that place blew up and then when it did explode I had watched from the loneliness of my own living room, feeling envious of these guys pulling that place apart. I could very easily envisage the junkies in their raid of the dispensary, and then wanting sweets and tobacco, and the violence freaks wanting to attack the sex-offenders for their fix. I just knew there would be carnage in there, and inwardly wanted to be a part of it. And now, November '91, here I was back on remand with no more than fifteen other guys and prison staff who were being uncomfortably polite to us. We were given medication of our own choosing when the remand section of the jail first reopened. I went for Diazepam, Temazepam and Valium, and spent each night sound

8   WILLIAM L WHITE, PATHWAYS, HAZLEDON PUBLISHING 1996

asleep, with each day feeling mellow as mellow can be. Life was actually quite good in the there and then, but ahead of me there was only darkness. I chose to rapidly wean off the medications and then had a bit of a bad time of it but I was fearful of a continued chemical dependency. Once the withdrawals were over, I began to develop and come to terms with a horrible reality of having an inner fear of release. I was scared of getting out even before I had a sentence to speak of, and there was a corner of my mind that could see how sadly insane my state was. My family had washed their hands of me, society's rejects had rejected me, and I truly believed myself to be unemployable.

A ray of hope came in the strangest form when I got a letter from Sue ending the relationship once and for all. She was not angry—she had just lost all hope of any reconciliation. And as I read it I felt a strange sense of liberation. I started thinking that this could be exactly what I needed to finally start getting real about myself, to myself. I also knew that it would mean severing all ties with Stockport for a period, and that would mean not writing any letters or receiving any from anyone.

Poetic Expression

On H Wing, a remand wing of Strangeways, I was at a total loss for which way to turn for the future. Rehab had been a waste of time, and my record was worse now than last time when 'prison was unavoidable'. But even more worrying for me was, 'what am I going to do when I get out?' I could not forget feeling relieved when I got arrested; not wanting to submit an application for bail and now I was in touch with a deep seated fear of release.

I was in a terrible place.

A headline on one of the daily papers leaped up at me in my cell one day. It said:

'Boy George, Heroin Addiction'

I can very clearly remember thinking 'welcome to the club'. I did not bother reading the article; I just brushed it off.

I was back in the gym each day, and this time I applied for education classes. It seemed that the attitude of the prison staff had changed and they just wanted a quiet life. I wanted to use my mind on something so I applied for and was accepted for education classes where I was asked what I would like to do. Without thought I simply said, "I'll have a go at poetry". The tutor pointed me toward a pen and paper and said, 'Tell me who you are in a poem'. I sort of got the impression he had said this once or twice before.

I sat down and without a pause of any kind I wrote this:

How It Is

The prison gives me 'thinking time', my life, my children, me
To think of all the wrong I've done, and what I'd like to be
To lie awake and ask myself: "why lead this kind of life"?
Of using drugs, of stealing things, of life without a wife
Throughout the day I scan the prison, a mission to find a sorter
That's not the way of a grown up man with a lovely son and daughter
Life on the out was just the same, out stealing things for drugs
Trying to be something I'm really not, with gangsters,
thieves and thugs
I've really got to sort things out or I'll just end up dead
Another fool with an epitaph "He never used his head"
I've made our lives a misery underneath a huge black cloud
By forever doing what others did by following the crowd
But that was life behind a front, that's not the real me
I'm Colin Garnett, I'm better than that, just you wait and see.
There'll come a time when once again I'll walk with head held high
But take nothing for granted friend by the grace of God go I.
Because I lived fast on smack and speed, on morphine, dike and coke,
I showed my body no respect; life was just a joke.

I took the rides in the ambulances, woke up on the heart machines,
Filling my spike with too much drug for darkness,
if you know what I mean.
So before you tell how bad life is, sit down and have a think
How truly precious life would seem if you were on the brink
Believe me man life ain't no joke, and neither is taking drugs
You'll spend your life behind a front with gangsters, thieves and thugs.
Forget the buzz of making out; forget the sense of danger;
Just keep in mind your kids will grow to you a total stranger.

I called the tutor back over and passed it to him. He thought I was being flippant because it had only taken me 10 minutes, but as he read it a smile began to crack on his face. He was smiling quite broadly by the time he finished and he questioned whether or not I had either had it pre-planned or had copied it from another source. I wasn't too put out because I knew the truth and I had actually enjoyed writing it because it felt like I was actually expressing myself, truthfully, for the very first time.

He threw a gauntlet down. With what I would consider to be a patronizing tone, he said: 'Ok then, write one for me about something we can all identify with, something from recent news'. I instantly knew what I was going to write about, The Strangeways Riot, what else? I sat down, took up the pen and within 15 minutes had written this:

The Strangeways Riot

As years passed by in Strangeways jail, tension grew and grew;
Inmates' protests got no response, so what else could they do?
The threat of grief was always there, but no one knew the truth;
Bad attitudes by all concerned cost Strangeways jail its roof.
The nineties dawned, the summer came, and then the day of fools?
The day the prisoners went to pray, with blades and wood for tools
The Chaplain Proctor blessed the men, "The Lord God be with you"
Then a voice rang out "now's the time" and they all knew what to do
The prison staff fled, they surely knew to fight would mean defeat

So one by one they turned their tails and beat a swift retreat
Now the prisoners sensed a victory, and each man lost his frown
For now the time had finally come to pull that prison down
The prisoners then fled from the Church; each one prepared to fight
'Till silence fell and someone said, "There's not a screw in sight"
At this some felt disconsolate at loss of chance to feast
Then someone chuckled "Oh never mind, come on let's kill a beast[9]"
But many cons had other plans, and went for things they'd seen
Like morphine in the pharmacy and sweets in the canteen
Elation grew as the men were given the prison on a plate
They stormed the landings, opening cells, releasing all their mates
Now this blew up on April 1st, through ignorance and rules
But who can say they did not know? The government? The fools!
The TV made the most of it, with radio and press
They revel in all the misery, enjoying all the mess
The public went to stand and gloat and watch that prison burn
And hustlers made the most of it as a chance for them to earn
Whilst in that jail some skulls got cracked and many minds got scars
By sights of paedophiles being slashed or kicked and beat with bars
Upon the roof some thought it fun, stood waving to their mates
And picking police off hid below, bombarding them with slates
For 4 long weeks those prisoners kept that prison under guard
With the police at bay, and the April sun, it wasn't very hard
And now in Strangeways with changes made and attitudes improved
The cons can claim 'we made a point, we made the system move'
But that's not to say, "All is well" or "happy ever after"
Because in that jail you'll often hear an evil wicked laughter
That laughter comes in the dead of night and chills you to the core
And everyone knows, it's a case of 'when' we wreck
the place once more

I hadn't noticed but the teacher was watching me this time and when
I looked up, three or four other guys were watching too. My heart
was pounding in my chest and I was actually quite breathless by the
power of what I was writing. I sat back in a rush of adrenalin and
started laughing. I wasn't in the least bit interested what this guy,

---

[9] *A BEAST IS PRISON TERMINOLOGY FOR CHILD MOLESTER*

or anyone else said or thought about my work. I knew it was mine and I knew it felt brilliant. Not only was I was expressing myself, and not only was it truth—it was extremely liberating and factually very accurate. Something else very significant also struck home to me but no one else mentioned it: God had made an appearance in both poems.

The tutor looked very seriously at me and said; 'Colin did you really just write this'? But he knew. Not only did he watch me write it, he saw my reaction to it and that could not have been pre-rehearsed. I heard him mumble the 'F' word and he sat down as if he had just opened the winning lottery ticket. He then said to me, 'Colin, people are making millions for poetry nowhere near as good as this', but he was missing the mark, money was of no interest to me; drug addiction was already killing me. Wealth was the last thing I needed; I was more interested in rewriting it and selling it to other prisoners for cannabis, and/or to prison staff for cigarettes.

The tutor challenged me to write something purely fictitious, 'something right out of the blue'. I went away to my cell and made my mind up to write it that night. That night I sat at my table and took up the pen and waited for the inspiration but none came. I eventually threw the pen down after an hour or so in despair. This went on for three days and nights; it simply would not happen. I could not get my mind out of the prison or out of the urge to express reality.

Then on the early morning of the 5th January, I woke up and without getting out of bed, I reached for the pen and paper and this is what came out:

From Prostitute to Nun

'Twas long ago on a star-filled night that the horseman came to town
Sat tall upon a horse's back beneath a silky gown
His hair was golden, eyes were dark, beard; trimmed and clean
The town's folk knew without a word he was the strangest ever seen
As children slept and the old folk dozed they knew that he was there

Because with this rider came to town a breath of clean fresh air
Yet no one spoke or said a word; I think they probably knew
Who this man was and why he came and just what he would do
The way he sat so tall and proud some said he had a glow
Of radiance and elegance and his horse knew where to go!
Some old folk said as he rode by they felt a surge of youth
Was this the one they've waited for? Was this the man of truth?
So a silence fell but goodwill grew and they followed him into town
And each and every one of them sensed hope beneath that gown
The procession grew and with it joy, some said a sense of love
Was this the man they'd read about come down from up above?
The night chill seemed to fade away and a comfort came to all
But still the stranger sat aloft, still radiant and tall.
Now in this town there lived a whore who'd had her share of woe
A bastard child born from a whore, the lowest of the low
Some menfolk swore they'd never touched this child of ill repute
But all agreed she had lovely breasts and her smile was kinda cute
The truth was though, she took her men, she took a man at choice
She simply had to purse her lips and use her sexy voice
This night she sat up in her room alone and feeling down
That was until the horseman came to the centre of the town
That night her whole life brightened up, her heart filled up with pride
The joy she felt she could not quell, the tears she could not hide
For in her sleep a voice once said 'one day a man will come
To put an end to your life of woe, He'll shine without the sun
With tear-filled eyes she looked at him and he looked back at her
This was the man she'd waited for, of this the girl was sure
At this point some men turned their heads to glance upon the whore
They knew their 'fun' was over now they'd use this girl no more
Throughout the town there grew a fear stirred up by shame and guilt
For each and every one of them had been beneath her quilt.
Now the horseman cast his eyes upon the menfolk of this town
But none of them could hold his gaze, in shame they all looked down
Then from the heavens there came a flash, the town fell into prayer
Then silence fell and then they saw the girl was sitting there
Upon this horse the young girl sat with evil in her eye
The menfolk feared the tide had turned, it was time for them to die

The town wives begged 'please spare my man, please lady let him live'
The whore just sat and laughed at them 'you want me to forgive'?
Its 'lady' now my man has been, before my name was 'whore'
You called me what you wanted to but that's finished now no more
I've had your men, every one of them they've
begged between my thighs
They came to me to satisfy their fantasies and lies
But truth be known I had my fun and adultery is a sin
I've been the baddest of the bad by letting your men in
So I'll forgive if you'll forgive and we'll get on with our lives
And you can take your husband's home and be their loving wives
But hear me now and hear me good, don't curse my name again
Because the horseman gave me power you see, a power over men
They did not know that horseman said 'don't use
this power for wrong'
Spread goodness girl, have faith in God and the
power of prayer and song
You've lived your life as a bastard child on shortages of fun
But heartache leads to wisdom, child, so now become a nun
Go preach to men, plant seeds of love and try not to seduce
For a person's fate is determined by the fruit that they produce

I walked up and down that cell that morning with my heart pounding
in my chest and the excitement actually gave me a dull headache. I
was totally amazed that something like that could come out of me,
and once again, God had crept in. I was more than aware of how God
had been included in everything I wrote, and it sort of spooked me. I
felt that I had no right to use Him in any way, but also felt confusion
because I never intended to.

My court case date came through for mid-February. Two weeks
before my court case, Boy George was back on the front page of the
paper, with a headline reading something like:

"BOY GEORGE BACK ON TRACK"

There was an article about how he had spent two months in a certain clinic and how everything was now hunky-dory for him again. I raged in my cell and picked up my pen again and wrote to my doctor in Stockport. I simply said: 'what has Boy George got that I haven't? Is it because he is rich and I am poor that he can live and I have to die from the God forsaken problem? What kind of country is this? United Kingdom? My backside!

Apparently my doctor sent that letter to a sister clinic of the one Boy George had been in and they analyzed it and then wrote to me offering me a bed with them for their intense therapy programme. Normal funding was 12,500 pounds per month per person; I was being offered it for free.

In Manchester Crown court, when the possibility of the clinic was suggested, all the Court dignitaries were considering my case, and talking about me as if I was in another room, but all I did was set my eyes on the judge until eventually she looked at me and I just spoke up. I looked her in the eye and said very politely: "Your honour, prison is not working; it does not hurt, I need help now".

Within two minutes she had made her decision. She said, "I want to reserve your case to come before me in six months' time from this date; at that time, we will pass sentence for today's charge and you will be judged in accordance to the progress you make".

Ten minutes later I was in my probation officer's car on my way to a very luxurious Clinic for Addictions in Lytham St. Anne's for what turned out to be one of the most significant periods of my life.

Secular Therapy

The change from sharing a prison cell, where the toilet was open plan within a meter of the eating space with a toothless and heavily tattooed heroin addict, to thickly carpeted hotel type room with a bell for room service, with a lawyer and *en suite* facilities, sent me into a severe culture shock, to say the very least. I was swept from one extreme end of the social scale to the other between a.m. and p.m., and was greeted at the door by several middle and upper class people wanting to hug me and carry my brown paper bag for me. People were saying things like 'Hi, I'm Simon, I'm here for coke addiction' and 'Hi, my name is Aveen and I'm an alcoholic'. I was shown into a huge rest room and offered a cup of tea.

I think for the first time in years, I actually began to feel a sense of safety. People kept telling me they were 30, 60 and 90 days clean or sober, and they had their own jargon like 'but it's just for today as long as I keep it simple'. I started to think it was one of those cult type sects that one hears about in life. However, my reality was that I was comfortable in prison, worrying about being released; so I thought it best to do what I did best, blend in. Two guys sat with me and started to talk to me about 'willingness'. "It depends on how willing you are". My opening line was, "If I'm told to drink gorilla snot in order to get clean, I will." People were visibly shocked, but I meant it and felt no desire to apologize or impress. I was a threefold mess: physical, spiritual and emotional. I could not deny the sad state of my heart any longer. My daughter was a 40-minute train ride away, and I knew no one could stop me if I opted for a runner. I also knew that if I allowed my love for my daughter to rule my choices, I would be dead by Christmas. I had to cling to this truth: go back now and Hayley will have a dad for a short time, or stay away, and we could develop a relationship for life. I wrote to Sue explaining what I was trying to do, and she in turn told my family. I wasn't particularly interested in what anyone thought, though. I was dying a slow death, and every attempt I had made to clean up had failed. Opinions meant nothing to me; I needed the right advice and guidance.

A guy who introduced himself as my counselor told me that it was going to be a rough road ahead, calling for every ounce of honesty and courage I could muster. He then said the weirdest thing to me, 'And we can have a good look at all that anger', and with that he walked off. I was speechless. Didn't he realize I had just come from

Strangeways Prison? Could he not understand how happy I felt to be out of that hellhole? I thought 'what is he talking about'?

I was up first the next morning because of the silence. It was deafening. Alex, my cellmate for four months, had snored like a rhino. Now it was so quiet I could not settle.

Yesterday I had had porridge from hell for breakfast served by a tattooed pig from Rochdale, and now this morning I was offered a variety of cereal, fresh coffee, fresh orange juice, a mixture of fried goodies and toast, by a lady who seemed to genuinely care. I couldn't handle all the choice and started to feel like I was in the way, so just scooped a major portion of cornflakes and orange juice and sat down. My social skills were non-existent and I found that I did not have the inner confidence to ask what I was allowed to have. I felt like I was stealing. It took me something like two weeks before I felt right helping myself, but I failed to see how significant a role my lack of confidence had played in getting me this far. I created my own confidence, from a platform of 'at the end of the day if anyone challenges me I'll fight them'.

The day was built around group and one-to-one counseling sessions, from 09:00 in the morning through to sometimes 09:00 at night, talking about feelings and motives, being forced to look at the consequences of one's addiction on the family and the other community members. Every sentence was stripped down and analyzed by pretty much everyone. It was in-depth examination of the way we had lived and our motives were tested each day. I bumped into my counselor on the stairs and he stopped to greet me and we had a quick chat. As he left he said, 'we will talk about your anger soon'. I was dumbstruck once again. I looked around to ensure he was talking to me and then laughed into empty space, 'that guy is weird'.

Group sessions were really deep and heavy with both men and women talking about rapes and men talking about raping. People sat crying from pain of their own and through compassion for others. I felt as if I fitted right in with the group's therapy sessions and it was often pointed out that I could pass as a member of the counseling staff. Whenever the Director of Treatment took the group, everyone acknowledged a sense of feeling intimidated and people were on the edge of their seats. I could see why people found him intimidating as he was very spiritual and had an extraordinarily keen eye for spotting and exposing behavioral distortions, but at no point did I feel intimidated by this guy; in fact I often looked at him and thought to myself, 'I can do what you do'.

In the group situation he would read people and anticipate their manipulative thought life, and somehow manage to cut a long story very short. He would expose and go directly to the root of the problem illuminating to everyone how the alcoholism or the addiction would gather strength within manipulations and he would leave people with no alternative option but to concede that they were being dishonest.

It took me a couple of weeks of treatment before I started to feel vulnerable. I wrote to Sue about my vulnerability, and asked her to help me by visiting me with Hayley, and that was the start of my decline; because I was starting to feel vulnerable, I turned to someone to fix me. My counselor saw what I was doing and again suggested how 'it might be time to get honest about your anger instead of looking for a meeting with your daughter to take it away'. As he walked away from me, I followed him and we ended up in his office. As he turned to sit down at his desk he then realized that I was in his office and as he sat down I leaned on his desk and growled at him, 'you say that once more and I am going to break your jaw'. He sat back, gave me a lovely warm and friendly smile and he simply said; 'There it is Colin'. I was caught breathless by both his smile and his tone of friendliness; it threw me because this was my best attempt at intimidating him.

This guy had gone to work on me as soon as he set eyes on me two weeks earlier, with a very professional motive of getting me to a place where I would have no defense. He was right—I was one of the angriest people in that establishment yet I had managed, over the period of my lifetime, to develop a variety of skills in hiding it from everyone, including myself—behind bravado, a false confidence and a sense of humour.

I was due back in Crown Court for sentence on August 1st 1992. I think the original plan was to put me through a 28 day primary program and then see how I should progress but my stay ran into seventeen weeks.

During our clinical examinations, all our beliefs, our relationships and our funny little quirks of character were pointed out, examined and responded to with direct honesty. I was told to stop telling jokes and to stop writing poems, which left me feeling inadequate regarding how to communicate and how to express myself. I had to learn how to do these things in a mature and honest way and while that might sound quite natural for many people, for me, it meant that I had to unlearn many deeply ingrained ways before I could start to make any real progress.

Each week the whole house would gather at one or two graduations to give someone a 'final peer assessment' before they moved on to the next phase of their recovery. The graduate would sit in silence and simply receive all the love and support that their peers could muster as a final word of encouragement.

I noticed how everyone seemed to receive the same feedback around the question as to what they should do next to further their recovery. Unless the graduate was exceptionally mature regarding their addiction and their home circumstances were safe, the group feedback would always be: 'you really need to consider going for extended care'. I gave that very same feedback week in, week out to almost everyone whom I saw graduate. This last group always got very emotional.

After seventeen weeks of between ten to fourteen hours a day of therapy, seven days a week of soul searching and brutal honesty about myself, my final peer assessment group dawned. I went into it feeling reasonably secure because my group work had been impressive and my one-to-one sessions had grown into a really honest relationship with my counselor. Two guys had actually commented that when I walked into group-room they felt the same type of internal reaction that they would feel when they would discover that it was the director of treatment taking their session. PJ McCullough was a spiritual giant, with a stature one can only attain through suffering of the extreme kind. He was gentle, yet firm, quiet and wise, and every one respected him. When PJ sat in the group sessions, every one expressed a dread of what he would see in them, but I knew, 'I can do what he does'.

I felt one hundred times better than I had done sixteen weeks previously when those weirdos met me at the door. I had no inclination toward drugs, and actually felt a sense of compassion toward all those guys in prison who were not getting the opportunity I had been given. I really felt better about myself now that the addiction was over and excited about life ahead.

As we walked into my final group, I noticed there was a slight difference in format to all the others that I had witnessed. It was customary for the counselor of the graduate to come right alongside and sit next to them in the group. As I followed my counselor into the group room, I saw another counselor right behind me and although he smiled at me, I found it quite disturbing and I knew something was going on. I was told to sit with my hands on my lap, which threw me because I had my own way of sitting—with my hands behind my back of my chair, as if I was being interrogated. I felt as if I was in control sitting like that for some strange reason.

The group started as normal with everyone giving me their honest feedback about how they had seen me change and of how brave I had been. I was told that my courage had given them courage and many people said they stuck at it because of how they saw me stick at it and as many tears flowed during that group I really started to feel loved.

Then as it came to the time for my counselor to give his assessment, usually the one where the floodgates really open, he took a diversion from the norm and quietly said, 'Colin, let's talk about your mum'. I was rocked, it was like getting slapped across the face in dark room; I had no idea at all that this was coming and I remember shuffling around in my seat and mumbling something along the lines of 'o.k. if you want to' and as I said that I tried to put my hands behind my back, but my counselor would not let me.

Before I had any opportunity to defend myself, my counselor quietly asked me to imagine my mum sitting in the empty chair a few feet away, and he very lovingly asked me, 'what one word do you want to say to her?' A few seconds later, I heard myself quietly saying 'I'm sorry', and with it there came an eruption of emotional turmoil bursting up and out of me.

I started to weep, which turned into a sob, and I sobbed and sobbed, and I even began to kind of howl and wail. I could hear strange noises coming out of me and I actually thought to myself at one point, 'is that me?'

My knees came up to my chest and I folded my arms around them so that I was sitting in a ball on the chair where I sat and wept into my own lap for what I think was approximately fifteen minutes. It just poured out of me; years of bottled up grief and sadness and loss and injustice was finally given release and I was aware of repeating the word 'sorry' over and over to my 'imaginary' mum. I did not feel as if I was sorry 'to her'; it was more like I was saying sorry 'about' her, about her passing, about never really getting to know her, about the assumption that she would always just be there and about the hundreds of times in my life where I had reached a point of need and confusion where no one else could have comforted me but my mother, and all I wanted to cry was 'I want my mum. I miss my mum'.

As it started to subside, I started to become very aware of two things: one was how my jeans were wet through from the tears and snot, and the other was of how the room had fallen absolutely silent.

Eventually, like a tortoise coming out of its shell, I put my feet back to the floor and I started to straighten up, and as I did, I noticed that most of the people in the room were not really paying any attention to me. They were holding each other and hugging each other and it was then that I noticed that most of them were crying. They were not crying for me—these guys, my friends, were crying with me.

All the women were crying, some of the guys were too, and the nursing staff and the counseling staff, it was really really special, everyone was crying, and right at that very moment I received a very deep healing. I was alright, I knew I was alright, and not only did I know that I was loved, I knew that it was also alright for me to let go of my mum's hand now and finally lay her to rest.

The format of the group resumed its normal pattern, and these beautiful people began saying goodbye to me.

Then the time came for each of them to ask me what I thought would be the best thing to do next. In a flash of an instant I realized we were fast heading toward July, and I was due back up in court up for judgment in August. It was as if I did rapid mental survey of my options and I was now at the moment of truth. I knew in my heart that I had changed and that I had received several layers of healing in my time there. In my heart of hearts, I wanted to go home and make a new start at being a daddy to my little girl. As I looked around that room I saw love and respect from everyone, and I knew that they each held hope for me to make the recovery focused choice. When it came time for me to speak, just before I spoke, I folded my arms behind my chair and then replied, 'I think I should go to extended care' . . . to which the whole room erupted with applause and people ran to hug me.

I got lost in all that emotion for a little while, and really enjoyed the accolades, but within my heart I knew that I had just been dishonest. I wanted to go home and truly believed I could make a go of it, but I said 'yes' when I meant 'no' in order to please the people, and that was the root, cause and engine room of my whole addictive bondage. At that very moment of time in my treatment I started to relapse.

Relapse is never an event, it is always the end of a long process, and I went into that process as soon as I started to deny the truth of my heart through fear of rejection. I made contact with Sue again to let her know how well I was doing because my relapse was in motion now and I started to rebuild bridges back into addiction.

The Cotswolds is undoubtedly one of the most beautiful parts of Europe's countryside. The valleys around Stroud are green, the people are warm and friendly and the general pace of life is perfectly suited for early recovery. Early mornings are the most spectacular as the mist rises up from within valleys and one can see trees sticking out of the top of the mist as it rises, and on occasion, a cottage on the other side of the valley might give out a stream of smoke from its chimney stack. It is absolutely gorgeous.

I travelled from Lancashire to the Cotswolds on the train, deeply disappointed in myself because I wanted to go home, but did not have the gumption to risk saying so in the group situation.

I actually went through Stockport on the train, and as I did so I applied 10 seconds of thought to my daughter less than a mile away. Immediately following this line of thought I spent the next 20 minutes thinking about the heroin supplier who lives between the station and where my daughter was, and a craving was conceived in me.

The Hijacking

I followed through on my promise to go to Nelson House, hoping my heart would get back into recovery mode, but by the time I got to Stroud I knew exactly what I was going to do. I had manipulatively primed Sue in Stockport for my return and she was ready to have this 'new' Colin back, all that remained now was the quite simple task of getting myself thrown out of treatment.

I got a taxi from the station to Nelson House, and I knocked at the front door where a young guy appeared wearing between twenty to thirty studs in different parts of his face and sporting a Mohican hairstyle. I can remember thinking from behind a painted smile, 'Oh wonderful, a zoo'.

I was judging people before they had spoken a word to me because of the way they looked and I knew that it would only be a matter of time before I got into a fight. At night I was lying awake listening to love songs on the radio, and dedicating the really romantic ones to an imaginary girlfriend. I knew all the words of all the love songs but had no one to sing them to. I stayed one week, and totally rejected anything anyone said to me in-group.

People were trying to love me, but I was set on getting them to reject me and I was trapped in the 'Oh that might be alright for you' syndrome, sitting in arrogant judgement on everyone. I had failed to see that the craving I had stirred in myself a week earlier was now dominating my attitude toward recovery. I was given good sound advice and I just threw it out without consideration. The impending judgement on August 1st meant nothing to me either by this time and after one week I sabotaged a group session with talk of extreme violence and cruelty to the point of causing people to get up and walk out of group. I then left and accused them of rejecting me; grabbing my pre-packed bag of clothes I walked out.

Less than 200 yards from that home of rehabilitation there was an entrance to an industrial estate and as I approached it I had to stop to allow a truck out. As the passenger door got level with me I opened it and jumped in. I said to the very startled driver, 'drop me off near the motorway mate'. Waving his arms in the air and slamming on his breaks he gestured for me to get out of his truck and said, 'I'm not going near the motorway'. I looked him right in the eye and spoke through tear filled eyes and clenched teeth; I kind of growled very slowly, 'take me to the ##*#**# motorway'. The poor guy went white and just said 'alright, calm down, I can go that way'.

The rest of that journey is a blur to me, but as soon as I got back into Stockport, I just walked back into Sue's life, unpacked my bag, and the very next day I went back to injecting heroin. I went from Mr. Recovery to full-blown addictive attitude in the blink of an eye. Within two days, and with just over a month to go before judgment, I was injecting heroin and amphetamines and breaking into houses in broad daylight.

Now my thinking was, 'I've just been in one of the best addiction clinics in Europe, and it has not worked for me'. I then believed that my addiction would be the death of me.

I somehow made it through the month before court without getting nicked again and during a burglary I found an old man in an unconscious state in his bathroom. He was lying face up and just by instinct I checked for a pulse and spun him over onto his belly. He made a very dim groaning noise so I knew he was alive. I wanted to help him but I needed a hit, so I took his wallet and called the police, giving them his details, before spending his money on heroin and using his credit card to get myself some new training shoes for the jail.

Once again I made the front page of the Manchester Evening News:

'BURGLAR WITH HEART SAVES MAN'S LIFE'

Having been in treatment and managed to paint a very hopeful picture for everyone around me, I had won the favour of my dad again. However, just before my Crown Court date, dad came to visit me. On his arrival I was in the bathroom injecting sleeping pills following a night on amphetamines. I'd been high for three days and needed sleep. I had just injected seven sleeping pills and then heard Sue calling me to tell me my dad was there. I quickly stashed my drug paraphernalia and skipped down the stairs two at a time, thinking I could manage to influence the sleeping pills. Just as I saw my dad, I collapsed at his feet and it looked like I was going to die, I was rushed to hospital once again. I woke up in intensive care wired to that very familiar sounding heart monitor, surrounded by several medics, with a drip in my arm and my hand and both my dad and I stared into what looked like hopelessness.

Dad's heart was shattered, again.

More Prison

August 1st 1992. Judge Bracewell sat in her cloak and funny wig with her glasses perched on the end of her nose. She had good reason to look puzzled. The probation reports on me could not be traced and I spoke up without invitation and said 'there are no reports, ma'am; I did not report to the probation office; I did the treatment thing but I've relapsed and I'm back on drugs'.

'You will go to prison for 30 months'.

I went to the cells at Manchester Crown Court and it was just like the last six months had been a crazy dream. I lay back down on one of the benches, folded my arms over my eyes, crossed my feet, and began once again, to think prison. The pain of prison was immense, but it was less than the pain that I was causing within the hearts of my family as long as I was outside and on drugs.

The faces of all the people at the clinic kept me company to begin with, but they soon started haunting me. Now I was back in among the animals. I smoked a weed that night with a guy who could see the state I was in but the pot did nothing for me. It slowed my mind down, but it could not reach the emotional torment and sense of failure that I had within me. In my heart I resolved to end my life at the first available opportunity.

Suicide Time

Because the main prison at Strangeways was still being renovated, Manchester prisoners were sent all over the country to serve time. My second night of the 30 months was spent in Nottingham police station where I silently planned my suicide. A guy doing a lot of laughing on the wing walked past my cell and passed a comment about heroin addicts which I took personally. I was a dead man walking and had nothing to lose so when the guy went into the loo I just burst in on him and beat him up as he sat there, leaving him not knowing what day it was. I then returned to my cell and sat there trembling with fear and rage.

Once the door was locked for the night, none of it would matter. I considered writing notes to my dad and Alan and Linda, but believed they had no interest. I thought of writing a letter to my little Hayley, but I could not think of anything of any value to put in it.

I therefore found myself at life's end, totally alone and so convinced that there was no other way out. The misery felt strangely peaceful as I counted down my 'lasts'. The last cup of tea; the last head count; the last door slamming; the last sliding spy-hole cover; the last bolt.

I tore a strip of sheet off my bedding and sat staring at it for a while and I knew I was going to make front-page news again. As the place fell silent, I sat on my bed with the sheet in my hand and weighed up the pros and cons of opting out against trying again. I weighed less that 50 kilograms as opposed to my normal 75, I had empty sunken eyes with the darkest of rings around them, I had track marks from injecting, a string of broken relationships and over 10, 000 shattered dreams and broken promises. And it was then, right at that moment in time that I believed that this was as good as it was ever going to be for me, and I decided 'now' – and with that I put one end of the sheet between my teeth and wrapped the rest of it tightly around my throat and quickly got under the sheets and blankets of my bed, fully clothed.

I started to slowly slip away and I knew I was slipping away. It got to a point where I could not hear anything and I did not know if I was breathing or not, I felt like I was almost floating. I remember thinking my face was going to explode and the madness was added to by the sight of dots or tiny psychedelic bubbles floating around inside my eyes, as if I was looking into a weird kaleidoscope. It was then when I knew that I was going to die very soon, but it no longer felt like I was going to die, it felt as if I knew that my life was about to leave the dying shell, the prison and the misery, and an immense sense of self-pity came over me. I then experienced a word. I'm not sure if I saw the word, or heard the word or if I had thought the word because it just sort of appeared within my mind's eye. One word simply overwhelmed me, the word GOD.

A bolt of fear shot through me. I somehow managed to roll off my bed and jump up and remove the sheet with a deep sense of panic. My thoughts were, 'I'm not ready to face God, I am simply not ready to face God' and all suicidal thoughts were abandoned from that time on, even though I slipped into an ever deepening sense of depression.

Most people around me had come to think that 50 to 55 kilograms was a normal weight for me because of the amount of drugs. Whenever I went to prison the kilograms would pile back on as I would eat and eat and I would shoot back up to 75 kilogram. This time, my weight stayed down at 50 kilograms, and this time I knew that it was stress and depression related. I could not eat properly and my sleep was down to one or two hours a night at best.

The next few days in Nottingham were a personal hell for me, and then I received a letter from Sue. I opened it with a sense of dread, knowing I could not pretend anymore and I could not start the promises again. While I knew that I would be unable to love without the will to live, and despite the fact that I just wanted to be left alone and be forgotten, on opening the letter, I sank to a new low: she said 'Colin it is over, I am not going to visit or write, don't reply'. Her words were in line with my thinking, but it still felt like another kick in the soul, and this time I knew I was alone.

My appearance said more than I could and seeing my desperation, two guys gave me the Valium that they were getting from the police doctor. Now for a con to give drugs away is a rarity, but two guys saw my state and it even struck chords of compassion in them.

Compassion of Convicts

The next day the guys on the wing tried to comfort me with talk about parole and of how, if I got parole, I would be out in March. These lads really took an interest in my condition. I tried to apologize to the guy whom I'd attacked in the bathroom and he just laughed it off and we shook hands.

The guys on the wing did everything they could to help me out of the valley of death into which I had fallen encouraging me to focus on getting parole. I tried to but found myself slowly growing in confusion about the idea of parole. I did not want to live, but I did not want to die; I did not want to be in prison, but I did not want to be released; I did not want to be in a relationship with Sue but took umbrage when she rejected me. I felt as if I was at the very bottom of humanity with no desire for direction to speak of.

I was moved from Nottingham up to the North East of England, to a prison called Acklington. I was the only guy in there from Manchester. I hustled for cannabis every night and always managed to get some. One of the local gangsters challenged me one day about why I was in Acklington, suggesting that I was child molester or something because I was so far away from Manchester. Rumors like that have got to be extinguished straight away or a person could find himself seriously injured. Ten or twelve of the main gangsters would congregate every night in the cell of the one who challenged me, so when I heard what had been said I went to the cell. I gently knocked on the door and quickly jumped in and closed the door behind me without locking it. I was face to face with approximately ten pot-smoking gangsters in their own fog bank of cannabis. The main guy ignorantly said 'what?' I said to them, 'you lot are in here smoking weed while I'm out there with loads of other guys who have none. I do not get visits so there is no chance of me getting any weed of my own. I can sell for you and at the same time make a bit for myself.' There was an uncomfortable silence for a moment or two until one of them chirped up, 'how do we know you are not a child molester? If you have been sent up from Manchester there must be a reason.' I was waiting for it and wondering who would say it. I simply said, 'There is only one way you can find out whether or not I'm a nonce. If you want I will get my depositions sent from my solicitor and you can read for yourself about my charges. I do not mind doing that, as long you don't mind getting yours sent in for me so that I can check you out, because I don't know what you are really in for; some of you might even be grasses for all I know'. I held the main guy's stare for a long time, until I winked and he smiled and simply shrugged. He started to laugh and he said: 'Manc, you have got some front'. I said 'it's not front—it's a need for weed'.

I came away from that cell with a pocket full of weed for sale throughout the prison and from that point on I became known as 'the Manc', and the locals (Geordies) were coming to me, in their own jail, for drugs. I was one month into my sentence and a whole world away from the lush clinic and everything those guys had taught me. However, in the quiet of the night I would ponder on every face and every hug and every colourful meal, and everything I had lost forced me to sink even deeper into a heavier depression.

I was working out in the gym and playing soccer, but the sadness within me—together with the heavy sense of failure—was slowly all getting mixed into an absolute dread of the future.

The longer this went on, the more drugs I needed and I started to rob the cells of the drug dealers I had befriended which would probably mean getting my fingers broken when they found out, but it was as if

I couldn't stop. By mid-November I was running riot in my attempts to get drugs.

Two detectives from the Greater Manchester Police force came to the prison to interview me regarding unsolved crimes in the Stockport area. This happens to pretty much everyone and includes going through a list of unsolved crimes from police files and then if a prisoner confesses to any of them, that crime is removed from the unsolved shelf boosting statistics, but no charges are made. The crime is written off. These two detectives had travelled almost 300 miles to interview me and I immediately saw an opening and went straight in for the kill. I sat down and said, 'this has been a waste of your time because I'm not even going to look at your files. However, if you come back tomorrow with ten pounds (sterling) worth of tobacco, I will empty your shelves'. They started getting all moral on me, asking me if I expected them to smuggle contraband in one of Her Majesty's Prisons but I just got up and started to walk out saying, 'that's not my problem, that's up to you; if you turn up tomorrow with tobacco, we talk', and I walked off the visit. I went straight back to the wing and visited one of the main dealers who had some amphetamine powder and I bought an eight-ounce deal from him and a two-ounce deal of weed, on the strength of the next day's police visit. I was now in serious debt, and if the police did not turn up my time in that prison was about to get very painful.

One of the drug dealers I was running for was a little guy, who was by no means a gangster; he just happened to be in the position of having a wife who brought him weed every week. I tolerated his bravado to meet my own needs, but I was slowly starting to resent this guy because of the way he spoke to me. The other guys often sat with me and smoked a weed with me, but this little character did actually believe he was better than me.

On the night of my buying the amphetamines, he passed a comment in front of twenty or thirty guys about me having a police visit. I just laughed it off and came back with a sarcasm that left people laughing at him because most of these guys knew me by now and knew I was just an everyday thief. But as the amphetamines took over my mind, I started to imagine what could become of a comment like his, and a horribly dangerous resentment started to stir in me and I resolved that somehow, I was going to get this clown back.

The police turned up the next day and I sat with them for over an hour. They brought me a file to look at within the corresponding dates of my last release from prison, and I started to flick through the burglaries. I was astounded at the number of burglaries I recognized and I went through ticking those I knew, or even suspected, were my responsibility. It worked out that from release from my third sentence until the arrest for this fourth sentence I was responsible for somewhere in the region of 400 crimes in the greater Manchester area. I found myself getting more and more emotional as I went through the list of crimes being accredited to my name. The reality of it all was actually proving quite painful.

One of the detectives said, 'We believed you when you said you would sign the files but we did not expect you to literally clear our shelves, why are you doing this'? My response came from my heart when I said, 'I just want to say sorry to someone'.

I left that visit feeling as if I had done as much as I could at this point to make amends to some of the victims I left in my wake. I got my tobacco and cleared my debt with the amphetamine supplier; all that remained now for me was to get this pseudo-gangster back. Although I was full of bad feelings about myself and my situation, this guy occupied center stage in my thoughtful theatre of revenge.

Solitary Confinement

Christmas was coming and I started to want a move back closer to Manchester, just to be around some familiar faces and maybe see if I could manipulate a visit from Sue for me to see Hayley. I applied for a transfer to Risley or Strangeways, which was flatly refused without consideration and the prison officer laughed at me as he threw me out of his office. I knew exactly how I was going to do it.

It was Thursday lunchtime, 'pay-day', when everyone gets to go to the canteen to spend their wages, the day when drug dealers and runners are at their busiest. I had packed all my personal goods into a pillowcase: my radio, toiletries and letters; I threw the pillowcase over my shoulder and then went to every drug dealer in the prison under the guise of having 'a guy on B Wing who wanted a sorter'. I was well trusted by now, so almost everyone who had weed gave it to me and then I went to the plastic gangster last. The pillowcase over my shoulder was a normal sight for Thursdays because it was also the day we changed towels and underwear, so I looked quite normal. The truth was, everything I owned in the world was in that pillowcase.

I approached the guy who I considered to be 'muscle-mouth' and made it sound as if all my customers wanted his weed. I was going to sting him for everything he had. Sadly, for me, he brought two deals out of his pocket and said, 'this is all I have'. I said I could sell them for him 'right now if you want' and he fell hook line and sinker; and just to twist the knife a little bit I really smiled at him and said, 'I really enjoy working for you'. Oh, the ego just exploded in front of me and he promised me a treat when I brought him his tobacco.

I went to the canteen to purchase my own tobacco, finding myself in possession of a handful of cannabis, three packets of cigarette papers and two ounces of tobacco. Feeling like Richard Branson, I very casually walked across the prison yard, took a slight diversion from the norm, walked straight up to the door of the solitary confinement block and booted it with the sole of my boot before leaning on the bell.

Within seconds two prison officers were at the door expecting some sort of trouble, they found me, a tired and lonely thief, dying behind dark eyes, with my pillowcase of worldly goods thrown over my shoulder, looking for help.

I noticed that there was a governor of some sort standing in the confinement block and I spoke over the officer's shoulder so that he would hear me and I said,

'My life is in danger, these guys are going to kill me.
I need protection'.

They had no choice but to respond and I was ushered in and put straight into a solitary confinement cell and the door was very quickly slammed behind me.

I stood there for a minute or two, listening to the sounds of the mainstream prison through my window and comparing it to the silences of the solitary confinement block outside my door. I erupted with howls of laughter, punching the air and jumping on and off my bed whooping with a twisted form of delight. I bounced up and down on my bed like a six year old and doing a dance that would have looked more fitting in Saturday Night Fever than in a prison cell. I was lost in the euphoria of what I saw to be a successful plan out. I had a pocket full of drugs—enough to last me a week at least and I was confident that I would now be shipped out and back to Manchester by Christmas.

I felt very smug about looking muscle-mouth in the eye before ripping him off and I roared with laughter and raised my middle finger in the direction of the main prison from that solitary confinement cell. With a pocket full of drugs and a new journey to look forward to, life was good.

The next day was Friday so I knew not to expect a ship-out before the weekend as they only happened on Tuesdays, but my sights were set on being in among familiar fools within a week, with many embellishments to my stories of 'ripping a whole Geordie prison off' and 'blackmailing the police for drug money'.

By 2 a.m. I had smoked all the drugs that I had come in with and despite knowing that I was smoking a decent standard of weed, it was not actually having any effect on me. My internal frustrations, failures and fears were impossible to quell. I had a deep and painful remorse continually stirring in me regarding my past. I hated being where I was, and the future was non-existent, and then all of a sudden, I was out of drugs.

Deafening Loneliness

I slept very little on that first night of solitary and the next morning seemed to suddenly appear. My cell opened and I was absolutely stunned by the shock of seeing a Roman Catholic priest standing in my doorway with a prison officer. I immediately said, "What do you want?" thinking a member of my family had died. He began to explain his role in my life as a prisoner in solitary confinement and got as far as telling me that 'God loves me and if ever I needed to talk to him (God) all I had to do was say so and he (the priest) would be the first face I would see the very next morning'. I cut him off at that point by pushing my door closed and telling him: 'Go and play with yourself, mister, you'll be the last person I talk to'.

I felt as if the only way I could talk to God would be as a second class citizen needing someone to speak on my behalf and I would not agree to it.

The door was quickly slammed from the outside and I was suddenly standing with my back to it finding myself inexplicably wanting to cry. I had resolved in my heart not to talk to 'these clowns', while I was in solitary confinement, because (a) they were child molesters and rapists, and (b) if I persisted with an aggressive isolation it would also speed up the ship-out.

I had a little radio for in-house entertainment with a new battery that should last me until I get out of that hellhole, and there were several books in the cell for me to read. I would not use the daily one-hour exercise time, because that meant interaction with the perverts. I tried to make the battery last so that I could have the late night love song station on the radio to torment myself by reminding myself that I had no one to dedicate any of the songs to.

It was in those times that I started to feel something very heavy bearing down on me. It was like a very long, wet, heavy trench coat was being placed on me, but always getting heavier and heavier. I would walk up and down my cell and get a crushing sensation all around me. I had no drugs to sedate me, and no one to talk to, and then the penny dropped: it was the silence and the loneliness that were crushing me. My past was continuously attacking me with memories both good and bad. I had the faces of the most recent circle of friends from the clinic flashing through my mind, quickly followed by names and faces of guys I had bonded with who were all now dead from drugs. I started making a list one day of the names of the people I had known that were now dead from addiction. I abandoned it after thirty minutes or so because I was afraid of forgetting someone. I knew many of these guys from before their addictions had progressed to a state of degradation and it haunted me to know that this was where I was heading. It was the thought of no one turning up for my funeral that ate away at me the most. Thoughts and pains around my mum resurfaced and seemed to twist what felt like an emotional knife in my heart. I had not passed one weekend of solitary yet.

Tuesday came and went and there was not even the mention of me being shipped out. By Thursday I was longing for someone to talk to. I was bursting with nervous energy and started to run up and down my cell, on the bed, off the bed, kicking the door and yelling all kinds of obscenities at the world. Whenever a screw came to the door I would stand against the door, panting and sweating and totally enjoying his interaction with me. I would get called all kinds of names by the screw, but just laugh them off with enjoyment at being recognised as existing. I would then swing from this crazy euphoric high to sitting on my bed with a pillow pressed up against my face in an effort to keep the sobbing noises down to a minimum.

After one week of what felt like total solitude, I took up the offer of going out into the 18-feet square exercise yard with the two other prisoners. One of them was obviously missing a slate or two and unable to hold a two-way conversation. The other was a bald headed guy who looked quite normal through eyes starved of people, and I got alongside him. We walked in this stupid circle for a full hour and both of us talked the whole time. We spoke over each other. He was having one conversation about his life and I was having another about mine. Loneliness does the strangest things to a man's mind. Toward the end of my self-centered hour, I managed to get a response from him when I asked how long he had been in solitary. He looked at me through unnaturally grey eyes, the same colour as his skin, and said, "14 years, on and off". I was dumbstruck. One week had nearly crushed me, and this guy had made a life out of it. It turned out he could never settle in mainstream prison because he was a baby killer. That night I sat staring at the wall for hours and I had to concede that this guy had, from time to time, seemed very normal to me. I actually thought to myself that there was very little difference between him and me, and I began to see that this individual's circumstances had twisted and crushed and moulded him into what he had become, and it was only a matter of 'pot-luck' that it was he and not I; and that being the case, what on earth was I becoming? I was bad enough when I came to prison—where the hell was I going next? Especially having now sunk to my current depth of self-hatred?

The future went from black to blacker still. My parole date was three months away, and my full-term release date was fifteen months away. The thought of release scared me, but it was from the possibility of parole that I got my only sense of hope. Christmas seemed to gallop toward me, and I asked if I could have a phone call on the grounds of not having had a visit. I had started to accumulate phone cards from my first week in solitary with a view to buying weed with them as soon as I joined mainstream jail again, and offered to surrender them for a chat to my daughter on Christmas day. I was given the phone call and allowed to keep my cards. Hayley and I simply said we loved each other over and over again, and that night I slept very soundly. I had no promises to make her, because I really did not know if I was going to live through this sentence. The New Year crept in very quietly for me although I was lying awake listening to the main prison erupting in whistles and howls as the midnight minutes passed. 1993. Would I see it through?

Shortly into the New Year my cell opened and one of the staff looked into my cell and said, 'Sorry son, your parole application has been turned down', and he closed the door very quietly. I fell onto my bed and released a huge sigh of relief. I felt a huge burden lift from me, and I relaxed for the first time in months. I could actually see the insanity of my wanting to stay in prison, but that was just the way it was for me. My past was too painful to look at. My present was a constant struggle for survival. My future was non-existent. I did not want to live. I did not want to die. I hated prison. I feared release. You work it out.

Mainstream Prison

My transfer came not long after my parole refusal and I was slipped back into mainstream prison population. I wanted to talk to everyone I met. My phone cards lasted me two days. I used one to call Hayley and the other six went on weed. Before I left solitary I signed the wall. It is a prison thing. I wrote my name, where I was from, what I was in for and the jails I had been in. I then noticed that I had been in eleven different prisons in my relatively short prison career. I felt a deep sense of sadness about my miserable journey so far, not knowing that it was about to get much worse. I had had a lot of thinking time in solitary and could see quite clearly that I had to change my circle of friends, because every one of my current friends was drug-involved. I felt inwardly sure that if I could just get a new start somewhere away from the madding crowd, I could make a go of it in life drug free.

The fact that while I was having these thoughts I was saving phone cards for a weed as soon as I got back into mainstream prison, fell victim to a very selective amnesia that I regularly used. I had progressed not only to making the right noises to impress other people, but I also made them to impress myself too. I actually believed all my intentions would dictate my behaviour. I knew there was a prison on the very

South coast of England, and fantasised that this could be where no one would know me and I could escape the trap of reputation and the pull toward the drug culture, from which I was an outcast.

I started heading back toward the North-West England prisons, stopping off at several places like HMP Armley in Leeds and Walton in Liverpool and finally ending up in Wymott near Preston. Arriving at Wymott created a new pit to my emotional and spiritual valley. I went to a new low at this point. My dad visited me and asked me to release my part of the ownership of the house we jointly owned to my step mum. Dad and I had purchased the house while I was still in the army, for my future. When dad and Maureen announced that they were going to get married several years earlier, I said to Alan "she will get the house from me". My robbing them gave her all the ammunition she needed and now they wanted to sell and to move to Portland in Dorset. I felt an immense sense of guilt and loneliness about them selling that house. I knew that I had spoiled it for them as a home by robbing them.

As I signed the deed over to them, I tried to catch my dad's eye to maybe offer some sort of apology, but he avoided me. I just scribbled on the forms. It meant nothing to me anyway; I just hated the fact that it was her influence behind it all. I was extremely resentful toward Maureen and made no secret of it to the rest of my family. But then I realised that I could capitalise on my dad living in Dorset if I played my cards right. If I keep writing to him at his Portland address, as if everything was sweet between us, I could apply for a transfer to that area of the country on the grounds of place of residency on release.

WYMOTT stands for: Where You Must Obey The Tannoy. There is a marked absence of prison staff in Wymott because prisoners cannot escape the Tannoy system and are called for if and when needed. This pretty much meant that the prisoners ran the prison as they wanted. I witnessed several vicious beatings in the internal drug wars of Wymott. One could visit a guy in his cell before supper and all would be well. On return after supper he would be lying there unable to move because rival gang members reaping revenge for some drug-related or woman-related issue had smashed his knees and ankles. There was no telling who would be next. I was very nervous in Wymott because I had been in solitary, and many prisoners often put two and two together and come up with three. If these characters find out I've been down the block, someone will arrive at me being either a nonce or a police informer, and I could be next. Wymott was a mix of mainly Manchester and Liverpool prisoners and there has always been a vicious competitiveness between these two cultures. I suppose it is because of the two cities holding four of the main soccer clubs in the English premier league; but it spreads into prison politics too.

I was in with eight or nine guys from our area of Stockport and we were pretty much left alone and respected. We had a serious thug in our crew who was one of the most feared bullies ever to come out of Stockport. This guy fell just short of a professional boxing career because he failed to cope with guys actually hitting him back, and so he transferred his 'skill' onto the streets where most of us were 15 or 20 kilos underweight. He became known for his jaw-breaking punch and was quoted as saying 'I am going to knock everyone with a reputation clean out'. He was training in his garden one afternoon and I was holding the medicine ball for him to work out on. The guy was big, strong and fast and following one of his training sessions he flexed himself in front of me and then said exactly what was in my mind: "All this (muscle) would not stop a bullet would it Col" and he faked being shot. He is now buried in Stockport cemetery with the Epitaph "At Peace in God's Kingdom" on his headstone because some young guy drew up alongside him at some traffic lights one day in Stockport and blew the side of his head off with both barrels.

Stabbing the Bully

A similar type character came onto the scene from among the Liverpool contingent in Wymott shortly after our bully had been released. This guy was nineteen or twenty years old, 6 feet 2 inches tall, he had the body of a world-class athlete and the speed of a professional fighter. He was frightening even to look at, and he was on a rampage of taking drugs off people by force. No one could stop him. I had only been at Wymott approximately three weeks and was still in the process of settling in and one night I went to the cell where our little gang met to smoke together. As I walked in, someone said to me, "Colin, you could take this guy out if you put your mind to it". I knew who they were talking about, and without thought, in the heat of the moment, I agreed with them. The truth was that I was 15 kilos underweight and even the thought of this guy had kept me awake more than once. But what came out of my mouth was the exact opposite of the truth. I simply said, "I'm going to", and in a split second of hot air, I committed myself to a mission impossible, one from which these guys would not let me back down.

I went back to my cell that night and wondered why the hell I had said it.

The next day I knew exactly what I was going to do. I was doing a welding course at that time and I saw this guy most mornings. I gradually started going out of my way to let on to him with the jail style of respect every time I passed him. He, obviously desperate for friends, returned my greetings with an equal amount of this prison counterfeit admiration. I knew I had him and I put a plan into motion. I told no one what I was doing, but he slowly became an obsession for me. I took a piece of metal from one side of the welding shop and another piece from the other, and I welded them together in my secluded welding booth. I then sharpened one end until it was extremely sharp. I hid the 6-inch blade in another guy's cell without him knowing, and went about my day like everything was normal. Eventually I was openly greeting this guy and had even approached him for weed on a few occasions. After a few weeks I knew I had him. I got the blade to my cell, and took it to work with me the next day. My plan was to get up alongside the guy that evening when the workshops had finished and everyone was out and about, and I was going to get him behind him on what was known as the M1 – a long and busy stretch of passageway. I was going to ram my blade in behind his knee and yank it up to the buttock, making sure he would not be able to chase me, while simultaneously ensuring that if he died it would not be murder because of the place of entry, and ensuring he would never return to the mainstream prison population. Only I knew. I had the blade up my sleeve, knowing that I had him the next time I saw him. I actually felt very calm, similar to the way I had felt about my suicide before God had interrupted. As I was looking for him, there was a skirmish on one of the wings and bells started to ring. We were all returned to cells and when the storm passed there was a buzz all over the prison. Two guys from Wales had jumped my target and almost put him on a life support machine in the prison hospital.

I found it difficult to walk back to my cell because of my trembling. I felt physically sick with the release of tension and as I sat in my cell, I was cold with anger at myself. I was going to stab this guy, 'for them'. I was going to end up with a possible 15-year sentence, 'for them'. It was all 'for them'—for the approval of the crowd.

The next day I went into the wing office and I asked for a transfer. I had to get away from this shit-pit but the screw just laughed and said 'a transfer to where?' I said 'The Verne'. This was the jail on the South coast of England. The screw actually laughed at me, he said, 'Son, we would all like to go to The Verne, but Dorset prison service and county council will not take a heroin addict from Manchester to be released into their community, especially two days before Christmas'. Everything he said made sense, but as he finished talking I said, 'Am I allowed to apply?' He said, 'Oh, you can apply.' I said, 'I want to apply'.

I made the application and stayed off work that day to have the second interview with the governor about the request. I was called into the governor's office and asked to make my case known. I was asked 'why The Verne?' I looked straight at the governor and said to him, "Sir, your prison is full of heroin. I am a heroin addict and I am not changing. I have to get as far away from this part of the country as I possibly can and am trying to build a new relationship with my dad. I have only just starting writing to him again in recent weeks; I write to him regularly now and would like to go and live with him when I get out. I am doing everything in here that I have been doing outside for the past seventeen years and it is killing me from the inside. Sir, when this prison goes up in flames I want nothing to do with it or the people involved.'

I welled up with tears at this point because of the truth within my fabrication, I really wanted out of this lifestyle. The room went very quiet so I said, 'I know in my heart, sir, that if you could see the turmoil in me, you would take the hat of officialdom off and the gentleman in you would give me this break and you would let me go'. He sat quietly for the best part of a minute. I simply walked out before he responded. I could not quite fathom why I had mentioned the prison going up in flames, but giving it some thought afterwards, realized it could not be ruled out. Wymott was a pressure cooker always on the boil.

I knew from experience that a prison transfer request takes between eight and twelve weeks. The application is studied and considered by the sending prison, including checking where my letters have been addressed, and then the application considered by the requested prison; then the forms are sent to the Home Office in London where they join a pile waiting to be considered before they are stamped 'yes' or 'no'. Then they are returned to the sending prison.

I came out of the governor's office that day and I just knew in my heart that I was going to The Verne. As I returned to the wing, the laughing screw was standing in his office doorway, but now it was me doing the laughing. I said, 'ask me who is going to The Verne', but he wouldn't ask. I did wonder what was going through my dad's mind as he received all my letters of reconciliation, but knowing him, I guessed he would know that I was up to something.

I went into work for the remainder of the morning; I was also on afternoon education classes at this time where I took an English exam for fun. I really enjoyed using my brain and I actually got a distinction for one exam.

As I returned to the wing that same day for lunch, two hours after my governor's meeting, the governor called me into his office. He sat me down and simply said, "your name is on the list for transfer to The Verne for next Thursday. Do not ask me how or why, but your name was already on this list for the bus to transfer to HMP The Verne" and he gestured me out of his office.

I went back to my cell that day very slowly. I spoke to no one. I simply strolled back to my cell and as I was sitting on my bed, I knew— with a deep and really weird sense of assurance—that a miracle had occurred in my life. My mind very nearly drifted toward God again, but that was ridiculous and I snapped myself out of it, but not before thinking that I would have actually gotten the transfer, even without the manipulative mail games – maybe honesty could work.

We were in May of 1993 now; the summer was just around the corner, and one week later I would be climbing onto a nice clean southbound minibus. I had a whole new feeling come over me from that point: hope. I somehow knew that something unnatural or supernatural had happened for me the day I cried out over my hopeless condition and desire to change in the governor's office. Although I had no clue what was going to happen next, I knew one thing—life was drifting from black to grey. It was almost starting to look better.

The journey to Dorset was a long one and we stopped off at five or six other prisons before we got to Winchester for a final stop before The Verne. I had smoked a weed on the way down with some guys, but felt a sense of shame about it. My heart's cry had been 'I am not changing', and here I was being given a chance and I still wasn't changing. I had a single cell for my brief stop at Winchester, and all through that night I was preparing myself for my arrival at The Verne. I must avoid the drug culture; maybe get involved in Church and the gym; do education classes; either find clean friends or have no friends. I was deeply excited because I felt inwardly different this time. I knew I could do this. I'd been in good rehabs and Europe's finest clinics—now it was up to me. I had seven months left to serve, and with this final glimpse of hope, all may not be lost.

On the bus to The Verne the next day, I was handcuffed to a guy who was returning there. He was a lifer and had been to London on accumulated visits. As we got going, for some weird reason I asked him, "What is the Christian fellowship like at The Verne?" He smiled and said, "On fire". I started to relax.

Fear of Release

Travelling to Portland, the island sticking out from Weymouth in Dorset on which The Verne is located, I was feeling inwardly sad because of my memories. As a family, before all the madness started, we used to come to Weymouth for our annual holiday. Mum, Dad, Alan, Linda and myself; and now here I was cuffed to a lifer, heading for my 26th prison, seventeen years into an unstoppable intravenous heroin and amphetamine addiction.

Reception at The Verne held one officer and three prisoners who did all the booking in and kit-issue. The prison officer spoke with a lovely soft Dorset accent, and his attitude was much softer than the Northern screws. He spoke to me and offered suggestions, where the Northerners spoke at me and barked orders. One of the cons asked me where I had come from and when I told him Wymott, he asked if I was one of the rioters? I asked him what he meant and he explained how it was all over the news that Wymott had exploded and had been burning for the last three days. I was very close to saying 'thank God', but that was ridiculous.

When the prison officer had finished reading all the in-house rules to me, he asked me, 'do you prefer a single cell'. I was mind-blown, but the best was yet to come. I asked for a single cell and was given the wing and cell number written on a piece of paper, and a key! I thought I was on Candid Camera. We had our own keys! The door into the main prison was then opened and the officer said, 'go and find your cell, get unpacked and settled in, then tomorrow go and find yourself a job or a training course'. I thought I was being set up but I wasn't—I had entered a whole new world.

The Verne is a training prison and offers training in different areas and skills. I walked around the jail, unchallenged, until I found my cell. The windows did not have bars, guys had curtains up and plants on the window sills; and not only was the place clean, but we could see the sea from the wing. I found my cell and started to move in. The rest of the wing was at work, so I started cleaning out the cell from the last guy. As I emptied the drawers I found an abandoned cannabis pipe hidden right at the back of one of the draws and without thinking I looked through the barrel of the pipe and found it was thick with oil. Within minutes I had snapped a length of thread from my bed cover, tied three cigarette papers to one end, passed the other end through the pipe, warmed the barrel of the pipe for a few seconds and then pulled the papers through. What came out of the other end were three cannabis oil saturated cigarette papers, and I proceeded to roll a joint.

Within five minutes of being in my new cell, with my new plan of a new life and of avoiding the drug culture because it kept leading me astray, I was smoking a joint strong enough to knock over a donkey. When the rest of the guys came back to the wing for their lunch, they were met by a fogbank of cannabis coming out of my cell, and the drug culture gravitated toward me.

The insights and information about addiction during my time at the clinic started to resurface in me at this point and although I had failed to stay clean, I started to use clinic terminology among the guys who were coming to my cell to either sell or find weed. I started to talk about 'dealing with the feelings', 'considering the consequences of drugs' and 'taking responsibility for past actions and reactions'. But all the time, I was ensuring that I had a little sorter for bedtime. I got myself onto a painting and decorating course and tried to occupy my mind in that way, but each day I would have to walk past the main gate just as that day's discharges were leaving the prison, and the fear of release started to stir within me.

I had gravitated toward a certain table in the dining room where a guy from Scotland used to sit on his own. It turned out that this guy, Steve from Motherwell, was a regular Churchgoer in the jail. Steve liked a weed and from time to time I would go to his cell and have a smoke with him. Invariably the conversation would drift toward the Bible and I would question him from behind a fogbank of weed, and analyze the answers with arrogance and cynicism.

Haunted by the Holy Ghost

On the 17th June 1993 however I woke up at the normal time of 7:30 am, but something was different. I could not pin down what it was, but something was different. I was trying to get up and get dressed, but my mind was continuously attracted to the name of Jesus. I could not think of anything else other than the name of Jesus. I did get up and get dressed, I shaved and cleaned my teeth, but all the time I had the name of Jesus going through my mind. I went down for breakfast and held conversations with people but all the time, going on in my background, I could hear the name of Jesus in a very quiet but never drowned out whisper, Jesus Jesus Jesus Jesus, on and on, over and over. I went to my painting and decorating with it: Jesus Jesus Jesus Jesus. The Golden Hour was on Radio 1 for all of us to listen to as we decorated our allocated rooms, and the daily norm was for us to sing along and guess what the year was. Most of us identified tunes by means of what jail we were in when it had come out, but this day for me was different. Jesus Jesus Jesus Jesus. By lunchtime I was almost used to it and was quietly enjoying something no one else had experienced. It was weird to my mind, but kind of soothing to my soul.

I took my lunch to my cell, and after eating I went for a walk to Steve's cell. I was in no way expecting him to give me an answer, because it did not take a genius to work out that this was something beyond the standard man's understanding. However, I approached Steve with it. I explained everything to him from the moment I had woken knowing something to be different. Steve had a beautiful glow about him as he looked at me that day, and as he did so, he seemed to speak right into the very soul of me when he said, "Colin, Jesus is calling you".

Steve's answer cut right through me and from somewhere within my empty existence, I just knew he was right. Just like I had known that a miracle had taken place, and just like I had known that I was going to The Verne, and just like I had known Wymott was going to go up in smoke—beyond my human mind, I knew Jesus was calling me.

I had grown up with a dad who ruled by the tone of his voice, and felt his wrath many times. I had been up before a couple of Military Court Martials in front of the most frightening of disciplinarians and felt their wrath. I'd been bullied by the toughest military gym instructors that the British Army had to offer, and very nearly been broken within their torture. I'd seen the whites of the eyes of IRA terrorists in Belfast, and virtually smelled the stale ale on their breath as they smiled at the idea of my murder. I'd broken into gangsters' houses, even stood at the side of their beds while they slept, and then walked away with their gold. I'd robbed a police station whilst the police were attending a traffic accident outside their station. I'd gone on one-man missions in jail that no one in their right mind would even consider. I'd been shot at, shouted at, and shit on by the best in the business. Fear actually energised me, but nothing struck fear into my soul like the idea of Jesus Christ inclining His attentions in my direction and actually 'calling' me.

This brought home to me the fact that simply by virtue of my attitude and lifestyle, I was His enemy. I agreed with everything I had heard about Him and the things He had said in the Bible, and I sympathised with how He was crucified and all that stuff, but I had absolutely no desire at all in me to get personal with Him. I was comfy with Him at arm's length, or in the manger at Christmas, but no more. Steve said to me, 'There is a baptism in the chapel tonight, are you coming'? I walked off shaking my head, actually having to hold the wall in order to walk in a straight line. I was steadfast in how I was definitely not going to the chapel that night. In fact, it was Thursday and I was the organiser of the Narcotics Anonymous group, so the chapel was a no-no!

The rest of that afternoon is a blank to me. I cannot recall whether or not the Jesus Jesus Jesus thing went on into the afternoon. However, what did happen that evening will never leave me. I left my cell with a box of literature for the N.A. Group, with the view to setting up for the meeting. Now what happened to that box is a mystery to me, I can only imagine that I gave it to someone to stand in for me, but I do not remember. As clear as crystal, though, I do remember walking toward the chapel that night, and seeing Christian prisoners from each corner of the jail walking to that house of God in two's and three's. It was one of the most beautiful sights I had ever seen. It was so peaceful. I had actually reached a point of my life where I cared very little what was about to happen, because the glimmer of hope of which I had caught a glimpse in recent months was slowly fading with every joint I smoked. I walked into that chapel that night a desperate soul in need.

Conversion to Christ

As I entered the chapel, I was shocked to see a bright blue industrial rubbish bin sitting in the corner of the room. It was in the wrong place. It was usually reserved for the backs of factories or shops, and wheeled out on refuse collection day. It dominated my view as I walked into that chapel and I went and sat next to it out of curiosity. I lost all interest when I noticed it was full of water; obviously it was not meant for me to know. I sat down and just tried to blend in. Steve was in there with a big daft smile on his beautifully glowing face and I purposely avoided his gaze. Off to my right, there were between twelve and fourteen prisoners, including the lifer I was cuffed to on the way in.

It turned out that we were waiting for the Prison Christian Fellowship to arrive with guitars and tambourines and hopefully some biscuits. There was an uncertain silence in the place until a huge black guy stood and started to talk. I made an instant judgement on this guy as being 'ugly'. He had nothing going for him in my eyes—he was black and he was ugly. However, when he started to speak, I had to check it was his voice. His voice sounded really comforting, almost silky. I was astounded. He said, "We are waiting for the Christians to arrive and Jesus Himself is here". He then started to sing the most wonderful song. It went from wonderful to heavenly when the rest of the guys stood up with him and joined in perfect harmony. They were singing 'Majesty'. It seemed to fill the whole room and was quite tear provoking.

The PCF arrived in the midst of the singing and initially crept in to listen to the guys singing, but soon got caught up in it themselves. I suddenly became an observer. Steve was as caught up in this rapturous worship as everyone else, but I stood watching, feeling left out and left behind. As the worship grew in volume and adoration, I grew more and more distant from the whole evening.

Twenty minutes or so into the evening a guy, who turned out to be the preacher, stood up and went to the front to deliver a message. He started to talk and read from the Bible, and what he said gave me reason to think that Steve had spoken to him about me, because everything he said pointed to me. I sat there feeling like everyone knew he was talking about me and I tried to catch Steve's eye, because I wanted to tell him he was out of order talking to these people behind my back. Steve knew all about my failed attempts at cleaning up and what I addressed as 'the clinic failure' and it was more than obvious that the whole night was pointing at me.

Even the preacher was in on it and he read Romans 7:15 ff:

'I do not understand what I do,
for what I want to do, I do not do; what I hate, I do'.

Straight away I thought 'Oh, very funny' and I tried to catch Steve's eye. It went on:

> 'I know that nothing good dwells within me,
> that is in my sinful nature, for I have the desire to do right,
> but I cannot carry it out'.

A lot of it went over my head, but a lot of it hit me in the very depth of me, and then when he said:

> 'Who can set me free from this body of death?'

I had to concede that not only was he speaking the language of my heart, it also slowly dawned on me that this had been written by some guy in the Bible, 2000 years ago, 2000 miles away, with the exact same problems as me. I was stunned by the truth, and the truth seemed to ask me, "Colin, who is going to rescue you from your body of death"?

From a room in the corner of the chapel, a guy from Jamaica was brought out with a bathrobe on and he was walked toward me. As he got closer, several Christians got up and followed him over to my corner. They were all smiling and hugging this guy, and he then removed the bathrobe. He was wearing a tee shirt and shorts, and he climbed into the bin right next to me and knelt down. Christians crowded into the corner, around the bin and me, and they started to pray for him. After a short time, the preacher guy said to everyone in the room:

> "Our brother Earl has lived a life displeasing to both God
> and man. But tonight Earl is openly turning his back on his
> former lifestyle and turning to God for forgiveness in Jesus' name".

He then focused on Earl and asked him these three questions out loud:

Do you believe in your heart that Jesus Christ is The Son of God,
that He was crucified for your sin, died and was buried and
after three days was raised from the dead?

Earl openly confessed this to be his belief and deep within my heart
I said to myself, 'I've always believed that'.

The preacher continued:

Do you confess your sinfulness before God and
before the people here tonight?
And do you now turn to God with your life in repentance
and ask for forgiveness in and through The Name of Jesus Christ?

Earl tearfully nodded his head, and the minister immersed him in
the water 'baptizing him in the name of the Father, and of the Son
and of the Holy Ghost' and the Christians exploded with praise and
applause. It was something deeply moving.

I had no problem with my sinfulness and from deep within me I was
somehow crying 'Jesus is Lord, He took my sin, I am the guilty one
not Him, I need to know this God'.

I knew I had never made a personal invitation or commitment to
Jesus. In fact, my last genuine interaction with God was back on the
school stairs, when I aggressively threw my so called religion in to
the bin.

I was in a stunned silence. The Christians started to disperse back
to their seats, and the preacher went back to his Bible from where he
threw a gauntlet down to me when he asked:

'Is there anyone else in here tonight who feels the need
to receive Jesus into his life as personal Lord and Saviour?'

The question had not completely left the minister's lips and I was
standing up and taking my jeans off. I heard myself saying:

"I do. That is exactly how I feel, I need to know Jesus".

The whole congregation turned to look at me and as they all looked at me, I felt an inner urge to turn it all into a joke and to sit back down. But the truth was I could no longer live my life under the influence of what I thought other people might be thinking of me. I looked at them, and in a moment's clarity of heart, I knew: 'I cannot allow these guys to define me any longer'.

I simply said; "I need to know this Jesus for myself".

My jeans went one way, my shirt went another, and I climbed into this trash can of water and tearfully fell to my knees. I suddenly found myself up to my armpits in water. I looked at that wall directly in front of me and thought to myself; 'If this does not work now, I am dead'. However, after a very short pause I conceded that within my heart, 'actually, I'm already dead'.

Within minutes I was openly confessing my belief that Jesus is The Son of God and that He died on The Cross for me and that God raised Him from the dead. I was openly confessing myself sinful before God and man and openly turning to God with grief in my heart over my sin. I turned to Him for forgiveness and readily confessed my desire for Jesus to be my Lord.

I was then immersed into the waters of baptism.

In the waters, I placed my broken and sin stained heart at the feet of God.

To summarize, I said:

'Lord, there is nothing in me of any value. I come before you tonight not knowing who I am or where I am going. I need you to show me who I am, and I need release from this inner drive toward destruction. If you are willing, and you make me clean, Lord Jesus I will serve you with my whole being for as long as you want me to live and I do not care what that might mean.If you release me, I am yours lock, stock, and barrel. Lord, I know and accept that in truth, you should actually turn your back on me and if you do I have no argument.

But before you do, I want you to know this much, I am truly,
and deeply sorry for the way I have lived my life'.

And that's where I, the junkie, met Jesus—exactly where I had left Him, in the trash can.

As I came up out of that water it was as if a heavy wet trench coat was removed in that instant and I knew, deep within me that I had just been saved.

I was a free man. My addiction ended right at that moment. It was removed.

I simply knew it was over. I knew I was free. I knew in a second that I had been changed from within and I knew without counsel that I would never have to take drugs again and that my life was never going to be the same again. I looked towards a guy standing nearby and I genuinely expected him to say 'I saw that', such was the feeling of release.

I knew that I had been born-again, with a rebirth taking place in my heart, in the very soul of me, and that I had literally been transferred from darkness to light.

Christians wanting to pray for me surrounded me, and to begin with it was quite nice, but I must say that my only desire was to be alone with The Lord.

A little old lady with eyes alight for God took me by the hand that night and whispered in my ear, 'Barnabas, son of encouragement'. Mrs. Irene Long from Weymouth Baptist Church made a special point of bringing me worship tapes and giving me my first Bible, and she was a primary source of wonderful blessings as I started my walk as a new man, in a personal relationship with God.

I somehow removed myself from the chapel that night and made my way back to my cell. I noticed that the light was still on in the education block and that the N.A. group was still running. I went in just as it was ending and made my first confession of Jesus. I apologized to the group for not fulfilling my duty, and then explained that I had just given my heart to Jesus, and would be serving Him from here on in. The guys seemed very pleased for me, but I instantly picked up on how my mention of Jesus actually disturbed them.

Repentance Fruit—Removing Porn

I went to my cell in a bit of a hurry, because I had a job to do. As I left the chapel, I simply knew what I had to do. My cell wall was heavily stained with worldly pictures of women and I had to remove them and get my heart right with God. I suddenly felt embarrassed about the pictures on my wall. I did not look at any of them when I entered my cell. I kept my eyes lowered, and systematically removed each picture, praying for each girl in each photo as I did so. Oh boy, had I changed!

I asked The Lord to forgive me and to touch the girls in the pictures that they too may come to repent and be saved. My whole vocabulary had undergone a radical transformation, and my mind had immediately joined a process of renewal. My innermost desires had changed and I felt a deep and wonderful sense of peace within the very core of me. It was as if a raging storm had been replaced by a clear and still pond.

I sat on my bed that night and simply sat with The Lord. I just sat in the silence, knowing that I was in the presence of The Lord Jesus Christ Himself, and that He had been awakened in my storm and commanded the waters 'be still'. I suddenly saw how He had actually inspired every detail of my life in order to secure my move to the

Dorset prison, in order to get me into that trash can. Even losing ownership of the house which was for me one of the final straws that broke the camel's back, was a divine idea to save me. As long as I had any ownership of that property, I had some measure of control over my life and over other people's lives. It all had to be removed, in order to get me to my knees.

I was free. Jesus had set me free. It was true. That night I got into my bed at approximately 9:45 pm, and I prayed for ten or fifteen minutes and then I went out like a light and slept right through the night to 7:15 am. I woke up and lay very still. I wondered if 'it' had vanished in my sleep, but I was immediately aware of a wonderful bright new day and a song of joy in my heart. The sky looked different now, because I knew the architect; the scream of the seagulls sounded totally different now that I knew their designer. It was so fulfilling to wake up free.

I then realised that I had slept for a full night without interruption. I could not remember ever sleeping right through the night like that, not even as a child; but now I was free. As I washed, I noticed my eyes had changed. I stood staring at myself in the mirror. My eyes had changed in some way—they were different, and there was a very warm smile within them. I bent to wash and I kept popping back up to check my eyes out because they had changed. My entire thought life, as I prepared to go into my decorating course, revolved around Jesus Christ. He had actually thought about me, and knowing me, He still saved me! I was saved and in Christ. I was born again by the Spirit of Christ. His life was and is in me and He was now giving me newness of life and it was a life that no one could take away. I felt different, but I did not feel like a different person. I felt as if I had become the person God had intended me to be, and suddenly I felt a wonderful peace about myself. I was still Colin Garnett, but now I was the true Colin Garnett, born of the spirit of God.

It went on all morning and it was absolutely wonderful. Halfway through my first new day, I prayed to The Lord the most wonderful prayer, 'Lord, should you desire to remove your spirit from me later today, I would not concern myself about it at all. I have met you, I know you are alive, and I know you have paid the punishment for the salvation of my soul in the eternal scheme of things'.

That night I was still free.

On the Sunday afternoon, as most of the prison slept, I crept into the television room and turned the TV on and with the sound down. I was answering an inner compulsion to see the name of Jesus on the television screen. I knew Songs of Praise was on, and I knew they gave subtitles to all their songs. His name caused me to well up with an immense joy. Just the sight of His name on the screen caused me to want to cry. The sight of the singing Christians made me to want to run around the room and punch the air as if I had scored the winning goal in a cup final. I sat there with a celebration beyond description taking place in my heart. I sat panting and breathless, from simply seeing the name of my Saviour Jesus on the telly, and my new family celebrating Him. I belonged, and I knew deep within my heart that I truly belonged, at last and forever.

Guys saw me in the TV room and came in to see what was on, but when they realised what I was watching, they would simply stare at me, and then walk out. Some guys went away and came back with one or two others to see this guy from the drug scene with tear-filled eyes, staring at a silent picture of the Church. I wanted to try and explain about the power and grace of Jesus to save sinners, but I simply did not have the vocabulary to do so. Collectively they started to mock me. But as individuals, 95% of them came to my cell to see what had happened to me. All I could tell them at that point was: "Jesus has set me free". I could not back my statement up with anything academic or any more theological than that; I simply said that which I knew: "Jesus the Son of God had tracked me down to my state of nothingness, in a trash can, and liberated me from my body of death, even while I was still sinning"!

The academics tried to explain it; the cynics tried to trash it; the philosophers patronized me; and the Muslims simply watched with disdain. The prison staff said 'Oh yeah, another parole scam' until they checked my file and saw that my parole had been refused six months ago. I was already free, and every one could see it.

Three days into my new life, I woke once again with something going on in my cell. A song woke me up. It was such a beautiful song, that it caused me to snuggle down into my pillow like a child under the loving stroke of a parent in bed at night. I started to stir from a deep slumber as the song invaded my heart and mind. I am truly inadequate in explaining. I started to think 'what is that wonderful noise, or sound, or song'? I could make no sense of it. It was gloriously simple. Two words, repeated three times. "Sanctify him; sanctify him; sanctify him", and then it evaporated. As it lifted from me, or my cell, or whatever was going on, I sat up to try and grasp it, to try and take ownership of it. As soon as it left, I could not recreate it. It was wonderful, yet gone. I sat still. The wonderful peace within my heart was still there, like a river flowing deep and slow, underneath all the trappings and noisy hostility of prison life, and the impending release, and the following homelessness, a Peace that transcends ALL understanding remained undisturbed by it all.

I started to entertain the word 'sanctify'. Not a word greatly used in my context. I said it to myself over and over, 'sanctify'. I felt like I almost knew what it meant, but just fell short of a tangible explanation. It was no real problem, though, because I had met The Lord Jesus and there I sat on my prison bed, trying to process all that had happened to me, and trying to make sense of this Jesus Christ making Himself known to me, and now trying to piece together why there should be a song in my cell. And in the midst of it all, I had totally lost any and all desire to use drugs.

My whole desire system had been affected by my conversion to Christ. It was not that I had made a new decision to stop taking drugs; I had simply lost the inner urge to find, use, and repeat that destructive cycle. I had not stopped—God had removed the desire. Eventually, when the day started to break, and the birds started to sing to me, I ran down to Steve's cell and stood at the foot of his bed.

I twisted his big toe. One has to be careful doing this sort of thing in prison. One can end up severely beaten or married! Steve sat up with an astonished look in one eye, the other would not quite open, and he thought something was wrong. I asked him, 'what does sanctify mean'? He sort of grunted something. I repeated my question, "what does sanctify mean?" There followed a long silence and then an intake of breath and a beaming smile, and he said, "It means to set apart and purify".

I walked away from Steve's cell that beautiful June morning, and I knew from deep within me that Jesus Christ was on my case and that He had begun the process of cleaning me up for His glory. I did not need anyone to tell me this, and I did not seek out anyone to confirm it. I knew that The Lord was at work in me. I inwardly seized Jesus and felt an enormous eruption of excitement at the potential for rescuing souls from the devil's grasp. I saw the truth that Jesus had been with me right throughout my dark life. He was there every step of the way. Right through the dark and dirty valley of sin and shame, Jesus kept me alive for such a time as this. I sat on my bed and looked at my life as one might look along the Grand Canyon. It was deep, long and frightening. I then looked to Jesus in my heart and said in absolute sincerity, "Lord, I want to go back in, there are people in there dying without knowledge of your wonder".

A prison officer was walking toward me one morning and I simply said to him, "Good morning boss". He stopped and looked at me for a few moments and then in a really friendly tone replied, "Good morning Garnett". I believe he not only saw a difference in my smiling face, he heard a difference in my voice, because I truly desired that he should have a good morning. This was going to take a lot of getting used to, for everyone.

The lifer I was handcuffed to on my way to The Verne stopped me outside the chapel in that first week of my conversion. He and another lifer asked me to approach the chaplain and request a book from him. I was more than willing to agree and I went into the chaplain's office and asked him for the book. He motioned for me to go into his office and as he passed the book to me, he kept hold of it until I looked at him. He then questioned me with what I thought was a cynical tone about my experience that week: 'So what happened to you, then?' As he questioned me, I remembered that he was actually in the service that night and I remember catching his eye as I was being prayed for and it actually flashed through my mind that he did not like what he was seeing. I actually thought he was jealous of me, but I dismissed this thought as being my arrogance.

I left his office feeling saddened and confused. The two lifers did not look at the book; they were more interested in me and then one of the asked me, "What's wrong". My thumb pointed over my shoulder to the chapel and I had to say, "He is". They both then embraced me and said, "You've been converted by the Spirit of God".

They then explained that the chaplain was suspected of being unconverted and the book thing was to test me, and we agreed to take the unconverted chaplain issue to prayer. I saw the chaplain five years later when he visited Bible College and he was alive with Jesus.

One of these lifers took me aside later in the week and spoke gently into my heart. He said, "Listen, brother, you've been grafted into the Bride of Christ. There is going to be a honeymoon period, and then your ministry will begin. Do not rely upon the Church for answers or sustenance, because they will let you down. They will not trust you and they will hurt you. Stay intimate with Jesus Himself".

My heart's response was one of strange excitement. I nervously said, "Satan is imitating the Church, isn't he?" There was no need of a response. There was love for me in his smile, and my love for him almost brought tears to my eyes. Later it transpired that my God-given insight had startled him.

We did not interact again, but his words etched themselves deep into my heart, and I was going to need them in the next few years.

Therapeutic Thuggery

I had visited sixteen prisons on that sentence. The process of prison transfer is a process of degradation. Being stripped and searched where the sun fails to shine, pulled and pushed, talked at like an animal, and shifted around without identity or opinion. It had all reduced me to an internal state of nothingness with no identity and no hope, and yet it all had to be that way for me.

My circumstances crushed me and forced me to the feet of God and He then gave me new life with identity, reason, purpose, hope and glory. Not only could I now look toward my release—I had the inward knowledge that it was not the prison system releasing me—Jesus had set me free. I started to think that if this continues, they are going to be releasing a free man! None of it made sense, yet it all made perfect sense.

My prayer life was a tearful and passionate time. I spent the first two weeks confessing and rejoicing that He had set me free and my internal state became a constant meditation on God: His character, the mercy, the nails, the cross, the blood, the truth, the freedom, the joy, the hope and the peace. My heart simply flicked from one of His attributes to the other. I was holding conversations with guys around me, but the wonders of Jesus never subsided.

It regularly came to mind that I had less than six months to serve and so toward the end of June 1993 I wrote to my dad. I had not heard from any one of my family in over sixteen months, and the sound of their disowning me still rang loudly in my heart. I wrote to my dad and I simply said, "If you could see your way clear to visiting me, I would love to talk to you." I sent him a visiting chit with the letter. Dad was sitting opposite me in the visiting room within three days. It was lovely to see this giant of a man again. We simply sat and stared at each other. I broke the silence with, "Dad, I have become a Christian". He leaned forward to hear me again not trusting his hearing and said, "Sorry, son, I thought you said you'd become a Christian then." I knew it was too much for him because of our

Catholic background so I tried another route. "Dad, I have been born again, and I was baptized." There was a flash of apprehension on his face and he nervously asked, "Have you kept your name?" I felt myself grow in stature as I said; "Dad I am your lad, Garnett through and through, and gratefully proud to be your son and mum's son and Alan and Linda's brother; but now Jesus Christ had saved me and my life belongs to Him".

We both sat back and totally relaxed. We held hands and we got tearful, and then once again just like when he would carry me up to bed he said: 'come on young'un, give me a squeezer', and we stood up and hugged and hugged and hugged.

From that time on dad sent me books, money, letters, tapes; he visited me and each time he did, he held my head and looked deep into my eyes. He regularly did this as his way of seeing and remembering my mum in my brown eyes, but now he was confused with what he saw because he saw Jesus in me.

I had no inclination to live with or even near my dad: as much as we loved each other, he had his new wife and my uncle living with him and I was now chemical free and needing to grow as a Christian.

I grew more and more aware of not having anywhere to live on my release and my prayers were along these lines: "Lord, I know you hold the future. I need you to tell me where you want me on my release". Each morning I got before Him and asked, "Lord, where do you want me?" One morning, I sat before The Lord and gratefully declared, "Lord, if you desire me homeless, I will declare your name among the homeless, and I will gratefully go. In my heart of hearts I offer myself for cardboard city, with relish". I said this prayer with fervour and tears in my eyes as I sat quietly in the early morning time of prayer. I then got up to wash and shave. During my shave, I stared at my eyes and thought of the change I could see and I then thought of the prayer I had just said. I dried my face quickly and sat back on my bed, and in a very childlike manner I simply said, "Lord, if it is alright with you, I would prefer not to go to cardboard city". Heaven smiled back at me.

It was in one of these deep and meaningful quiet times that The Lord made a startling revelation to me, about me. I was seeking His desire for me for when I got out. 'Where do you want me Lord and what do you want me to do?'

After my prayer, I sat quietly, and within my heart I suddenly knew; 'do nothing for two years'. Of course, I dismissed this as totally ridiculous. Two years? I was raring to go now! Then on a visit from dad he asked me what my plans were on my release. I saw he was nervous because I had ripped them all off so many times and he had the fear of me wanting to go and live with him. Their trust was severely damaged and I thought about the question for a moment before telling him, "I am going to write to Nelson House in Stroud, and ask them if they would consider taking me back for me to try again". This answer was like a revelation even to me, but as soon as I had said it, I knew that The Lord would have me return there in humility and make my amends to the people I had hurt, and to try again. I also knew that He wanted me to 'do nothing for two years'. I did not try to explain the two year thing—that was between God and me at that point. Dad took my face in his hands and with tears in his eyes he spoke my favorite three words, 'That's my boy'. In a prison visiting room this sort of thing would have normally embarrassed me, but not now, no more.

I was his boy and I was no longer enslaved by ego. I'd missed this man in a way that words could not describe.

I wrote to Nelson House and applied for re-entry. They sent me a condition that I attend a Therapy Group being run in another prison in Surrey until my release. This style of therapy, similar to the clinic I had been in, was a prerequisite for residence at Nelson House. I then applied for yet another prison transfer. The wing officer looked at my file and the fact that I had been transferred sixteen times already, and he laughed at me. He asked me if I thought I was on a milk round. I smiled back at him, made my application and left his office.

Once again, within five hours, I was standing before a puzzled prison officer who said, "Who do you know?" I was formulating a Gospel message response when he continued, "Your name is on the list to be transferred next week". I went back to my cell and lay on my bed. In my heart I looked to The Lord and had to say, "Lord, just take it easy with the Grace please; slow down a bit; I am not sure I can handle it". Heaven smiled back at me.

In my heart I was also aware that I had been given a wonderful window of Gospel opportunity when the officer said, "Who do you know?" and I missed it. I considered how if, that guy died and went to eternal hell, I would feel as if his blood would be on my hands. The severity of not knowing Jesus dawned clearer and clearer by the day for me, and a burning question haunted me: 'How can I keep this to myself?" My prayer life intensified.

I arrived at HMP Downview, onto The Addicted Prisoners Trust Programme, in late August 1993. I had four months of Group and One-to-One Therapy to negotiate and it was time to make my stand for Jesus. I had been handcuffed to a guy claiming to have a chunk of weed inside him, and 'we' would get stoned as soon as 'we' arrived at Downview. I saw him the next day. He was rolling a joint by the gym and I purposely went and stood with him until he started to smoke to joint and then when he passed the joint over to me I quietly said, "No thanks mate, I don't need it".

Up to this point, since my conversion, I had smoked several joints of weed. I had smoked it, but it did not get me stoned. I had smoked with the circle of guys I was in with at The Verne. In fact, since my conversion, they went out of their way to smoke in my cell. I smoked, but nothing happened to me and then the day before I left The Verne, these guys produced 10 liters of home-brewed booze and a chunk of weed. I sat in with them until they were all stoned and drunk, but I remained stone cold straight and sober, and they all knew it. It was difficult for me to grasp that even smoking weed was over, and it was still strangely difficult for me to say no to these guys who had become my friends and party hosts.

However, once I had moved to Downview and I quietly declined the offer of a weed, the freedom I had been given seemed to intensify. I was set free at another level, and I truly walked away from the drug scene at that point. I was still smoking cigarettes though but it did not bother me because it was not me who had stopped the drug using. The Lord Jesus had set me free. So when He removes the cigarettes, I will stop smoking too. I was, however, able to give half of my weekly tobacco allowance away to strugglers around me. I accepted that there was no point in judging them, because if Jesus does not do a work in them, then I have no right to 'expect better' from anyone. I have no doubt in my heart that Jesus had released me from the nicotine addiction, though, because I no longer enjoyed the taste or the smell of the smoke, my faith was young and I was actually afraid of not smoking. I had always enjoyed a cigarette; it had a calming effect on me. I could not grasp that I no longer needed them.

The desire had been removed, but the courage to change the behaviour pattern needed development.

The Therapy group consisted of approximately ten other guys. In that group I came face to face with heavy gangsters who had fallen prey to heroin. They were aggressive and very confrontational. I was clean from narcotics and I started to accumulate 'clean-time'. I can remember it like it was this morning—the first time I reached seven days clean. I was actually clean, in prison. I had a thousand justifications for smoking weed, and yet there I was, seven days clean. I had no inclination to boast at all because I had not done it, He had. I was amazed that my life could function 'clean'. In-group I became the butt of some very venomous sarcasm, and the whispering and laughing plucked at the chords of shame in me which had been instilled in the classroom over twenty-five years earlier when everyone around me pointed and laughed at me. The shame was still deep, but I knew I now had the fortune to take hold of it and take it to my Lord; everything the devil threw at me I took to God and He did some wonderful healing work in me, once again, among the unbelievers.

Everyone else in the group was still using weed, and my being clean threatened every one of them. They each tried to get me to smoke with them, and they collectively rejected me for being 'teacher's pet'. They attacked me verbally every day in-group. I just sat and took it, acknowledging the fears and the injustice of their cruelty, trusting God to see me through. It was very hard to express these fears and struggles, but every time I did, I grew. It was hard, because every time I said, "I feel hurt by your cruelty", it was like a red rag to a bull and I would be bombarded with abuse and ridicule. But I slowly grew in an inner maturity and the handling of these situations. I started to recognize how the pain of the verbal ridicule never lasted if I answered with the truth of the pain.

Sometimes, though, some things were said and the pain would not go away as easily. I would even wake up with the pain the next day. I then started to see that, in among the 'abuse', there was very often some truth about me that I would have to get before God in prayer about. I was unknowingly developing discernment between good abuse and bad abuse. Some things were said to harm me, which was bad abuse. Others things were said and they hurt, which was healthy abuse, because it pinpointed needs of change. The truth will regularly hurt, but it never causes any lasting harm. Slander and sarcasm is designed to destroy.

Looking to God's Word for guidance, I found this text in Hebrews: "Solid food belongs to those who are full of age, who, by reason of use, have had their senses exercised to discern both good and evil" (Hebrews 5:14 NKJV).

I realised that good advice does not necessarily mean it has to be good 'sounding'. It may hurt, but the content could be very nourishing if digested, like most medicines. If medicines all tasted like honey, spiritual medicines like constructive criticism would always get rejected.

Slowly, over the next three months, I could feel myself growing, confirmed when each group member came to my cell individually to apologize and express respect, some even asking me to pray for them. I was puzzled as to why I had to endure such hostility and was starting to feel very sorry for myself. I was of the opinion that this group needed me more than I needed it, and although I sat in the therapeutic group circle, I was not actually a part of the group. I knew that I had to stay focused on God and keep turning to Him at every available quiet moment, and He would sustain me, and attract them to Him in His way.

During the darkest hour of the persecutions at Downview I sat on my bed in the early hours of the morning, preparing for another day of it; turning to God's Word, my attention was caught by a section of Scripture:

Jeremiah 15:16-21(NASV)
"I have been called by thy name, O Lord God of Hosts.
I did not sit in the circle of merrymakers, nor did I exult.
Because of thy hand upon me I sat alone, for thou didst fill me
with indignation. Why has my pain been perpetual,
and my wound incurable, refusing to be healed?
Wilt thou indeed be to me like a deceptive stream
with water that is unreliable?
Therefore, thus says The Lord:
"If you will return to me, then I will restore you
before me you will stand.
And if you extract the precious from the worthless
You will become my spokesman.
They for their part will turn to you,
But as for you, you must not turn to them.
Then I will make you to this people a fortified wall of bronze.
And although they fight you they will not prevail over you,
For I am with you to save you, and to Redeem
you from the hands of the wicked".

I actually felt sorry for these guys, because they had no idea who this God was who they were up against when they attacked me. There was one guy who was ruthless in his mockery of Jesus. He died of an overdose one week after his release.

My personal counselor, a Kiwi guy called Eddie, actually ended up receiving my counsel about 'the peace that transcends all understanding' and he said, 'I am jealous of the quality of spirituality you have'.

My clean time grew, and my personal time with Jesus went from depth to depth. I was in a single cell, on a section of the jail dominated by Yardies (Jamaican gangsters). I was one of three white guys on that section of prison.

Next to me on one side was a heroin and dope dealer, and on the other there was an ex-IRA terrorist. The dope dealer had nothing to do with the therapy group but the terrorist was very heavily into heroin and was a dominant member of the group.

A hot water pipe ran through the length of the wing and if we wrapped a towel around the pipe and placed our head on it, we could see each other and chat away. One night as I was chatting to John, the terrorist, I asked him why he was so hostile towards God. His response blew me away. He said, "Colin, I was chased out of Ireland by the IRA. I was running amok. I got such a high from killing that I used to kill IRA members, and then go on revenge killings, killing two for every one of us. One night they (IRA) came for me, but I escaped".

I wrote a prayer out on some toilet roll and slid it through the wall to him. John went quiet for twenty minutes or so, until I heard him quietly weeping. He wept for the rest of the time I was awake. The dope dealer on the other side tried to get involved by offering me some free weed! I quietly declined, telling him I had no need of it. The silence from his cell was also strangely deafening.

I knew The Lord was revealing Himself to some very heavy criminals around me. I had a deep burning desire for these guys, because I knew that, just like I had been only five months earlier, they were addicted and heading in the wrong direction.

Love of the Word

My hunger for God's Word was insatiable. I had two or three Bibles open all the time, comparing texts in different translations, and writing notes. I had notes all over my cell, piles of them on different verses and translations.

At something like 4 a.m. one morning I was wide awake and singing praises to God. I had been sent a Walkman by my dad and a worship tape by Irene Long and there I was, tearfully worshipping The Lord on my knees in my cell. I heard the night officer coming onto the wing to do what would be his final head count for the night shift and I was aware of him approaching my cell and looking in. As he slid open the eye-hole of my door to look in, the light would shine in from the wing corridor. This was usually a 3 second thing, but on this occasion I noticed that the light in my cell changed for something like 10 seconds before it went back to normal. I smiled in my praise and simply asked God to bless him. A few seconds later, he came back and watched me again for something like 20 seconds as I worshipped God.

I was singing loud enough to be heard, but not loud enough to disturb anyone else. The Prison Officers were being reached too and as I considered how this guy could be from among the ranks of the doomed, I became very aware of what I was singing, and the depth of theology within the words. Fortunately I was singing 'You laid aside your majesty', and I felt secure that it had attractive truth within it. I seemed to have suddenly developed an acute awareness of the potential damage Satan could cause within a man's heart with counterfeit spirituality and by twisting the truth of God.

It was during one of these worship sessions that I broke down on my bed and started to cry again, "Lord, I have to take this testimony right into the enemy's backyard".

I was haunted by the thoughts of all the men and women I had known who had died from addiction, and of all those in the rehabs and treatment centers who were desperately wanting to be clean, but who were being guided by, and left seeking in, the wrong directions.

Heaven smiled back at me, I was already in the enemy's back yard. I had to learn how my internal sense of security and joy could actually blind me to the darkness around me.

The only mentoring I had received thus far had been from the lifer in The Verne and it left me with quite an anxiety because the insights and what could be described as 'revelations' that I felt was experiencing were quite frightening. I joined a Bible study group run by the chaplain and following a testimony around what had happened to me and about the need to be 'born again'; he asked 'so where does that leave me?' I lacked the courage to tell him that he would be "lost forever without being born again into Christ", because he was wearing a dog collar and I was wearing stripes!

The Christians visiting from outside were also astounded by what was taking place in my life and I think some of them just came to have a look, a bit like a zoo, but it was really nice. I was approached by one of them and asked if there was anything I needed and I instantly knew that it was time for some humility on my part. I was in need of shoes. The shoes I went into this sentence with many months earlier were falling off my feet, but I struggled to ask. I felt pride and shame all at the same time. I had to ask myself, 'if this person was my brother and he was in need, would I not want to help him?' and off the back of this I assured myself that I was now actually talking to a brother-in-Christ, and so I pointed him to my need.

Within a week I was walking around the jail in a new pair of training shoes. It was an awesome time for me. I had something new, and there was no desire within me to sell them for drugs. I felt a true sense of appreciation even though they weren't a top brand name, which took my ego a little time to adjust to but I got there.

I saw myself now wearing an unknown brand name of trainers and saw two things: first, at this rate I could be wearing 'frumpish' from head to toe within six months, and second, there was still an image issue that needed to be addressed.

I went on to learn that as soon as I took ownership of my image problem, and arrived at a place of being truly grateful, even for the possibility of becoming known as 'frumpish', the image problem lost power over me, and brand names were no longer a problem.

I did, however, make a mental note of how I had unknowingly labeled Christians 'frumpish' from within my unregenerate state, and how that label had kept me away from any attraction toward them in my days of struggle. I mentioned this in one of our discussion groups, and most of the visiting Christians (frumps) inwardly smiled and pointed out how 'Oh, that is pride, and when Jesus is in your life you are set free from pride'. I said 'I know that now, but in my unregenerate state there was absolutely no reason at all why I should see it as pride, and was it not the Christian's responsibility to be an attraction to those who are lost rather than a symbol of ridicule? I was met with a warm but very loud silence and I started to think that I could be catching glimpses of the truth of Jesus turning tables over within the belief systems of His people.

I was silently intrigued by the fact that I was getting into bed at night and falling straight to sleep because every night since my conversion I had slept straight through without disturbance. Regarding my approaching release date I had been down to the 'only three months to go' place several times before so I was expecting 'gate fever'; the minute by minute counting down of months, weeks, days and hours. I should have been tossing and turning the night away, planning my future, where I will go, where I won't go, what job I will get and how different life will be this time out. It all starts to churn through the imagination at approximately three months left to do so I was actually waiting for the gate fever to take hold; but, it simply did not kick in. Each day was a day connected to and in the company of Jesus, and each night was peaceful and calm, all without drugs. I slept every night in perfect peace. My mind regularly drifted forward to my release date, but only in wondering if I would sleep the night before my release.

Two days before my release the Rehabilitation of Prisoner's Trust awarded me their Certificate of Completion as I came to the end of their prison treatment programme. Although Jesus was within me at this stage, the stress of being drug free in prison, and my impending drug free release, my weight remained down to 59 kilograms (I was 15 kilo underweight). God did not remove the stresses; He empowered me to handle them, and at the end of the day I knew that any 'normal' person would be underweight and stressed in the same set of circumstances. I was 'normal'.

My clean time grew, as did the resentment toward me in those group sessions. It was a terrible time of emotional bullying and suffering, but now I was suffering for belonging to Him, and that I could live with. It was healthy suffering. I was asked by one of the group if I would urinate into a container for him so that he would get through the random tests we were subjected to as a part of therapy. I declined, but another guy claiming 'clean time' said he would do it. I knew in my heart that he should only be claiming 'drug free' time, as opposed to being 'clean' because although the drugs were absent, the behaviour remained the same. As it turned out we were all tested, and these two characters went through the urine-by-deception routine, and yet they both still tested positive—for alcohol. It was the funniest thing: when challenged as to 'why did you tell me you were clean', the other guy just shrugged and said, 'I am clean from heroin and cannabis but nobody mentioned alcohol'.

It was good to be free. I was so glad that I had been given the opportunity to bin the other life. Although I grew in gratitude that Jesus had set me free from this worldly caliber of relationship, it was all I had ever known, so I knew I was going to struggle in the relationship area.

I reached my release date six months clean. The night before I got out, sure enough, I got into bed and slept like a log right through the night. I was free indeed. I was released the next morning and given my release grant of £52. Two other guys were released the same day and I felt a deep sense of compassion for both of them as I listened to their pre-release plans to conquer the world and 'never to return to their addiction or prison'.

I'd been at that point five times before and I knew they still had lots of jail left in them.

I my case, I knew they were releasing a free man

Bondages of Freedom

I had money in my pocket for the first time in two years. It was only £52, but it felt like a mountain of money to me. It was two days before Christmas and I felt a distinct pull toward Manchester for a very brief moment, but I knew that I would not fit in up there any longer. On the platform at the railway station, I inwardly underwent a grieving type of experience because I could see the train bound for Manchester and I knew I could be with Hayley within three hours if I chose to. The pull was almost physical until I turned to The Lord in my heart and said something along the lines of "Lord, you know exactly what is going on in me right now. I am going to leave that chapter of my life in your care, and turn my back on it all unless you make it plain to me that you want me to return". I boarded a train heading in the opposite direction and once again my freedom and peace went to a new level. I posted £35 to Hayley for her Christmas box, bought myself a chocolate bar and a coke, and caught the train to The Cotswolds. I had actually browsed through a few shops first, but saw nothing that I wanted. I had everything I needed—a train ticket to a new way of living, all the human help I would need, and Jesus as my Saviour.

I was elated because I had given my daughter her first honest Christmas gift, it was not stolen or bought with stolen money, and I felt an inner peace about the whole future.

On the train I saw humanity in its hopelessness, and a burden to cast His light started to grow rapidly within me, but I could not escape The Lord's two year time-out period. I did not understand it, but I now knew that there were many things beyond my understanding that I simply had to go with. The train ride from London to Stroud took me through some of England's finest countryside. It was winter and the fields were white with frost. I was in absolute awe at how God looks after the land, suddenly knowing that the frost was equally as important as the sunshine for the farmers and the crops and I saw God's hand everywhere. Even in the suffering people, He was working to fulfill His purpose, just like He had in my life.

I arrived at Nelson House by midday and the moment I met the lady who ran the program I saw that she stepped back with a puzzled look on her face and then said, 'Your eyes have changed'. I said, 'That's down to Jesus'. Mary had seen me at my worst on my last visit to Nelson House and she knew all too well what I was like and what I used to look like.

On my previous visit, I was told that it was forbidden to leave the house alone for the first two weeks, but within two hours I had gone out to the shop alone. I reasoned that I had been in jail three months, and primary treatment for three months. I needed writing material for letters and I needed some space from being escorted everywhere. I simply had to have some stationary in order to write to my daughter. At the shop I found I was short of the right amount of cash to buy a pen, pad, envelopes and a stamp so I slid the pen up my sleeve and paid for the rest. At that time I did not see it as a major problem because in my twisted world I was above the rules of the house and still thieving as a matter of routine. I also failed to see how I was using the name of Hayley and my 'imagined' relationship with her as a means of justification. I had made it sound as if I had a wonderful relationship with Hayley, and in many ways I did, but on the whole it was stained by crime and disruption and was very damaging.

This second time at Nelson, though, not only did I fall in line with house expectations—I actually wanted to. I had a new kind of battle taking place within me about being at Nelson House this time, but made it a conscious act of my will to yield to their regime. My confusion was, "I now know Jesus as my guide and counselor. He is my all-in-all. Why do I need to attend a secular rehab home if I am now confessing Jesus as Lord?" I did not allow this argument any expression. I simply waited, knowing that The Lord would reveal to me His wisdom in His time.

I enjoyed waking up early each morning and sitting with The Lord, listening to the birds singing and watching the winter. It was awesome. My restriction period passed quite quickly and I ventured out alone for the first time. I walked by the canal and talked to The Lord about where I was and why. I ended up outside the shop where I had stolen the pen. I went into the shop and bought myself some chocolate. I also bought the same pen again, only this time, after paying for it, I returned it to the shelf. I left that shop feeling 'approved of God' and I knew that that was exactly how human beings were supposed to feel. I knew His smile upon my life, I felt truly close to Jesus Himself.

On a high, I decided to travel into Stroud by bus. I had forgotten to get change for the bus ride and only had a five pound note; I was taken completely by surprise when I got on the bus and approached the driver with my money because, suddenly, my confidence just drained out of me. I just suddenly felt extremely vulnerable did not know how to communicate with the driver who was impatiently waiting for me to pay. I heard myself say: "Is this bus going to Stroud?" The driver came back with an 'ask a stupid question get a stupid answer' tone of voice and a look of contempt on his face and said: "What does it say on the front?" I nearly exploded. I felt a surge of energy coming up from within me and I suddenly found myself wanting to slam this guy's head into the ticket machine and to drag him off the bus. I actually lost my breath because of the eruption of anger in me toward this guy. I gave him the note and said nothing more. I sat on that bus and knew in my heart that although The Lord Jesus had saved me out of the world for Himself in an instant, it was going to be a long process of getting the world out of me.

Life started to look like too big a task for me; if I had actually felt 'vulnerable' in this, the simplest of social situations, and reacted with that amount of aggression, how was I going to cope throughout life?

An instant lesson for me was: as soon as I start to feel good about life and about 'how Christian I am', I become susceptible to lessons in humility from the old nature rising up in me.

It also became a reality for me that there was a lot of making right to do in my life—particularly in the everyday relational issues—and that that would take time. People had heard my apologies year after year; now it was time for Colin to actually change and let the people see my sincerity. Nelson House had many guidelines and expectations. One of them was regular attendance at Narcotics and/or Alcoholics Anonymous meetings. I had attended NA for several years at this point, but never quite managed to get clean. Now I was clean and free in Christ, but it was slowly now dawning on me that these groups had many diamonds and pearls of wisdom essential for my context of recovery and reintegration into mainstream society. I was deeply in love with Jesus Christ, and everything belonged to Him and I knew He would never abandon me, even if I was making a mistake going to the world for guidance.

I attended two Church services in my first two weeks of freedom and came away feeling terribly confused. At my first, I walked in expecting to find joyous passion and a prodigal son type of greeting. It was a Methodist Church with the younger members being in the late 50's to early 60's age group. The visiting speaker made claims of having 'seen Jesus face to face' and of having 'received special instructions from Him'. My heart sank. I looked around the 20 or 30 strong congregation and it just looked like death's waiting room. I walked out of that service thinking 'thanks, but no thanks'.

At the second service I attended, everyone was sitting around talking in whispers as if we were at a funeral and once again I was totally disgruntled. I wasn't so disturbed by their style of meeting and worshipping, what bothered me was the fact that I was actually getting all my emotional and psychological needs met by the 12-Step recovery world. But my deepest need, that of Christian fellowship, was proving to be a disappointment.

NA has this thing about not flying deity-specific flags in their meetings. Jesus was not to be proclaimed as Saviour, because of the 'each to his own' ethos. They offered 'a god of your own understanding' and each individual brought in their own interpretation of whom or what God was 'to them'. I refused to be put off, threw myself into these meetings, and saturated myself in their 'recovery' literature. The more I attended these meetings, and the more I shared one-to-one fellowship with NA members, the more frustrated and disconnected I became. I was identifying myself at meetings, sometimes up to 9 times a week as: "I'm Colin, I'm an addict". Every time I said this I had an inner belief that I was in the midst of believing a lie. I was actually creating an identity that would (a) fit in and (b) make sense of all the years of active destruction behind me. I then started to see that people were not actually creating a 'god of their own understanding'; they were creating a 'self' of their own understanding and it was just another version of the (addiction) problem. A cleaner, safer version, but it was all just another version of 'following the crowd, just to fit in'.

First Christian Role Model

At Nelson House one afternoon I got a phone call and a guy with a local accent on the other end of the line asked me if I would like to "share fellowship at their Church this Sunday?" From deep within me I knew that this guy was a part of the answer to my prayers and that my Christian needs were about to be met. He said, 'we are a small charismatic fellowship and this Sunday is fellowship lunch, do you fancy coming along?' I agreed to join them and as I replaced the receiver to its cradle, my heart started to pound within me, because I knew The Lord was sending someone to guide me into the next chapter of my life.

That Sunday morning I was up and ready by 7:00 am. He had arranged to collect me at 9:30, so I sat looking out of the window like a little boy looking for Santa Clause. It was really weird. I was only going to Church, for heaven's sake, what was there to be excited about? At 9:30, a guy knocked at the door of Nelson House. As I met him he stretched out his hand and smiled straight into my eyes and simply said, "Hi, I'm Andy Morris". That was pretty much the sum total of this guy's introduction, but something happened inside of me that I would never be able to explain. I just totally relaxed around this guy. He was of a similar height to me, and a similar age. In fact, as it turned out, Andy was born a matter of hours before me in the same year. Andy was born on February 4th 1959; I was born on the 5th. My initial thoughts were: 'The Lord has sent me a role model'. I had a lot of street and prison image to get out of my system, and I knew it; but what I did not know was how and with what would I fill the void left by all that had to be removed? In Andy Morris I instantly saw enviable godly characteristics worthy of emulation and I saw what I wanted to be. I saw Jesus in Andy and felt a healthy envy of him and I knew I would be spending time with this guy in the coming months.

Within ten minutes of leaving Nelson House that morning we had arrived at Minchinhampton Christian Fellowship, a social club type building used by the local youth for Friday night youth club. In my eyes, we were lost in the deep dark outback of UK and I found myself right in the thick of typical English country life, yet for some strange reason I felt at home. People came and greeted me. They were relaxed and wearing bright colours. Children ran around and made noises like they should; people hugged each other, and there were cakes and biscuits, soft drinks and guys around my age. It was totally revolutionary to my mindset. I did not know Church could be like this. Then when the worship started and I simply released my inhibitions unto the worship of my Lord and Saviour and we worshipped Him as one. I was in 'fellowship'. I felt at home. I felt safe. From time to time I looked around the gathering—we were something like 75 in total and I was amazed to see people worshipping the same Lord I had met in jail, in just the way that I had worshipped Him in the early hours of the morning in my prison cell. Free.

I caught people looking at my tattoos from time to time and then smiling embarrassingly, not knowing what to make of me. The cultural contrasts were stark: a hidden little fellowship out in the countryside consisting of school teachers and shop owners; and me, an extremely heavily tattooed ex-intravenous drug addict of seventeen years, having just been released from a brutal lifestyle and prison, yet now fired up for God. This was going to be very interesting to say the least.

I sat with Andy and his lovely family, and simply melted into Minchinhampton Christian Fellowship. As the weeks started to tick by, I actually picked up on a sense of apprehension from some of the members at Church. I felt they were afraid of me, and began feeling a sense of rejection from them.

My second week at Minch included going to Andy's parents for lunch, where we all sat around a table as a family to eat. It was the weirdest thing for me to sit in a quiet family environment to eat. Feeling like a mongrel among royalty I caught my first glimpse of a new meaning to 'family life', one in which I saw how the posh people live. I grew up with my plate of food on my knee in front of the telly (and I wouldn't swap it), but this was all polite and proper and inside I was as nervous as hell, and yet laughing away to myself at my own ignorance. I had to learn all the basic social norms like which knife to use and to avoid belching but I have to be honest—I was tempted to belch simply to see what the reaction would be—but I resisted. I had it in my mind that they all wanted to belch too, but they were far too posh to fulfill this desire. I was being all proper and polite on the outside, while laughing at them and at myself on the inside. Not in any venomous way, it was simply my way of coping with it all.

Then one Sunday morning the strangest thing happened. As I sat listening to the message, I had the strangest feeling that I was not alone. As I looked to my left I found a little boy aged 18 months or so, standing and staring at me. The natural thing to do was offer my open hands for him to give him the option to climb onto my knee if he so wished. He held my eye contact with a very slight hint of a smile, and for a moment it felt as if he almost recognized me, and climbed onto my knee and within 5 minutes he had fallen sound asleep. I felt as if I had stolen him and I looked round to find his family. They were all sitting two rows behind me, all watching, all smiling unconditionally at me. His mum and dad just shrugged and gestured for me to let him sleep.

In my heart I knew that The Lord was saying something to everyone in that service.

The majority of the Church was quite rightly reserved about me, but this little man, representing those closest to Christ, was totally relaxed with me. I started to think that my involvement at Minchinhampton was not just for my betterment—it was for those around me too.

When the young man started to stir I felt a sense of panic welling up in me. He will be expecting feeding, and I was simply not equipped. I was starting to panic because he would want to see his mum, but see me and he would surely panic. When he awoke, he sat up and got his bearings for a moment and then turned to look at me. He looked straight into my eyes. We held eye contact for a beautiful moment until he smiled and went straight back to sleep. I cruised past the point of no return at that exact moment and I knew that it was time for me to fit in.

I went back to Nelson House that afternoon and sat in silent awe at how God had communicated His heartbeat for me, to me. I was invited back to the little man's home the following week for lunch, and fell safely in love his whole family: Peter, Vanessa, Joshua, Jordan, Amy and Laura Record.

It was an amazing thing to sit in among 'normal' folk and actually feel a sense of belonging; and how wonderful it would be if I could draw this testimony through to a close at this point with 'and we all lived happily ever after', but not so. The more they loved me, the easier it was for me to allow my masks to drop, but the more my masks dropped I found the weirdest thing started to happen in me.

34 Year Old Teenager

I had joined the addiction culture decades earlier primarily because of a need to belong and an inability to be honest about how I felt about myself. The addiction further exacerbated that seedling problem and because I had lost the ability to express my feelings in an adequate manner, I had adopted a way of self-governing my emotional realm. I was either funny or angry, with very little in between. So now, as I started to relax in this new life, the suppressed emotions started to surface and to confuse me. I was 34 years old, feeling inferior and unsafe with adults and strangely attracted to and safe around teenagers. It was just an inner safety that I felt around the younger generation. I mentioned it to some of the guys around me and they hinted that it could be a 'call to youth work', but I just knew that it was more than that. I knew that I had to be secure with adults before I could ever lead the youth anywhere.

In His providential mercy God gave me an awareness of what was happening to me, and the 'two year time-out' period started to make some sort of sense.

I also started getting in touch with a very deep desire to be with a woman. I would sit in in-group sessions at Nelson, and find myself inwardly yearning to be in some sort of contact with a woman. No one specific, I just yearned for some feminine input. I had been in a macho all-male environment for so long that the feminine felt really attractive to me. I was afraid of my feelings by this time and started keeping them to myself again. It was safer, even in Church, to stay in denial. I prayed for someone to understand where I was at and for them to approach me, but everyone around me just smiled, clapped and praised God week in, week out.

I knew that I was loved, but I was stuck with a trust deficit. I feared that my growth had stopped and I started to feel cynical about this Christianity thing. I was getting more identification and understanding from the local secular self-help groups than from my brothers and sisters in Christ. I started to remember nights in prison when I would sit feeling excited about the prospect of having my character flaws and my stained soul cleansed when I got in among children of God, and with those memories I started to miss the prison.

Inadequate Discipleship

It was during this season of suppression that my imagination started turning the innocent hugs from sisters in Christ into sexual fantasies but I did feel it safe to express my problems to my mentors. I started to feel disloyal to my new friends and ultimately to God when I shared my disillusionment about Church in the secular groups and within me, I was slowly growing in turmoil. I then found that I was developing a masturbation problem. I could not stop my imagination until I masturbated, and secondly, it became a means of release for me from the internal frustrations which continued to build up.

I felt deeply ashamed of myself.

I tried to talk to one of my elders about it because I somehow knew that 'the light' of the truth was the only solution for this darkness of soul. I started to confess to one of my leaders about the activity within my heart and my shamefully corresponding behaviour, but I instantly knew that I had made a mistake. As I got to the point of wanting to break down over my condition, I got cut off with an aggressive 'you must turn to The Lord' and he proceeded to cast out the 'demon of masturbation'. I was so disappointed.

A hand was placed upon my head and an unintelligible noise came vomiting out of him as pushed me backwards. I'd seen similar things in some of the Churches I had visited and I had seen people falling over. So, not wanting to nullify or disrespect my leader's authority, I fell over. I chose to fall over. It was not God; it was me, by my own choice.

My elder then started to weep over me in prayer because he believed God had used him. He was sincere in his efforts, and in his belief, but I felt nothing but embarrassment for my part in the playing of this game. I was disappointed in myself, but not personally strong enough to confess or to challenge anyone about what had happened.

I truly desired to respect my leaders as leaders, but I had to inwardly concede that I was struggling with these guys. I could not understand how, if I was a temple of Christ, in-dwelt by The Holy Spirit as I knew to be true, how a demon could live in me?

I eventually raised this question with one of my Elders and was politely told to just yield to the power of prayer. I loved them, more than words could adequately say, but my respect for them *as my leaders* in Christ was severely fractured, and a cynicism started to grow within.

It all sounded theologically correct: confess and turn to The Lord. But in all honesty, nothing was really changing for me apart from a growth in confusion.

Such was my desire to grow that I visited three different Church groups each week, one of which was a 'healing' service. My hope was to expose the lusts and distortions of my heart's motives, but each time I tried I could not get past having demons cast out of me and people 'prophesying over me' telling me how "God is going to do awesome things with your life".

As soon as people saw my tattoos, heard some of my testimony and saw me worshipping, they gave me this 'prophetic word of knowledge'. I heard myself regularly asking inwardly: 'how can you listen to me, see where I have come from, hear my testimony, and then say God '*is going to do* something special'? Anyone could work out that God had something special planned for me, given the details of my conversion, simply by means of common sense. To say He was *going to*, using a future tense was deeply saddening for me. God is Sovereign Lord, and I knew in my heart that if He chose never to use me at all after my conversion, I would still die grateful that He had done such a wonderful thing in my life simply by revealing Himself to me.

I tried to vent a lot of my frustrations at my home cell group. Once a week we gathered at Andy's home and shared fellowship and testimonies. I grew in love and respect for Andy and his family. I learned from Andy, even when he did not know I was watching him. Each week I gave testimony of people whom I had spoken to and had guided to a new knowledge of The Lord because it was happening every week. I had nothing else of any real significance to talk about, but I started to feel as if I was showing off because that was not the case for anyone else. Sharing the wonders of salvation and pointing someone to Christ seemed to be the exception rather than the rule. I could not grasp how anyone could go through a whole day without talking to a lost soul about this Jesus and when I was once asked; 'why do you think you lead so many to The Lord?' I could only respond by saying, 'Because that is exactly how I expect it to be on a day to day basis and nothing less will do. The Lord Jesus Christ has redeemed my very soul from the clutches of Lucifer himself, and liberated me from a daily nightmare into the glorious freedom of His light and truth.' My question was, 'how could I not, what right do I have to ever settle for any less, for anyone else?'

I was sadly amazed that folk could find interest in anything else after this eternally wonderful truth. Let any one of us win the lottery or experience personal trauma of any kind, and then try stopping us from talking about it; yet I was meeting people who professed the same freedom as I, yet could remain silent?

I started to drift away from the naivety of idealism into the reality of spiritual warfare having more casualties than the Church is prepared to take ownership of. Then one day a dear lady in the Church whispered in my ear, 'The Lord told me to give this to you' and she passed me a piece of paper. I immediately started to hope that it was money, so I was disappointed to find a piece of paper with "Romans 8:1" written on it.

"Therefore now there is no condemnation
for those who are in Christ Jesus"

I was perplexed.

That very morning I had been sitting in tearful worship with eyes closed yet seeing clearly how marvelous, how wonderful, is the love of God. I knew I was adopted and grafted in, I knew I belonged and that I would now always belong. I was singing and praying and thanking God for His amazing grace and adoring all that He is, and all that He had done and I was deeply excited about what He was planning to do. I knew that I was free and I knew that God saw me as His own and that I belonged to Him and to His family. So to be given Romans 8:1 made no sense and I started to believe that while it was probably given to me by the loveliest of Saints with nothing but the warmest of hearts and the purest of intentions, I started to think that I should be very careful not to buy into emotionalism.

As I looked at Romans 8:1 that afternoon I immediately had awareness that this text on its own means nothing because it begins with "Therefore now". So I went to bed really early that night in order to pray about it in the early hours of the morning, and it was then that I began to dread the unthinkable: that there were people within our congregation(s), who definitely knew and truly loved God, but when it came to handling His Word, they might not actually know how to 'handle the word of truth correctly' (2 Timothy 2:15).

I was getting the impression that 'Christian maturity' was developed through Church time sitting under the teaching of God's Word, passing verses around from time to time and sharing at cell group once a week. However, I knew that I needed more. I knew that the deceptive influences of evil was the problem, but I also knew that a superficial interaction with the Bible was not going to be enough to be the answer, yet to say this stirred up violent resistance.

I believed it then and I believe it now: inherent evil, although it may not be our 'fault', it is our problem, and personal ownership is our responsibility. The Bible, however, as it sits on our bookshelves, is not the answer.

The problem with evil is it has attached itself to the very fiber of our nature, impressing itself upon us to believe that (a) God's Word is not enough, (b) right is wrong and (c) wrong is right. Therefore reading The Bible is not the answer, because our nature is to distort it in order to achieve a path of least resistance.

I know from personal and repeated experience that every time I prayerfully study God's Word, seeking the guidance of The Holy Spirit and requesting the humility to accept by faith all that I read, my whole understanding of Him and of His holiness and self-sustainability and my understanding of man and of man's unholiness and dependency changes.

The broader picture clearly shows how deception is seducing the masses both outside and inside our Church buildings, yet Scripture equally as clearly shows how mass conversions and mass discipleship cannot and must not be seen as the answer.

Matthew 5:1
"Seeing the crowds, Jesus went up on to the mountain and
when he had sat down <u>His disciples came to Him</u> and
He opened His mouth and <u>began to teach them</u>."

Intimate, individual and small group discipleship is the only safe
and true answer. I found it horrifying to imagine that hymn singing
'believers' might actually be heading in the wrong direction. But here
was I, a heavily tattooed ex-junky and ex-con with no education—
what did I know? I'll tell you what I knew: I knew that I once went
forward with 20,000 other people at a Billy Graham concert and
for a very brief moment I prayed a version of the sinner's prayer to
Jesus, but no one followed up with me afterwards and I did another
four years of active addiction including another stint in prison which
nearly killed me.

I started going up to the top of one of the valleys between 4:00 and
4:30 in the mornings to sing to The King. Just simply for that sole
purpose of singing to The Lord, a debt of love from a grateful heart.
I would burst into rapturous choruses of "Thank you Jesus", and I
would sing and dance for The Lord Himself. It was awesome. From
time to time I would stop and look for the others who had been saved
and who were doing the same thing, actually believing that 'they will
be here soon', but no one came.

I started to listen intently to the messages we were getting from the
sermons and started to question in my heart whether or not we were
actually hearing what The Bible says, or just something our teachers
said the Bible says? Then one morning a sermon was delivered on
Jesus saying, "You did not choose me, I chose you" (John 15:16). It
was encouragement on top of encouragement about how special we
were and how He has chosen us, etc, etc, etc. It went on and on, and
people were steadily getting fired up responding with 'amen' and
'hallelujah', until it almost reached a fever pitch. I slowly started to
sink into a pit of despair in my heart, because the text was never at
any point completed. The text goes on to say "and appointed you to
go and bear fruit, fruit that will last, that whatever you ask in my

name it shall be given unto you". What we sat and listened to was like a lifejacket in the freezing Atlantic. It might keep you from sinking, but it will not keep you alive for long. People will naturally gravitate toward this form of teaching and worship because of its therapeutic value and the fact that it tickles the ears of its hearers. However, my fear was that when text is cut in half or taken out of context it would actually pacify people rather than sanctify them.

I was attending a lot of charismatic Churches where the worship was very often described as 'anointed', when I thought it was more of a therapeutic release for many at the end of a long week of frustrations. I was growing in a fear that psychology was playing more of a role in Christianity than Theology was. I saw similarities with my hooligan days. I used to find going to football and singing in unison with thousands of others to be extremely therapeutic, and on the way home I would always feel totally peaceful. I started to fear that this was what people were mistaking for 'God's peace', making it a counterfeit spirituality.

I was also growing into my theological standpoint during this period without realizing it. I did not even know that varying theological standpoints existed. In the first six months of life in Church, having witnessed unintelligible babble being spoken in various Church services, I came to a belief position that tongues were never intended to be an unintelligible babble; they were what God says they were, "a sign, not to them that believe, but to them that believeth not" (1 Corinthians 14:22). The early Church was given tongues (languages) as a means of equipping them for the impending missionary trips into 'all nations' beginning later in Acts 8. I did not believe, because The Bible does not teach, that tongues would go down through the generations and transform itself into unintelligible babble. I came to believe that they were given for a reason and a season, and then possibly even withdrawn. Similarly with prophecy and words of knowledge, they were needed in New Testament times, because the Bible at that point was not written in its fullness as we have it today and once the canon of scripture was sealed, nothing else was required.

If I'm honest I also feel it would be divine wisdom to remove these gifts at the fulfillment of their purpose, because they are so easy to imitate and man is so hungry with ambition and yet so gullible that Satan could have a field day leading people astray from sound doctrine into counterfeit spirituality and ultimately, hell.

I found it very interesting, too, that God was only using the academically approved and those in no need of self-examination to lead His Church, which, if you look, is actually inconsistent to His character, as can be seen by His appointment of the unschooled and broken working classes alongside the religiously qualified, in Peter and Paul.

Without knowing it, planning it or having been taught it, and in the midst of charismatic believers, I drifted into a cessationist view. I deeply loved being in fellowship with the Minchinhampton folk and it grieves me to write about that period of my life with what may seem to be a disrespectful manner, but I feel I have to stand true to that which I believe, because I feel The Lord Himself would have His people take an inventory of motives and ambitions. I also feel the Church is in danger of becoming unteachable when the package does not meet with what is unfortunately very often a middle class expectation. Because I had tattoos all over my body and had no academic muscle to flex, I felt it was assumed that I was unqualified for significance. I had a very poor grasp of grammar in my speech. I would say 'was' when it should have been 'were', and had no use of the letter 'H'. I was always 'appy', when everyone else politely emphasised that it 'should' be 'happy'. I would often wonder, 'why can't I simply be 'appy' and not feel like I am below expectation? The answer was obvious: it simply was not good enough for those with a 'proper upbringing'.

After two years of struggle, hurt and what felt like much personal failure as a Christian, I started to look toward God for a movement in my life. Minchinhampton Christian Fellowship carried me through many turbulent times in those first two years as a new Christian, and many souls have been found and converted as a result of their mentorship, grace and patience with me. I do not believe that my abrasive nature would have been tolerated in any of the more 'established' denominations. Within the first six months of Christianity then, and feeling further away from God than I had experienced in prison, I got before God and had to confess with resignation that if what I had seen of Christianity thus far was where I was expected to go, then I would simply rather drift into the background and get a job as a truck driver in the world and enjoy Jesus at a personal level, watching Him reach hitchhikers lost in sin. It had become apparent to me that my type would never really fit the criteria for leadership in the Church context. I would simply remain the trophy of grace that they could claim a ministry around, like some poor cousin. I did slowly make some progress, though. In no way did I see myself as leadership material, but the truth was that Jesus chose tax collectors, publicans and roughneck fishermen to head up the original Church, so why not me?

After six months at Nelson House, I started to feel a pull toward leaving. Every week in the Peer Evaluation Group, I got the same feedback from the whole house, "Keep on doing what you are doing", but in my heart I knew that I was starting to backslide. I had allowed myself to become emotionally involved with one of the female residents, and we were both starting to make it sound as if it was God's plan for us. I started getting involved in secret meetings with this lady, and even though nothing physical was taking place between us, flirting with the idea was under way. I did not have any means of protecting myself from this emotional involvement, and it became apparent that I not only had a lot to learn, but also had a great deal to unlearn. I had no skills in avoiding this kind of situation, and actually felt that I was sliding down the side of a wet embankment into a whole new valley of struggle.

I was inwardly heartbroken at my behaviour and eventually when it became extremely painful I spoke to one of my elders. I had chosen at some level to return to old behaviour. Unfortunately, however, I had another demon cast out of me. I felt out of options, and took my guilt and my shame to NA, and received some life saving feedback pointing me to extreme loneliness and a deep-seated fear of saying 'no'. Once again the Church told me to "turn to The Lord", but the world helped me to "examine my ways and test them". It took me several weeks to work through the confusions and the hurts I had both caused and felt. The Lord aided me to get my life back in line with His heartbeat and I started to move on. I felt an inner sense of fear and disappointment at how I had been handled by my new family, because I saw without doubt that they did not know how to handle me—either as an ex-con, drug addict or as a new Christian.

I went from Nelson House to sharing a house with a lady who had been in NA for over 10 years. I occupied the top of the house and she the bottom and we shared the kitchen. She had no name for her god. Whenever she hit hard times and struggles she made reference to her higher power, but would not give it a name. It was impersonal. I answered the door one day and almost fell through the floor to see my brother Alan standing there. Something was terribly wrong. There was a pregnant silence between us until he stepped inside and said, "It's Lin, she has cancer". I simply asked, "Is she going to die?" To which he took me in his arms and said, "Not necessarily".

I packed a bag and we were heading south towards dad's place within 30 minutes. Inwardly I felt God's peace within my soul. It was right then that I realised, once again, the miracle the day Jesus came into my heart on the 17th June 1993, because since then I had not had one desire to drink, smoke or use drugs, and I therefore knew that whatever the outcome of this crisis, God was within me. I had not once felt any pull toward using drugs of any kind, and it is His Name which deserves all honour and thanks. With smoking, I continued the habit despite losing the desire, but eventually, and with the prayers of Minchinhampton Christian fellowship behind me, I walked free from the nicotine habit too. I was expecting a long and miserable withdrawal from the nicotine, but felt absolutely no anxiety at all. I then realised that I had continued smoking out of fear. I was trapped by a conditioned reaction, that of being thoroughly miserable whenever I did not have a cigarette for any length of time. I had not brought this issue to Jesus. Now it looked like my sister was going to fall prey to the same fate that mum fell to years earlier. I started to wait for the urge to smoke or for a drink, but nothing came. I simply felt at peace with God, and as long as I was in His will, I would have everything I needed to handle anything life wanted to throw at me.

Dad knew something was wrong as soon as he saw Alan and I turn up at his home of the cliff edge of the South Coast of England. He met each of us eye to eye and simply asked us 'who'? We sat him down and explained that Lin had cancer. I instantly got in touch with what I can fairly claim to be Garnett denial. Dad instantly adopted the stiff upper lip, never say die attitude. I snubbed it and expressed my anger and fear of losing my sister at such an early age. With that, it seemed that everyone got in touch with the same feelings, and we were able then to rally round each other in a time of grief. At Linda's request, we did not all gather by her beside. I returned to Stroud, Dad stayed where he was and Alan returned home. We just sat and waited. I got before my Lord and placed my sister in His hands, but with willingness in my heart to worship His Holy Name, even in the event of Linda dying. I wrote Linda a letter and tried to reach her in her terrible state of desperation. I spoke of the desperation I had regularly felt being trapped in addiction, and of the inner knowledge that no one really understood how I truly felt. I then went to The Cross of Jesus, and wrote that in her loneliest and most desperate of moments, it is right at that point that Jesus will understand and respond if she should call to Him. No one could really understand, because Lin's cancer was of the most severe kind, at the entrance of her stomach, and there was a very low success rate for this type of operation.

That was in 1994. Today, 2004, I speak to my sister very regularly. She is now fully fit and working in health care herself, having come through with flying colours. Whether Lin turned to Him in repentance for the forgiveness of her sins and received Jesus into her heart for her personal salvation or not remains to be seen, but in our conversations she never refers to Jesus, so I can only assume not. That's the trouble with Catholicism: its members are inoculated with 'some' of the truth, and because they profess a love for Jesus, they see no need to be born again of the Holy Spirit, thereby actually calling Him a liar (See John 3:3). It is so ironic, that we can talk about any subject under the sun, but Jesus as personal Saviour.

Returning to Stroud, things soon took another turn for my growth. It was after six months of sharing the house with the NA lady that I went down to the kitchen to find her sitting in the dark weeping. Before I had an opportunity to say anything she started with, "Colin, I feel like I'm dying. You have such life and consistency, but I cannot get out of this darkness". The opening was clear, I said to her, "You are right, you are dying, and in your own choice of darkness". That night, after ten years of self-generated recovery, she came face to face with the truth of who Jesus is. I cannot say what she did with this truth, but I know that come judgement day, God will judge her for what she did with what she had been told about His Son. The next morning I knew my mission at that address was complete and it was time for me to move on, and that day I moved out and into a little bed-sit of my own and I just loved it. At night I would close my curtains and do stupid childlike dancing for The Lord. Often I would weep while dancing in the presence of The King I loved. I set Him a chair in the middle of the room and danced for Him, before sitting on the floor at His feet, and thanking Him for saving me. I had failed Him miserably, and took pleasure from being His enemy, and yet He still remained faithful.

I occupied that little flat for another six months. I had many non-Christian visitors, some of whom received Christ for forgiveness and Salvation, others who took the truth away with them. I delivered the message with every ounce of passion within me, and knew that it was then between the sinner and God. Often times I would try to get them to 'receive Jesus', but it never sat right with me. I knew that I was very convincing, but that God's Holy Spirit had to convict of sin. I therefore delivered the message of grace and mercy toward the ungratefully sinful.

I then heard of some new flats being built in a little village called Nailsworth. I got a good feeling about these flats as soon as I heard about them, and I felt that The Lord was waiting for me to ask Him and He would give me whatever my heart desired. I made visiting them my next venture. I had come from jail, to Nelson House; from there to shared accommodation, then into a single bed-sit of my own. I now just felt it was time to progress some more. I visited the building site that was to become new flats. I climbed over cement bags and upturned crates to get to the top floor. There were three flats on the top floor and I walked into the middle one. I just knew that this was going to be my next home. I took the number of the flat—number 7—and the phone number of the landlord, and rang him that day. I was invited to fill in application forms. I agreed to fill them in, but said to the guy, 'I want number 7'. He said, 'That's all good and well, but there is a waiting list that you will have to join first and we have to assess your suitability'. I said, 'Go ahead, but I want number 7'. He said 'why number 7?' I told Him, 'Because 7 is God's number, and I belong to Him'.

He came round to interview me at my bed-sit the next day and it seemed that he actually struggled to not give me the keys to number 7. He kept justifying why I should not have this flat. 'There is a 12 month waiting list', 'you have to follow procedure' and 'there are forms you have to complete'. I just sat there and prayed all over him. Then shaking his head in a type of disbelief, he gave me the keys to number 7. One week later, I moved into my own little flat overlooking the village of Nailsworth in the Gloucestershire countryside. My dancing before God increased, as did the tears of gratitude. I was speaking to my family regularly by now, and during one conversation with my brother, I said 'I would love a home of my own on the side of a valley', and we both chuckled.

I had been out of prison two years to within a week, when I gave testimony at a healing meeting near Cirencester. Following my testimony, a Baptist minister approached me. He asked me if I knew Vic Jackopson. I said I had never heard of him. He then went on to tell me how Vic was an ex-villain who had founded Hope Now Ministry and how he was going to Ukraine in the summer to visit prisons out there. I knew without a shred of doubt right there and then that I was going to Ukraine with this Vic guy, whoever he was. The two-year period was up and God was remaining faithful to the conviction He gave. I went to Andy the next day and simply said, "I'm going to Ukraine". I wrote to Hope Now the same day introducing myself with a seven-line testimony. I poured out my heart in those seven lines and expressed my frustrations with 'there must be more to this Church thing than setting out chairs week in, week out, and gathering in holy huddles'. Within one week I had received a response from Vic himself saying, "Ask your Church for support, but if they cannot help, I will personally pay for you. You are coming to Ukraine". God was about to open a new chapter in my life, and I knew with a deep excitement that this Jackopson character would be playing a significant role in my future. I thought that getting a passport might be a problem, but my application went without a hitch.

The minister who approached me in the healing meeting also had a profound effect on me, but in another direction. He rang me to ask if I would give testimony at two services he was leading in the same morning but in different villages. I agreed and he gave me his home address. I turned up at his house on the Sunday morning, to find a very disorganized man, rushing up and down stairs, and actually being, I thought, quite rude to his wife in front of me. We eventually got out to his car and we sped off to the first service. He was preoccupied, very nervous and driving very fast. When we got to the Church, though, a miracle happened. As soon as he stepped into the pulpit to open the service, he became very soft spoken, and very warm natured, smiling and endearing. I was shocked. He had been like the Tasmanian devil ten minutes ago! I gave testimony of how Jesus had mercifully redeemed me, speaking for fifteen minutes. The minister then brought the service to an end and we all had tea and cakes. Everything was typically English, with cups and saucers and dinkies stuck out during tea. I loved this glimpse of rural England and really lapped it up.

My minister friend was, once again, I thought, starting to get preoccupied to the point of rude, looking at his watch while sweet old ladies tried to relate to him. I saw what was going on and finished my tea in preparation for the next lap of the journey. We were due in the next village in fifteen minutes. He did it less than ten. It was like being in a police chase. I was holding onto the passenger door handle so tightly I got a deep ache in my shoulder and fingers. I had to hold on so tightly, though, because we were taking bends at 65 miles per hour in country lanes. Talk about temporary miracles! Tas was back. Then it happened again, as soon as he stepped into the pulpit, the same miracle took place. He was like Jekyll and Hyde. A lovely soft tone, especially tuned to titillate the ears and imaginations of extremely wealthy pensioners of the English retirement zones. I arrived back home that day, financially better off, but spiritually darkened. Two sermons in one morning, breaking all speed limits, and endangering lives to get from pulpit to pulpit? I wondered.

Hope Now

In two years of Churching, I had not been exposed to or offered any teaching on the varying theological standpoints, or the viewpoints around the tongues issue or any of the other gifts. It must have been taken for granted that I would fall into line with the surrounding school of thought, without voice of my own. But that to me was 'blending in', a reflection of my old life, and of the secular self-help groups that I was attending. I believed deeply that there had to be more to the issues of spirituality, and much more to me as a Holy Spirit-filled Christian than mere conformity. The impression forming in my mind was that my new leaders, and Church elders, had nothing wrong with them. I started feeling as if I was the only one who ever had anything internally wrong as a result of this sin issue. This placed me in a predicament, because I was unable to trust anyone who came across as having nothing wrong with them. I have always been incapable of trusting people until I have known them for some time and/or experienced conflict with them, but now here I was in a Christian context, wherein there never appeared to be any conflict. I loved the people around me, but I was unable to feel any real sense of trust toward them. As long as everything was kept at a superficial level with no one creating any waves, the ship would chug along at a relaxed pace.

At the N.A. Meetings I was attending two and three times a week, I felt it safe to challenge people and confront them if I saw that they were endangering themselves or others, because that was the level of intimacy we shared and the central ethos of the group. When I was out of line, they told me so. In Church, everyone was apparently alright all the time. It was the same people, week in, week out, crying and going forward for healing, and then falling on the floor and repeating it all again the next week. I was slowly growing disillusioned and feeling unsafe in Church. I had a lot of people around me with whom I felt safe. I knew that I could turn to most, if not all, of Minchinhampton Christian Fellowship if ever I needed them; but I had specific safe people to whom I just gravitated, like the Record family and the Morris family and a few other friends. I just knew in my heart that these guys were safe for me, but it saddens me to now see that these guys were in the minority. Missionary organizations or missionary trips were very rarely, if ever, talked about in our meetings, so the thought of me going out as a missionary was a totally foreign concept.

Of the many 'prophecies' spoken over me at the many Churches I visited, not one of them mentioned missionary work or the renewing concepts of education, ordination or marriage, which were—as far as I could see—all issues running consistent to God's heartbeat for His Church displayed in His Word. From time to time missionaries were prayed for by our fellowship, but they were an enigma as far as I was personally concerned. I had received no teaching on the principles within The Great Commission of Matthew 28 ("go, tell, teach and baptise").

Things were about to drastically change.

Off to Kiev

Correspondence came through from Hope Now and I suddenly found myself in possession of an air ticket to Kiev. I stared at it for hours, and kept repeating to myself, 'I'm going to Ukraine to talk of Jesus'. There was a team of Hope Now supporters going on the trip and we were called to meet at Whitton Baptist Church in London, the night before we were due to fly out. At Whitton, when people started to arrive, I started to feel a welling up of excitement. I felt a real sense of purpose, and all my struggles and frustration of the previous two years slid into insignificance. When Vic arrived, I saw an immediate presence to him. I saw Jesus in his eyes, heard wisdom in his words, and a gentle authority in his tone. A man of God. He shook my hand and as we held eye contact, we checked each other out and knew within seconds that this was more than just fellowship—it was kindred spirit, affinity of character. I knew that this guy, with all his godliness, would fit in on any prison exercise yard. He was neither a victim nor a hunter; he was at peace and I loved him from the first. He spoke across to me, as an equal.

The whole team sat in a circle in the Church hall and each member was asked to give a short testimony saying who he or she was and where they were from. We had schoolteachers, child minders, doctors, students, nurses, a few other folk and me. My heavily tattooed hand caught many an eye, and as I shared a very brief testimony, the room went from being quiet, to very quiet. But then Vic appointed me policeman over the baggage, and the irony brought an explosion of laughter. On the flight I found myself sitting next a female member of the team, and she looked terribly nervous about me. I believed that if I had yelled 'boo' at her, she would have had the plane turn around for her to get off and go home where she would be safe. She came across as very polite, but ready to run at the first hint of any mischief. Once again, Vic helped melt the ice when he asked this lady and I to count the money out into thousands of dollars. We were suddenly sat with a pile of dollars between us, and she went from being a bag of nerves, to a wonderful sister in Christ with the best sense of humour I have ever come across. Trish Jackopson-Hendy, Vic's one time sister-in-law, became my best friend before we touched tarmac in Kiev. So much so that she was nagging me before we reached check-in at the airport. "Come this way, carry this, go that way, nag, nag, nag, nag, nag".

I rejoiced in how God had given me such a trusting friend, which in turn told me that I could trust her. During the bus ride from the airport Trish, now totally relaxed, was chatting quite a lot. I waited for a pause and then jumped in with, "boy, can you talk". Trish, and several people sitting closest to us, went into a kind of amazed silence. I looked her right in the eye and said to her, "I'm betting you could talk a glass eye to sleep". There was slight lull, and then an almighty eruption of laughter. From that time on Trish and Roy, her husband, have been friends in the truest sense, who tell me exactly what I need to hear when I need to hear it. I could only thank God for the blessing of this nervous lady feeling totally safe with me.

The Lord was constantly making His heart for me known to me through His children. I found that every time I was asked a question, people seemed to hang on every word I said. Very often some would jump in to prove me wrong or dismantle my theological views; but on the whole, I seemed to capture respect. It was in Prison 62, Cherkassey that I received my deepest blessing since climbing into the trash can two years previously. The prison was in a shocking state of decay, and the prisoners blended in very well. They were thick-skinned and as rough as they come. Something like 300 men packed into the tiny chapel, and we spent some time singing praises to God. Following the worship, Vic took to the pulpit and opened God's Word. For the first time in my Christian life, I could honestly say that I was listening to God's Word, being unpacked by a man anointed and filled with God's Spirit.

I was suddenly being scratched where I itched, theologically. It was like having a cold shower. I felt totally refreshed by Biblical exposition. I looked to Trish sitting next to me, and simply said to her, 'He is sitting in my seat'. Trish was shocked and looked around to see if anyone had overheard. "What do you mean?" I shrugged my shoulders and simply said, "I do not know what it means, but I know that this man is sitting in my seat." Trish said, "You have to tell him". I avoided her idea. "No way, if it is of God, let God tell him". At that point, I knew, without need of man's approval, that I had to get alongside this little giant of a man, and sit at his feet whenever I could for learning. I started to watch him closely. Following his sermon, Vic turned to me and simply said, 'Colin, testify'. I simply took it in my stride, stood up and gave a twenty minute testimony of God's liberating mercy. Everyone felt how God rested His hand upon that meeting, and no one moved or said a word throughout the sermon and then the testimony. Vic took the pulpit again, and laid the truth before these men. We saw approximately 250 prisoners respond to an altar call for Salvation.

Team members were astonished, and actually looked surprised. I closed my eyes and got myself before God as best I could. At the response of these men, I inwardly and sin-wardly felt a sense of self-satisfaction and righteousness, as if I had achieved something. I sat before God and simply opened my hands before Him. Distorted motives are never very far from the surface. I received, however, a deep and blessed assurance within me, that The Lord Jesus Himself had drawn and saved the majority of these men that day. Colin had impressed many, and they came forward as a result of my persuasive testimony, but God was even at work on these men. God's Word, anointed by God's Spirit, connecting personal truth of Divine mercy to carnal frailty. The Word, carried by The Spirit, took souls into humility, and God then caused these weeping souls to be born again that very day. Not that God needs man to fulfil His salvation plan, but man needs to understand his frailty. I believe God said to me personally that day, "Colin, this is where I am taking you", and I knew that there should be no surprise by mass awakenings or Christian revivals when God's anointed path is followed. I was asked 'why do you think so many got saved?' Without doubt I answered, 'because it was exactly what we had expected'. Over and above my self-righteousness, and under-girding all my selfish ambitions, God remains faithful to His Word that 'He came to seek and to save that which is lost' (Luke 19:10). He does not save people because of me;

He saves them despite me, and that's the essence of grace and mercy. If God had to wait until His messengers were pure to save others, we would all be doomed.

The information and insights I had gathered in the secular treatment clinics had, in truth, empowered my testimony delivery more than the Church services had, and slowly the penny started to drop. I sat alone after that prison service and came face to face with some startling thoughts. While the secular world holds all the information and most effective methodology for 'examining man's ways', they have nowhere to take their findings. They then have to create an impersonal 'higher power' to satiate the spiritual element of its clients. In contrast, Church is 'turning to The Lord', without the required courageous self-examination, and is in danger of neglecting the emotional damage of its members. Therefore Lamentations 3:40, "Come, let us examine our ways and test them and return to The Lord" has actually been cut in half, crippling The Church in its potential to shine with men and women walking in healing and freedom. I believe that until we seek a healthy balance of the two, the world will continue to claim more converts to psychological reasoning than the Church can converts to Christ.

But herein lies a bigger problem with which our minds cannot, or simply will not, wrestle with. If this is true, then many of our Churches could very well be founded on a very attractive—and it must be said, a very nearly satisfying, but nothing more than a psychological—foundation. Should this be, then it follows that a multitude of 'converts' may not actually be converts from sin. Jesus warned us about leaders of influence, in among 'sheep longing for a shepherd', who will attract a following, and then go on to produce fruit of the same kind. Needs do get met, but souls go unsaved. I firmly believe that this is where programmes of mass discipleship like The Alpha Course have their roots. I have done two Alpha courses. I did the second one in the hope of evaporating the doubts I came away with from the first one. I twice sat among spiritually hungry people, and 'like sheep without a shepherd' was a perfect term of description: on both occasions I saw what I believed to be nothing more than carnal spirituality. I saw seeking men and women being impressed and convinced about God and Jesus.

This is not the work of The Holy Spirit. His job is not to 'impress and convince people about God and Jesus', His job is to 'depress and convict people about sin and repentance toward God in Christ'. I spoke out about this on both groups and was very professionally silenced. I have also spoken to friends who are very pro-Alpha and have yet to receive Biblical reproach from God through them.

Ants or Saints?

I was watching a lady inside the Church building recently as she sprayed all the plants within the building. In a very polite conversation I was told that the Mealy bug was attacking the plants in the Church and slowly killing them. Unseen by the untrained eye, the Mealy bug latches itself onto indoor plants, and slowly starts to suck the sweet life juices out of the plant. These juices soon attract armies of ants. The plant gets slowly sucked to death, before the Mealy bug and the multitudes of ants move on. The left over juice then slowly gets covered in a soot mould like a death sheath. One tiny Mealy bug, unseen by the untrained eye, not only kills—it opens the door for other untold carnage.

Carnal Spirituality, unseen by the untrained eye, will do exactly the same thing. Think of it this way—Sunday school. Most Sunday schools carry the same mission statement:

Proverbs 22:6

"Train up a child in the way he should go and when he is old he will not depart from it"

From that, infants are having it impressed upon their tiny, absorbent and very impressionable hearts and minds that God is their Heavenly

Father and if they confess their sins and repent He will take them to heaven.

But that is not what Proverbs 22:6 is teaching us, and it is not 'conversion born out of conviction of sin'. Proverbs 22:6 is telling us that by "the way" we "train up a child", is "the way" he will "not depart from when is old". "The way" we live—the example we set in our homes and how we are in our relationships with each other and in our personal relationship with God Himself—is the training we are passing on to our children.

We cannot 'educate' or 'theorize' our children into heaven; we can only set the example of being awe-full yet humble before this Holy God. Praise God if this is wrong, but my fear is children are being infested with a spiritual Mealy bug by, once again, well-meaning 'leaders'.

These are they who then go on to believe "Oh, I have been a Christian all my life". Next stop: Bible College and Church leadership—ants instead of Saints.

I turned to God's Word for confirmation and/or rebuke, privately hoping for rebuke and correction. The epistle of 1 John arrested me. Chapter 1 speaks clearly about walking in the light, by means of confessing our sins (Verses 5-10). In Chapter 2, John then makes this statement in verse 8: "the darkness is passing and the true light is already shining". I sat and stared, knowing God was telling me something. "Lord, why do you emphasise 'the true light is shining'? Why the true light?" I sat with this question until, in the quiet early morning and as clear as crystal, I knew. Because the darkness mentioned in that same verse, is actually false light. The darkness we are up against as Christians will not be that stupid or obvious as to appear and blow their cover with manifestations of the demonic. It is the false light, often peddled by those who are claiming 'victories' over the demonic, and gathering multitudes of vulnerable followers whose needs are never getting met in a true sense. I am not intending to discount demonic activity. I know it exists; God's Word tells me it exists. What I am saying is that it would actually be in keeping with Jesus' teaching about 'any kingdom divided against itself crumbling' in Luke 11:17 (and others). It would be accurate for the demonic to pose as light and cast out the demonic, because that kingdom is, in fact, by inheritance resentfully warring against itself and doomed to crumble anyway.

Consequently we are inundated by confused 'Church members' who are limping through their spiritual life, leading no one to Christ. They have not actually been converted from darkness to light. They have been converted from darkness to fog. Praise God if I'm wrong and I mean no ill intent at all toward Sunday Schools, I have children of my own who go to Sunday School. I know they do a good work, but scripture paints clear pictures as to how the satanic hates children. Look at how all the babies were murdered in the hunt for The Lord. I believe this is why God has the life of all babies in His hand. There are no children in hell. The abortionists did not take God by surprise. He has caught every slain infant soul from the beginning of time and will continue to do so until He returns. God has the dispensation of ignorance covered. Judgement waits for the likes of you and me who accept or reject His Son.

Back at the campsite that night, we sat in silent awe and prayed for God's new adopted sons in Prison 62. I kept my thoughts to myself, but the worship took on a new depth of sincerity and meaning for every one of us; we worshipped Him in spirit and in truth. As we worshipped, I saw much spiritual light around me. Most of us wept quietly before we slowly filtered off to bed against a cacophony of Ukrainian night sounds. Several team members got their walk with God back in step, too, at that time. God had not finished with any of us.

As that 1995 Ukraine trip came to an end I was asked, 'What are you going to do when we get back'? I had not thought that far forward, but without thought I responded, 'I'm going to get a job'. I'd been on unemployment for two years by that time, but things were about to change again. People's expectations seemed to be for me to go straight back into the mission field and evangelising, and I would have been happy to, but God had a few lessons in store for me before that was to happen again. Progressive Christianity.

Christianity in the Workplace

During a visit to a Christian bookshop I decided to buy one of those little fish emblems that many Christians wear. Mine had some Greek letters fixed in the middle of it. I could not work out whether or not I was wearing it the right way round, so I popped into a shop owned by one of my elders and asked him. He said 'Colin, is this the extent of your problems'? We chuckled, but that was actually the truth of the matter. However, on my return from Ukraine, that was about to change. I arrived back at my accommodation on the Friday night, knowing deep within my heart that I would be getting a job very soon. A few years earlier, I had chosen to allow my heavy-duty driving licence to expire. I had simply not renewed it. I had a terrible employment record and was blacklisted for numerous thefts from numerous delivery points and/or from my diesel tank. I had accepted that losing the HGV licence was a consequence of my former life style. I had been working part-time for the Morris family, driving a van delivering engineering parts. The part-time job helped me to keep in touch with employment commitment without too much responsibility too fast. The Morris family belongs to God and they are a very gracious bunch. They understood my need of slow growth, and allowed me two or three days' work a week. It also helped me to start interacting in the workplace as a new Christian, something else I needed to do gradually.

As I started to mature, I started to miss the truck driving with feelings of frustration because I knew 'I could do it honestly now'. When I woke up on the Saturday morning after Ukraine, I had the idea to phone the driving licence people in Swansea, just to enquire how to go about getting my licence back. It made no sense to ring these people because it was Saturday. I rang, though, deciding that the worst case scenario would be to leave a message on the system until Monday. I was surprised when the phone was answered, and I was even more surprised when the guy who answered the phone went straight into his computer to find my details, and within minutes he told me, 'Sir, your licence is current and valid; there is no problem with it'. I just stared at the phone in my hand, because this was unbelievable.

I left my flat that morning with an added spring in my step. I felt that doors of employment were about to open for me, and this time I could do it all honestly. I noticed a truck with a Stroud address passing through the village I was living in and decided to follow it. The thought of trucking was very exciting in a new kind of way. I had started to learn to manage my finances while on unemployment, to the extent of saving in a post office account. The banks rejected my applications as soon as my name came up on their computers. I accepted all these knock-backs with peace, embracing them as my consequences, and as something I would just have to live with. I had robbed from everyone around me, to the point of emptying my cheque book on electrical goods and clothes, knowing that there was nothing in my account. I had to find peace in my heart that my life may never reach anything like normal, and a willingness to face the banks about my former dishonesties. But first I had to be in a position where I could actually do something to repay, should they so desire. I was ready. I was prepared to work for nothing if it meant I could repay all I had defrauded.

I followed that truck back to its depot and was met by the boss of the company. Within two minutes of talking to him, he had employed me, starting on the Monday at 5:00 a.m. I could see that I was slowly getting back all that had been destroyed. On the Sunday night I was fired up with nervous anticipation and could not sleep. As the night turned into early morning, I started to grow in anxiety. "I have to sleep", was the thought that kept me awake. I was dreading having to read a map, find delivery points, interact with earthlings and handle a 16-ton truck. I was licensed to drive up to 30 tons, but because I had been off the road for so long, I went back in with the small stuff. The rain had fallen very steadily all night. Believe me, I listened to it. It was pouring down. I was gradually growing in dread to the point of thinking, 'I'm not going. I simply cannot do it'. I curled up in a ball on my bed and like a little child I said, 'Lord, I do not want to go to work in this rain'. At that very moment, it stopped raining. It had poured for hours, and as soon I got childlike before God, the rains stopped. I just knew God was on my side. In the midst of all my anxiety, I had forgotten. But there He was, just waiting for me to ask in the right way.

I got the sense that The Lord Himself had actually caused the rain to stop just for me. Not for me to testify about, because I knew, even in among Christians, this would be treated with amusement. This was not for testimony. It was God Himself interacting with me personally. As I curled up in a small ball on my bed, He took my heart to the truth of Sovereignty. And yet, in contrast to seeing Him in any position of power or dominion, I saw a tenderly swollen brow attacked by thorns, and muscles stretched beyond their limit. I saw a naked and twisted human form with its rib cage on show for the counting, and a slow rise and fall of a blood soaked chest in its final attempts for an air intake. I saw Jesus in a whole new light. I saw that all things had been created by Him and for Him, and that in His way He was reconciling all things back to Himself. I saw that He had even created the atmospheric dynamics that engineered the cloud formation that produced this rain, and it was at His bidding that the rain started and stopped.

I then saw another cloud formation, hundreds of years before Christ was born, in its infancy yet fast maturing and moistening to produce millions, probably billions of raindrops, more than man's most advanced technology could ever count or even estimate. Look at it this way—a million seconds is eleven days, but a billion seconds is thirty-two years—and in among this myriad of raindrops, one specific droplet was appointed to land upon one specific seed. That seed absorbed that raindrop, and a new form of life started its cycle and purpose. A tiny stem, slowly thickening and producing leaves. Years of growth, with varying seasonal climates and only God will ever know how many more raindrops were drunk by that seed. God produced the moods, means and purpose for the growth of that seed. Until, one day, believing the initiative to be his own, man cut down that tree. Then in accordance to God's foreknowledge and plan, they stripped and carved at that tree. Both lumberjack and carpenter had received their skills for this purpose from this God. Then finally, and once again for God's ultimate purpose, an instrument of torture was created from that tree. The Cross was made, even for the crucifixion of His own dear Son on Calvary. All preordained and carefully fulfilled in order for the likes of Colin Garnett to climb into a trash can full of water in a prison Chapel with his sinful soul, and go free from the bondages of sin and its life-controlling consequences of addiction. Even so, it could be argued, that I could curl up into a small ball on my bed in the early hours of the morning, and selfishly worry about going to work in the rain, in order to gain more depth of insight and gratitude.

By 5:30 that same morning I stood with my new employer, telling Him 'this is the day that The Lord has made'. He looked at me like I had no right to be so happy so early on a Monday morning, but I also detected a hint of envy in his eye. There was no way he could have known how I had been conveyed from a gory story to a glory story, but I could see that he saw something he liked. I left the depot that day with hitchhikers and the Gospel in mind. I was heading from Stroud to South Wales on the M5. I drew into the first service station five minutes outside of Stroud. I did not stop at the service station; I simply drove through and picked up a guy on the exit slip road. As he climbed into the cab, his body odour sort of just preceded him, a bit like an aura. I thought for a moment that he would probably have his own swarm of flies in the summer, that kind of 'aura'. He was very untidy, and not the best looking guy in town. His face was weather beaten and cruelly scarred by years of street life. By the time I had dropped him off on the other side of the Severn Bridge in Wales, I had delivered what I knew to be a very powerful and cutting Gospel message. The guy just sat staring at me and listening with an amazed expression on his face. I felt that my tattoos had become the backdrop of his expectations, but as I unpacked the meditations of my heart, the words of my mouth sort of hypnotised him. He simply could not make sense of it, and he looked like a rabbit trapped in headlights. He had nowhere to run.

Before he got out of the truck I asked if I could pray with him. During the prayer, the guy started to sob. I was sitting in the driver's seat, with one hand stretched across to rest on his shoulder. He cried for a good twenty minutes, about his failures and about his hopelessness, about his drinking and about his failed marriages. He spoke of rejection and loneliness in such a way that I could only listen and quietly cry along with him. In the end I had to anticipate the next lull and jump in to interrupt him because I had work to do. He turned to God that morning and humbled himself under the truth of who he is in relation to God's Holiness. As I drove away, I caught a glimpse of him in my wing mirror. He looked totally different to when I had picked him up just under an hour before, and I just knew his life was never going to be the same again. I could not help but think that even his posture had changed, as if now he had purpose and direction. He wanted a lift to Wales and I was able to get him to Wales. However, what he had not bargained for was going via Bethlehem, Gethsemane, Calvary, God's Wrath, The Sacrificial Blood, God's Satisfaction, Death's Disarmament, The Empty Tomb and Glory's Invitation.

The rain had started again on the outside of the truck and I was crying on the inside, and for some weird reason I turned the wipers on to fast, as if that would clear my vision. I had to pull the truck over to the side of the road because I was howling with laughter and joy, excitement and praise, and wonder at how God would use a toe-rag like me to redeem souls. I felt a deep excitement about being involved in the rescue of souls from the very clutches of evil and hell itself. I'd seen an awakening to the truth in Prison 62 Ukraine, and I saw the very same illumination in the eyes of my scruffy little hitchhiker just off the M5 in Wales.

The weeping subsided eventually and I was able to get on with my job. As I did so, though, a burden was sprouting within me. I knew that my scruffy little hitchhiker would be looked after, much in the same way as I had been in prison and the guys in Ukraine's 62 would. The question starting to grow in my heart was, 'Did The Holy Spirit convict him of sin; or did I just impress and convince him toward God?' I found direct rest to my question from what I firmly believe was of The Lord Himself. Man operates by means of impression and convincing, The Holy Spirit's primary role in the heart of an unregenerate sinner is to depress and convict. Before the 'thought' was over, I had started weeping again. I reached a point that day where I wanted to say to God something along the lines of, "Lord, will you back off a bit please, I have got to get this job done". Inwardly I knew that The Lord totally understood. I was struggling to understand Grace, to the point of not wanting any more. Many times my thoughts would be, 'Lord, just go easy on the Grace'. I knew Heaven smiled over me, and the scruffy little hitchhiker was the first of many.

I had worked for six months for this particular company, and on a number of occasions my boss set me a schedule which would require me to drive over the legal limit of hours. I had to stay within the law, and that meant I sometimes would not get the job done. I knew this would render me unpopular, even to the point of never making any progress in terms of promotion. I would always be last choice for any of the attractive jobs like overnight runs to Scotland. So before I knew it, I had gone as far as I was going to go in this job. Being out on the road each day gave me the opportunity to see who was who in the transport field. It turned out that probably the biggest transport company in the west of England had its base less than two miles from where I was stationed. I knew I could not work for this current employer much longer because—by standing firm in not breaking the law—I was growing in unpopularity.

It was early one Saturday morning when the bubble burst. Once again I had been set a task that was obviously legally impossible. I tried to explain that I would not get everything done within my legal hours. The boss just 'ordered' me to 'get on with it'. I threw the keys to him and simply said, 'No, you get on with it'. I walked out of that depot at 7 a.m. that Saturday morning. I visited the largest transport company in the west of England at 9 a.m. and started working for that company at 6 a.m. the following Monday. I felt that The Lord had honoured my desires for holiness and opened the door to a job close to the top in the haulage line. Within one week of starting, and being in the enviable position of working for such a company, I was inwardly feeling uneasy. Nothing can compare with sharing the Gospel of Jesus Christ with lost souls. I was now working for the type of Haulage Company that I used to dream about in my earlier miserable attempts at employment. I used to believe, 'If I could just get a start with a company like that, I would be alright'. But now, here I was, and all it offered was a worldly type of satisfaction.

I sat in a transport café one morning, with a nice new truck outside and a pocket full of money. All around me I could see men of the world. All they spoke about was speed traps, and roadworks, breakdowns and fogbanks. They spoke in a special kind of dialogue, and grew fat on greasy breakfasts. Hell was yawning beneath them, and ignorance was their best and only defence. Every time I rang my new boss back at the office, it seemed that he was not at rest until he had made some sort of disgusting sexual innuendo, and then roared with laughter at his own 'joke'. I found myself dreading the phone call because I would always find myself with dirty images in my mind and feeling abused. I resolved to try and give this job two years, but God had another plan.

I had heard nothing from nor made any contact with Vic Jackopson for the remainder of 1995. I just tried to concentrate on work. I then heard via a newsletter that another Ukraine trip was being planned for the summer of 1996. Once again I joined the missionary team for another summer camp. I had developed a special bond with Trish and her husband Roy, and once again, back in Prison 62, I sat next to Trish as Vic took to the pulpit. He did it again. Vic opened God's Word, and God opened the hearts of everyone in the chapel. Once again, I turned to Trish and said, 'He is sitting in my seat'. Trish took on a serious tone and said quite sternly, 'Well then, you have to tell him'. I knew she was right.

Once again we saw many men be saved and Vic baptised many of the previous year's converts. It was all very beautiful, but it all felt kind of surreal to me, because I knew I had to approach this apostle type preacher and tell him, 'I think you're sitting in my seat'. I was preoccupied for the rest of the day. That night I sat actually trying to avoid Vic. However, I saw that he was retiring for the night and I knew I had to get a move on. I gently tapped on his door, inwardly hoping he wouldn't hear, but he equally as gently said, 'Come in'. We sat opposite each other in a room not too dissimilar to an average prison cell in UK. There were two single beds. He sat on one and I sat on the other and we stared at each other. I could not help noticing that his feet did not reach the floor, but I saw a giant of a man before me. In moments of tension like this, I had an unfortunate nervous tendency of trying to come up with something funny to melt any ice. I went for it. "Vic, at worst I am about to make a fool of myself. Please hear me out, and let me voice my heart to you". I think I drank from the peace I saw in Vic's beautiful eyes, and with that I said, "I think you might be keeping a seat warm for me".

Vic sat back with a slow intake of breath and thought for a moment. He then said the strangest thing. "Colin, education is of the utmost importance. You will always have a message for the drunk, the prisoner and the thug. But the Gospel of Jesus Christ is aimed at the rich and the poor, the uneducated and the educated alike. Unless you sharpen up, you will lose many who need saving". I very nearly understood him. Then after a long apostolic stare and silence he said, "Have you ever considered going to Bible College"? I had to concede that I did not even know there was such a thing as Bible College, but it would make sense of where the majority of the 'unconverted' Church leaders got their qualifications from. Another pause, but this time there was an eruption of excitement building in me. As Vic very politely opened the door for me to leave, he simply said, "Try Moorlands". Before I knew it, I was outside his room and Trish was glowing with excitement in the corridor. "What did he say?" All I could say was, "I'm going to Moorlands Bible College". There was a beautifully musical type of "Amen" from Trish, and we both started to grow in excitement about my going to College. I had no money whatsoever, and no academic muscle to flex to anyone, but I knew I was going to Moorlands Bible College and that was that. I did not know where it was or what they taught, but I knew I was going.

The next morning I felt as if it was a ridiculous dream, and actually doubted God's involvement in it all. How am I going to find funding for Bible College when I cannot even get a bank account, let alone have any money to put into it? Trish once again put me straight. "Colin, that is God's business. Stop worrying, you will be going to Bible College". I considered asking my Church back in Stroud, but I knew it was a small fellowship and struggling with its own overheads. I was working and earning quite well, but the truth had to be acknowledged: my days of working for worldly people with worldly ways were over. I felt that The Lord had met the dreams of my heart in terms of wanting to work for a well established haulage company, in order for me know—without doubt—that the world had nothing to offer me. Souls were perishing in every street of every town I visited, and there was I trucking nationwide on an ego trip, keeping the very Word of Life secret! It did not sound or feel right at all. When I returned to work, I resigned my position before I had contacted Moorlands.

On my return from Ukraine, I found a court order in my mail. I was being summonsed to court for failing to pay 7 months worth of Poll Tax. I went into shock;. I did not even realise that I should have been paying Poll Tax. My bills had been sent to my previous two addresses after I had left. I had a bill for £350. That same week I appeared in the Magistrate's Court in Stroud. I was asked to take the Bible in my right hand and read from the card. I looked to the bench and quietly refused to do so. Once again my tattoos had created the mood, and the magistrate rolled her eyes and instructed me to explain myself. I said: "Ma'am, I actually belong to The Lord. Within this His Word, Jesus Himself made it plain that He did not want His followers to 'swear by heaven because it is God's Throne, but to simply let our yes be yes and our no be no'. Ma'am, He has my life in His hand, I can assure you, I will not be giving false witness".

I was excused the 'oath', and made a declaration instead. Regarding the £350 outstanding Poll Tax bill I was asked, 'Why did I have such an amount unpaid and what are my intentions?' I said, 'Ma'am, I can give you no excuses. That bill has grown through genuine ignorance and irresponsibility. I am prepared to repay this amount at your guiding. However, I feel it would be more beneficial if this bill was written off'. There was a growing unease in the courtroom. "Why?" I was asked. "Ma'am, I am in the process of bettering myself. I am walking with God and have been for the past four years. I am four years clean from over seventeen years of chronic heroin addiction. I am trying for Bible College this year. I could make you a commitment to pay this bill and lay aside College. Or I could make you a commitment to repay it from student status. I feel it would be a travesty if I were to lay College aside for a relatively small amount, and I also feel it would be naive to think I could honour dual commitments, when College is going to demand my all'.

The courtroom was the quietest I had ever heard a courtroom to be. The magistrate asked me, "What would you suggest?" "Please write off the debt, Ma'am". Without further question or thought, as if she had already made up her mind, the Magistrate placed my file back in its folder and said, "Outstanding debt in this case to be withdrawn, case dismissed. Mr. Garnett, I have a funny feeling you are going to do well, enjoy College."

I left the courtroom and walked beside a local canal. I was in a state of deep internal communion with, and worship of, God. I had not yet contacted College. I was so wrapped up in the very fact that God was always one step ahead of me—I was half expecting them to contact me. I rang them and made an appointment for an interview. I was very excited about getting back into a classroom environment, but not before I had interviewed them.

I went to Moorlands College in August of 1997 for an interview and it was much more than I had anticipated. Surrounded by beautiful countryside, in its own tranquil setting and within ten minutes of England's South Coast, I could not have asked for more. I sat with two of the lecturers and we just chatted at a very superficial level to begin with. I was asked what academic qualifications I had, because there were certain criteria that one had to meet in order to qualify for a Bachelor Degree course. I was mind blown by it all. I wasn't interested in getting a BA Degree; I just wanted to study God's Word and broaden my horizons of influence with the Gospel. The thought of doing a Bachelor of Arts Degree was simply too much for me to contemplate. I simply said, "I have no academic background to talk about whatsoever. (I gave a ten minute testimony). All I know is that I'm coming to this College." I was asked who had recommended Moorlands to me, and when I said Vic Jackopson, the meeting was adjourned 'for lunch'.

When we reconvened, one of the lecturers had a very reassuring smile for me. We sat and he explained: "Colin, in this day and age one does not simply walk into a College and say 'I am coming to this College'. One has to have a certain academic standard to begin with. Such is the demand for Bachelor Degree courses that one is required to have a minimum of two A-levels. We cannot, therefore, offer you our three-year degree course. How would you feel about doing a 2-year diploma in theology?" I allowed my heart to speak. "Sir, two years is not going to be long enough. It will take me two years to learn how to learn. What else can you suggest?" I was told to go away and pray about it and ring them the next day. I did not feel I had to pray about it. There were far more important issues to pray about without going over established ground. I rang Moorlands the next day. I was told: "Well, for some time now this College has been considering running a four year Degree course, starting with a foundation year, which would qualify one for a three year degree. It has to be said that your case has caused us to reopen this idea. In fact, we feel you are the catalyst for the introduction of this course and we would love to offer you a place starting in September". I did not need to pray or think any further than I already had, I simply accepted.

As soon as I put the phone down from that call, and without realizing how important it was to me, I rang my family and told them. The deep desire to impress them was still there. The only response I got from my dad was a swear word. He rang me back a few hours after I had told him, when it had sunk in and he said, 'Son, that is the best news I have had since your mum died'. I cried. It was lovely. I said, 'Promise me you won't die before I graduate'. He promised. My plea to God was 'please let him enjoy this'. Every member of my family was overwhelmed with joy and admiration. All the broken promises and failings of old suddenly meant nothing. As soon as I stopped promising and got real about myself for myself, I had to face the truth of my state. As soon as I faced the truth of my state, I had to turn to God. As soon as I turned to God, all the broken promises and past failings of old suddenly meant nothing. And now I was being offered a second attempt at school. I sat before God that night and simply bowed before Him for His goodness, grace, mercy, faithfulness, kindness and provision. I was sat silent before this awesome Father God and the eyes of my heart exploded with the light of His character.

Moorlands College

Sitting at my desk as I write, I have the first book I purchased at the outset of four years of Theological Studies:

"The Ladybird Book of Spelling and Grammar for Children"

On the wall directly behind me as I write hangs a certificate which reads:

"This is to certify that
Colin Garnett
Has been awarded the degree of
Bachelor of Arts
Having followed an approved Honours programme in
Applied Theology"

Hope Now Ministries met me, accepted me, trusted in me, loved me and wanted the best for me. They financially covered me for four years of Theological training, supporting me in the needs of books and a car. This was, and still is, active Christianity and faithful stewarding of God's funds.

I was warned prior to Bible College that theological study could destroy a man's faith. I had to bounce back with 'Group Therapy in jail should have broken me, but it didn't'. I had no worries about Jesus in me; I was just intimidated about joining a group of 'straights' for four years and how would I react to them. I soon realised that Bible College was not going to be the inner sanctuary that I was expecting. In actual fact, it was a prime target for the self-appointed who disregard personal holiness in order to get into the pulpit on time. But looking at it realistically, if I wanted to infiltrate the Church, knowing it to be of The Living God, the pillar and foundation of Truth, what better place to train unknowing infiltrators than Bible College? I'm not talking about people who wake up and decide to serve Lucifer and join Bible College as spies. I simply refer to the well meaning, yet unconverted. Would it be out of character for the father of all lies to 'impress' people toward Church leadership through Bible Colleges? I think it would be a very clever plan.

At the start of College, we were told that we had to reach a pass mark of 40% per assignment. For my first few assignments I was struggling to get 40%—45%, but I was getting there and I thought it was only going to improve. I set myself a goal, that if by the end of College I could be reaching the mid 50's, I would have made ample progress.

Being in the classroom environment was very refreshing for me. God's grace was very evident to me and I felt like I was drinking in every word the lecturers said. I was actually studying God's Word, all day, with the help of learned people. I soon started to realise how little I knew. But my learning circle did not come from the classroom alone. I had more bubbles of idealism that needed bursting. Basically, over a four year period I heard some of the most wonderful sermons from some of God's most heavily anointed men. I saw men weeping while praying over lunch. I partook in some of the most wonderful worship. I felt people loving me even when I was at my most unlovely, and I felt myself sinking deeper in love with Jesus the Nazarene.

My theological standpoint gained stability and growth, and my understanding of relationships took on a whole new depth.

The Beautiful Enemy

I would recommend Theological College to any one of the Redeemed. But Lucifer is not sitting back simply letting us gain theological strength. I am convinced that I saw enemy activity too. Remember who it is we are up against when we refer to Lucifer: it is not a horned being with a long tail and a fork—it is a one time high ranking angelic being who not only knew the presence of God in a past tense, but who actually has access to God's presence in the present, and who knew what worship was all about. Ezekiel 28:12-15 gives us a clear picture of who we are up against:

A spiritual being with the following description:
1. The Seal of Perfection (12)
2. Full of Beauty and Wisdom (12)
3. In God's Realm (13)
4. Anointed, Ordained and Blameless (14 and 15)
5. Position, Power and Prestige (12 – 15)

The aims and objectives of this evil influence are to distort and poison our motives.

Do you fit the bill?

Should we fall into the age-old trap of believing evil to be as obvious as something we might see on Halloween, we would free Lucifer's forces to infiltrate where he would least be expected and for him to slowly but very surely destroy what God calls Holy: Church, Marriage, Family, and Sexuality.

Look around, guys. The current professing Church, as far as I can see, has the potential within it to contribute more into hell's account than Heaven's.

Jesus said, "Enter by the narrow gate, for wide is the gate and broad is the way that leads to destruction, and there are many who go by it. Because narrow is the gate and difficult is the way which leads to life, and there are few who find it" (Matthew 7:13-14).

Could it be possible then, that more people will be going to destruction than to life? And yet still, for some strange reason, people seem to judge a church's health by its numbers. What we often fail to see though is how, while our congregations are often judged as experiencing 'God's anointing' because of the numbers and the noise, there are all too often 'leaders' languishing in positions of power and prestige, and very often having money thrown at them!

I will always have a deep sense of affection for Moorlands College, its lecturers and the guys I grew up with there, but I cannot find it in my heart to celebrate just yet, because I know that where and whenever God moves, as He is at Moorlands, Satan is more often than not right behind Him with a counterfeit plan, and he is quite active within theological establishments too.

Part of our Level 2 curriculum was to find a five-week, hands-on practical placement. The norm was to find a Church placement for experience of working in the Church context. I knew in an instant— with the same assurance that I had that I was going to Moorlands and that Jesus was calling me—that I was going to work in one of the treatment clinics where I had been sent by the court in 1991. It just went without saying; working in a Church never even entered the theatre of thought for me. I rang a same styled clinic in Manchester, Altringham Priory, and asked if they could accommodate me for five weeks while I undertook a fact-gathering mission. I acknowledged their programme and the wonderful effect it had had on me. I also said, "I believe that you boast a 70% success rate over addictions, but that the fees are extraordinarily high. I therefore believe that in charging so much for treatment, you are actually marginalizing 70% of the people you profess to want to reach in addiction and alcoholism. My long-term goal is to sit in and watch what you do and to learn as much as I can from you, so that I can go and do likewise for the marginalized free of charge". I was warmly invited to join their team for five weeks, on condition that I respect their 'freedom of religion' ethos, and that I do not preach Christ over any other belief system. For some weird reason, I knew God wanted me in there and I simply agreed.

I went up to Manchester and simultaneously invested in my family reconciliation. My family had been thoroughly ravaged by my addiction for a very long time and I knew that their healing was going to be a long process, and going to Manchester was all part of it.

I stayed with my sister and brother-in-law Ged. Years earlier, at the height of my addiction, I stole some cash from Linda's bedroom. Ged knew it was me, but I managed once again to convince Linda that I was innocent. Some weeks later, when the guilt weighed too heavily upon me, I went back and confessed. This was very damaging. Linda and Ged had argued over my guilt, and Linda had sided with me saying, 'I know when my brother is lying'.

My confession was not born in sorrow; I selfishly wanted them to forgive me so that I could be free from the guilt. Their marriage very nearly hit the rocks because of this and other similar incidents.

By now I had been clean for a few years and now studying at Bible College and the wounds were healing. They opened their home to me. At the clinic I sat in the small group environment and watched as the counselors systematically dismantled the denial systems from around the hearts and minds of addicts and alcoholics, by the gentle application of simple truth. I sat silently for five weeks. I spoke to no one about Jesus Christ. I returned to a feeling I had felt when I was in treatment. I looked at the counselors and knew in my heart that I could do what they do, and equally as effective, if not more so.

I returned to College at the end of my five weeks to find that my Placement Supervisor's report said: 'Colin does not have to preach his belief; he lives it". This came from a female version of PJ McCullough. Her name was Wynne Parry, a very spiritual lady who stood for no nonsense either from her patients or their families. She, like PJ, was the expert in her field. I was daily locked into one line of thought: 'This style of treatment would be ideal for making disciples'. It went direct to what are behavioural and motivating attitude-affecting roots, like pointing out pride and shame, fear and guilt, lust and envy, anger and fear. I foolishly tried this in Church and in Bible College, only to come up against explosions of rage and accusation. It was simply too difficult to contemplate. "Difficult is the way which leads to life".

During my final year of Bible College, Hope Now offered me the position of Head of Prison Ministry. I felt right to accept this position, even entertaining the possibility of starting prisoner treatment style discipleship courses, applying everything I had gathered in my remoulding experiences in therapy. Vic asked if I would like to visit South Africa, specifically Cape Town's Pollsmoor Prison. Hope Now was supporting two ministers out there and it was a steadily growing ministry. Suddenly, with the offer, I became the boss of people I had never met, so it seemed right to visit. The studies in the final year grew in intensity, but I was feeling inwardly confident that I was going to go the distance. My grades were over that which I had set myself, and it started to feel like a downhill ride.

In April of 2000, I went to Cape Town. The two ministers had prepared an itinerary for me that kept me on the go pretty much all the time. I gave my testimony in several different sections of the prison, and each time I finished, a very fiery altar call was made. Every time the altar call went out, 98% of those listening put their hands up to 'receive Christ'. I felt inwardly sceptical. Was it this easy? Is Satan so easily duped? The one who is described by God as being 'full of wisdom' being robbed of souls just like that? I also gave testimony at seventeen Churches in sixteen days. We went flat out and I nearly burned out. I found myself feeling deeply frustrated at giving testimony to the captive audiences of prison, whose motives are uncontrollably influenced by 'looking good in the eyes of parole boards' especially to be seen as becoming a Christian. But not only so, I was aware of being equally as frustrated at giving testimony to Christians. I started to feel like I was in the entertainment business. I grew inwardly confused.

Toward the end of the South Africa visit, I told my hosts that I was taking a break after speaking at Meadowridge Baptist Church. I had just over a week left and I had had no time out. I spoke at Meadowridge Baptist Church on Sunday the 9th April 2000. It had been said in the prison ministry office that week, "Oh, we must find Colin a South African wife before he leaves". I reacted by laughing it off and saying, "Forget it, guys, I don't want a South African wife, thanks very much". I often entertained the idea of marriage, but felt quite at ease with singleness if that was His desire for me. I was certainly not in the shop window. I had actually shaved my head and looked very thuggish, so I was adamant that it was not going to happen on this trip.

This was the night The Lord gave me a wife!

Unknown to me, I was supposed to speak for fifteen minutes at Meadowridge that Sunday night. I had given full testimonies at all the other Churches. I went at it for fifty minutes.

A very quiet, sometimes amusing fifty minutes, but I just went for it. The minister, Rev. John Broome, at the end simply stood up and said, "Amen and good night'. I left the stage exhausted. I had also become aware of a deep hypocrisy in me at previous venues. After each testimony, it was expected that as the speaker, I shake hands with sometimes up to 400 people. I was alright for the first ten or fifteen people, but then in my heart I was thinking one thing but saying another. I was smiling, but only on the outside. I was being false, and feeling forced into a position of prestige and power. It just happens. One inwardly starts to feel like something one isn't. I hated it. I found myself saying 'thank you' to the congregation members, but in my heart I was wishing myself to be somewhere else.

So after the Meadowridge service that night, I decided to avoid the crowd. I slid out of the side door and noticed a huge Cross on the outside wall. I inwardly smiled and sat at the foot of The Cross. I had gone from the pulpit to an inner attitude of sin. I needed The Cross. I had sat there for five minutes and was contemplating going back in when I heard the door open.

A lady walked out holding a Bible under her arm. We almost bumped into each other at the foot of that Cross. We exchanged polite nods and nervous smiles, me not having a clue what to say. The lady then said, 'Thank you for your testimony; I feel I have turned a corner tonight. I have been feeling far from God, but your talk has brought the reality of His love home to me again'.

I thought something along the lines of "Wow man". Not at her testimony—it was her eyes. I almost fell into them. We chatted for a moment and it came out that she was involved in a family business in Vehicle and Motorhome hire. When I heard Motorhome, I pictured a Mobile Home, the big caravan type home. I told her how the prison ministry was looking for a classroom for the young prisoners and gave her my phone number if she thought of anything they might have by way of helping. As she walked away, I confess, I quickly checked the chassis out before remembering the hovering Cross. I apologised to The Lord saying, 'Lord, I'm fine if you want me single, but if in your mercy you say I can have a wife, can I have one just like that?' We exchanged phone numbers and I found myself strangely smitten by her name: Deanna. I said it a few times throughout the next few days. I just said it, 'Deanna', but I heard nothing from her.

Then on the Thursday 13th April, she rang. I cannot remember talking about a classroom for the young prisoners. In all honesty, I could not have cared less about the prisoners at that moment. She rang me, she rang me, she rang me. Deanna very politely suggested that if I had any spare time during the next few days and wanted to get away from the madding crowds and see more of Cape Town that we could possibly go out for a meal. I said, 'How about tomorrow?' Deanna said, 'What about Saturday?' I said: "OK, Saturday too". I was flying back to England on the Tuesday, so some time out was due, and what better way to see Cape Town than with a very attractive local girl?

Deanna and I went to Cape Town's Waterfront for a meal. It was simply romantic and very romantically simple. We sat and chatted about the Waterfront, the various cultures, and the shape of the wine glass, the meal, and the pudding. We sat and chatted about 'things'. The simple things in life, and as we did so, I felt my heart getting warmer and warmer toward her. I was not asked one question about my past or me. Deanna was not interested in who I used to be or who I was being portrayed as by the Church—a wonderful living proof of God's Grace. Deanna was simply interested in me, Colin, and it totally blew me away. I got a break from me for the evening and I saw exactly what I was starved of, acceptance for who I was as an individual. Deanna and I left the restaurant and walked into the Waterfront.

Cape Town's Waterfront is one of the city's high points. Everyone who visits Cape Town visits the Waterfront. Deanna and I sat on a bench, facing the ugliest building for miles. It has to be said that we only had eyes for each other. It was during this part of the evening that I asked her about her family. With a little chuckle, Deanna told me that her dad is originally from Bristol. He was a policeman! It flashed through my mind that I had been set up and there was a camera hidden somewhere. We both just laughed. A copper's kid. Trust me. My testimony in Meadowridge Baptist Church, which should have only been a ten-minute thing, went on for fifty minutes and included all the violence, all the jails, all the drugs, all the overdoses, delivered with a shaven head, and I go out and meet a Copper's Kid, at The Foot of The Cross! I used to terrorise 'copper's kids'. This is what it means when it is said that the ground at the foot of The Cross of Christ is level. Names, histories, reputations and academic achievement, good or bad, mean nothing in the shadow of The Cross of Jesus Christ.

Deanna went on to tell me that she had studied and graduated in Law, and my life of poetic irony grew in colour and detail. Deanna could in no way whatsoever identify with the things she had heard going on in my life, but in a wonderful way, she identified with me. She could not relate to the sins, but could relate with the sinner. That night Deanna was reminded loud and clear that God loved her and was interested in her.

I arranged with my hosts that Deanna would be taking me to the airport for my flight home on the Tuesday. We prayed together in the departure lounge of Cape Town International Airport for God's will to be made plain to us. It was a very beautiful time, until I had to leave. I went through the final check-in gate and turned to say goodbye. As we said goodbye, Deanna made the move and walked away. I knew, right there and then, in the place that I knew I was going to Moorlands and that Jesus was calling me, that this was not goodbye. I did not sleep a wink on that flight home and Deanna was at the forefront of my thought life for every moment of the journey. I forced her out from time to time to pray, but I was smitten.

I rang Deanna two days later from England and asked her to marry me. I explained to Deanna that I could not get involved in a relationship with her for entertainment's sake and it therefore had to be with a view to getting married, if at all. I passed the ball to her then by saying, 'So the ball is now in your court'. It had to be the world's most feeble marriage proposal. Deanna was having none of it, though, and she immediately put the onus back on me. "What do you mean?" I closed my eyes and said, "Will you marry me?" With my eyes still closed I saw her face light up and she said she would. One week later, Deanna arrived at Heathrow airport, and we began our journey into the seasons together. We agreed to go through the seasons together before tying that knot. In my heart, I still had to confirm that the flesh was not the primary beneficiary in this contract, and that I could walk in relationship, worthy of Him who called me for His own.

The next twelve months was a whole new learning curve for me. Dee found a job in London and we got together each weekend, and we slowly grew to get to know each other and it was a beautiful time. My family in Manchester grew more and more secure in their love and respect for me. I had not yet met Deanna's family. All of a sudden their daughter/sister had jetted off to England to be with this guy who proposed after one week. This normally stoic and quite reserved lady, who had never rushed into anything her whole life, had met and accepted to marry an ex-con. A short time after Deanna arrived, and my heart resting in the love I felt for and received from her, I suggested phoning her dad to ask his blessing and for his daughter's hand in marriage. We went out for lunch one Sunday afternoon, and from the reception area of the hotel restaurant, I rang and asked, "Sir, I would like to ask you for your daughter's hand in marriage".

Derek Iles, once known as being second only to the Commissioner of the British South Africa Police (BSAP) in Zimbabwe, considered dragging me over the coals for ten or fifteen minutes of torment, but conceded that both he and his wife, Ethnie, felt at peace about the whole scenario, and he expressed great pleasure in handing Deanna, their only daughter, over to me for engagement to be married. We set the date for the following Easter season, 14th April 2001, at Meadowridge Baptist Church, Cape Town.

For my final year of studies, I once again had to find a five-week hands-on practical placement for myself, starting in February 2001. It seemed to go without saying, because of my new Hope Now appointment to Head of Prison Ministry, that Cape Town would meet several needs, the first one being that of getting to meet my new fiancée's family. As soon as College broke up for Christmas, I flew out to Cape Town once again and we all started getting to know each other and planning for the wedding. The Iles family took me in as one of their own right from the start. They converted what used to be a garage into a little flat for me, and I lived in it for the duration of my block placement. I was instantly amazed at how easy these guys were to get along with. We all went away for the Christmas period and I caught glimpses of beautiful South Africa, and started getting to know 'the folks'.

My college placement was due to start on the 5th January, and in all honesty, I could not find peace in my heart about working in the prison. It all sounded logical, considering my prison background, but it would not settle in me that this was going to be God's 'divine' plan for me. I kept getting images of everyone in the room lifting their hands 'to receive Jesus', and with that image came a deep burden as to the authenticity of these 'conversions' and what would happen to them next. I believe every conversion to Christ has to produce fruit, instant fruit. A change in attitude toward God, self and others. I felt these conversions were in the extreme minority. And so I sought prayerfully about what to do.

On Christmas day, Deanna and I, along with her mum and dad, went to a local Church service in Cape Town. It was a lovely service with a wonderful Gospel message, but during the service an announcement was given about a donation they had received for 'Beth Rapha', "our house for men and women who have been ravaged by alcoholism and drug addiction".

Once again, in that place where you 'just know', I knew. I am going to do my block placement at this Beth Rapha place.

After the service, I approached the minister who pointed me to another guy saying: 'Talk to him, he is running the place'.

I approached the guy and introduced myself, asking him if he was running Beth Rapha. He laughed and said, 'Brother, I'm not running it; I am just limping forward from day to day, waiting for God to send help'.

I gave him a two-minute testimony and in that time, I first saw the colour drain from his face, so much so—and such was the change in his expression—that I thought he had seen something behind me.

When I finished talking, he very quietly said: "Brother, we have been waiting for you, when can you start?"

That afternoon, Deanna and I took a ride into Observatory and found number 4 Grant Street. It was a rundown old house located in the center of a drug, alcohol, prostitute and shabeen infested area. I parked the car outside the house and inwardly froze. The front door of the house was open and I could see right into the lounge area. The floor had no carpet, the walls had no paint and the prospect of walking into this dark cave-like place caused me to tremble. I could see two men on the inside, both glazed from drugs, and both itching what must surely be fleabites and in my heart of hearts, I said: "Lord, please do not send me in there".

In all the glamour of travel and speaking at so many venues, and from climbing on and off various pedestals, I had forgotten something: it was during one of my earliest worship sessions that I broke down on my bed and wept, "Lord, I cannot comprehend what you have done in me, but I know I have to and I want to take this testimony right into the enemy's backyard".

Then right at that moment, standing outside that hovel, I knew that this was where I belonged.

I walked into that darkness without further thought and sat down. I was acutely aware of fleas and skin diseases, of blood on the carpets and of eyes full of manipulation and sadness. In every face of every person in that house I saw an inner desperation that I knew so well. I sat a while and listened to some of their hard luck stories, and their declarations of defeat from addiction, but it was the extreme sense of hopelessness that I saw that spoke to me the most. These guys had nothing, they had no one to turn to for support of any kind anymore,

because they had ripped off just about everyone they knew and this
was the end of the line.

In the ivory treatment centers that I had visited I had seen what I
consider to be the wealthiest failures anyone could wish to meet;
and so I knew that they too were all in the exact same state of
inner desperation and hopelessness as the men before me. They
had medical health plans and families of limitless funds, the guys
from Beth Rapha were from shop doorways, lengthy and chronic
alcoholism, prostitution, physical and sexual abuse, gangs, murder,
and rape.

And now there I sat, clean and free, having Christ within me, the
hope of glory, sitting with all the information any one of these
wretches would need to get clean and sober. If I could apply a tiny
fraction of what I had experienced and learned from my time spent in
treatment and training as a counselor, I could reasonably expect to see
at least four of these guys get clean. I had sat in enough group therapy
sessions with the likes of the infamous Irish guy at Pierpoint House,
and then again in my College placement at Altringham Priory, and
I had always known that I could do well in this type of setting, so
now, for me, it was 'put up or shut up' time.

I had told Altringham Priory, "My long-term goal is to sit in and
watch what you do and to learn as much as I can from you, so that I
can go and do likewise for the marginalized".

Now here I was, seeing firsthand how God had honored His side of
the vision, and the journey began.

I gave those guys a five minute testimony of who I was, what my life
was like as a heroin addict, what had happened to me and what my
life was now like. There was a very deep silence in that room as I
declared that Jesus can rescue anyone from the darkest of personal
dungeons, and these guys knew that this was more than a sermon.
It was a living and active testimony to The Grace and Power of The
True and Living God, and the power of The Cross of Christ and

the cleansing power of His Blood and the liberating power of God's Holy Spirit, bringing to life the truth of forgiveness in Christ—all the stuff that they had been exposed to at some point of their life's over the years in some Church service somewhere, the truth of it all was now here with skin on, in a life that declared Jesus was personal and alive.

The presence of God was something quite unusual and we all then just sat in silence. After five minutes or so I said, 'Now, if you want me to come and help you I will, but that has to be your desire and your request'.

In an instant I had received a chorus of 'please help us'.

Deanna and I then went away for a week with her parents for a holiday and in all honesty I did not think about Beth Rapha once during that week, I didn't need to, God had sealed His decision in my heart; therefore it needed no further prayer. I just had to let college know that there had been a logistical change of plan. Before we broke up from College for that Christmas break we were told that under no circumstances were we to change our block placement.

I rang College from Cape Town and gave my supervising tutors, Peter Kingston and Colin Bennett, a brief testimony of Beth Rapha and within a few seconds I was given permission to make the change.

Not long after our return, Deanna and I attended the same Church and I was asked to give a brief testimony in the evening service. I think it fair to say that everyone got a little bit more than they bargained during my testimony and Deanna and I received an invite for coffee by the Bishop of South Africa!

Over coffee, we chatted about how the Beth Rapha ministry was proving to be a bit of a problem for this middle class church to cope with. When I informed him that I had visited the house, he was delighted. He asked, 'What do you think we should do with it?' I said, 'Drop it. Get rid of it. Give it back to the world and take the

Name of Jesus off the door. It is a spiritual cesspit, a terrible witness and unworthy of such a great Name'.

I got the impression that he had already opened the same channel of thought and we sat quietly until he asked if I could think of an alternative. I simply said, 'let me run it for five weeks, if nothing changes, then get rid of it; but let me have it for five weeks and see what happens'.

We shook hands, and I knew that it was time for battle.

I rang Beth Rapha that night and told Malcolm, the guy running the place that I would be there fist thin Monday morning with one guarantee: change. Malcolm just gave me a very deep chuckle and quietly said 'hallelujah' before the line went dead.

Beth Rapha

I walked in to approximately fourteen expectant faces on that first morning at Beth Rapha. I did not have a plan and I did not have a clue in what direction it was going to go. I just knew that Christ lived in me, and that He had rescued me from this very same deep dark valley. I was back in the valley of death from which He had redeemed me. I'd told Him I wanted to go back in, and here I was, fleas and all.

So now what? I had five weeks to make an impact. However, God made a start that same day. I decided to start off as I meant to carry on and therefore told one of the guys in the kitchen to put the kettle on for a cup of tea. Everyone seemed to relax a bit and two guys actually set about making approximately sixteen cups of tea. As I watched, I saw an opening. One guy asked for five sugars! Five sugars? Then another asked for three and another asked for 4 ½. I had forgotten that when one first comes off the drug or hasn't had any for a few hours, two things wake up: 1. a sweet tooth; and 2. the sex drive. I sat the guys down and we started to chat. I steered them to a place of agreement that they were in a good place, where they had a bed, food, tea, hot water, cold water, bread and sugar. We started the daily routine of 'thank you therapy'. We started counting our blessings. These guys started to express a sense of gratitude when I reminded them of how fortunate they were to be off the street where people are dying of murder, hunger and suicide and the old and cracked faces of these young men started see things in a different way.

Two Sugars or Die

Then just as the guys were starting to open their hearts and minds to the truth of the poverty and decay around them, I said, "From now on, there is going to be a limit of two sugars for every drink of tea or coffee in this house". There was a deadly silence and a few nervous laughs. "The tea and coffee are there, but you are only welcome to take two sugars". I could see that everyone sort of sensed that things were about to change. What they did not know was, I was making it up as I went along; I somehow managed to make it sound like a recognized therapeutic tool, but it was all off the cuff. I continued telling them: "from this point, if you truly want to get free from the life-controlling influence of your alcoholism and your heroin addiction; if you really want to see your families restored and your children's eyes once again smiling at you; and if you truly want to see a Christmas without having to go to oblivion to 'enjoy' it, then it is all down to this simple rule: "two sugars" and with that I left for the day.

I went back to Deanna's place, changed in to my swimming trunks and dived in to the pool.

As I lay sunbathing all on my own for the rest of the day, I underwent several manic outbursts of laughter, as I slowly started to see what God was doing at Beth Rapha. Later that day, Malcolm rang me simply to say, "I trust you brother, and I think I know what you are doing", and with that we both laughed like crazy. I was 20 kilometers away, diving in and out of my future in-laws' swimming pool, soaking up the sun, without a care in the world, and I had a whole house of drug addicts, gangsters and alcoholics, staring at each other, not knowing what on earth this English guy was up to or what was going on.

I was now in a position of leadership in the addiction ministry.

I got there at 8:00 a.m. on the dot the next day and we started by having a group therapy session. We prayed for a few minutes and then a silence fell. After a few minutes, I started to stir up the urgency for honesty in this ministry. 'Whatever the truth is about your thoughts, your feelings or your behavior, the one conquering factor can and will only ever be the truth. Addiction has an engine room and it is dishonesty. As long as dishonesty exists, there will always be the probability of falling back into full-blown addiction, hospitals, mental institutions, prisons and eventually death. Dishonesty has been raping you and your families for years now; and as we sit here, they are at home, fearful of your return, and it's all rooted in and fed by your dishonesty'. I spoke like this with volume, urgency and conviction for 30 to 40 minutes, pointing my finger into the faces of individuals and throwing out statements like: "and what do you care? You care nothing, you only ever cared about you" and I pushed it and pushed it and pushed it. I knew that I would get one of two responses: they would either respect or reject me. Eventually I fell silent, exhausted from the tirade. We sat there in silence for 5 minutes or so, and very slowly, one at a time, heads dropped in shame.

Eventually, one guy started to cry, and then another, and then another. One guy stood up, in tears, and quietly asked 'how do I stop'? I let the question linger for a moment and then calmly explained, 'when you take up the struggle to do the right things for the right reasons, I believe you will experience God's support in your life. When you join planet earth and start to live in accordance to everyday rules, you will find God's favour on your life and you will start to grow and to heal and to mature. The secret is, you have to strive for this level of honesty in secret when no one can see you, because when you can be honest in secret—with tiny things—you will start to know a whole new meaning to the word 'freedom'. Now, has anybody been putting more than two sugars in their tea?'

One guy put his hand up and I quickly responded with: "I am going to give you the first of two warnings: if you take more than two sugars once more, I will put you back on the street'.

I got a very angry reaction from most of the residents, telling me it was a stupid rule and it meant nothing if a person had more than two sugars in their tea.

I then explained that God had a deep desire to transform their lives into something brand new and to give them sweet fellowship with Himself through His Son Jesus and to set them free, but He was unable to. He was actually disqualified from helping them, because He could see that when no one else was looking, they were being dishonest. I then promised on God's behalf that as soon as they could be honest when no one was looking, God would fulfill His purposes in their lives and they would go free.

I had spoken to Deanna the night before about one particular guy and how I had seen a burning hatred in his eyes, some long-term and deep seated wounds in his soul, and a very manipulative charm. He scared me. I had told Dee that I felt good about the task ahead, but felt totally hopeless around this guy. After what he had told me about himself I told Dee that I could not see any hope for me ever helping him. I could not divulge any specifics to Deanna about what I was being told simply because the contents were brutally disgusting.

In Beth Rapha that week, as we sat in silence after a long chat about Grace and the promise of freedom, this same guy very quietly started to weep. His face became contorted with immense grief and pain, and suddenly the tears burst out of him. He became a sobbing wreck. I wanted to believe that the Holy Spirit had unplugged his pent-up pain and that it was all now going to flow away. I had to stop some guys from trying to comfort him—he needed to cry more than anything else in life. He sobbed and sobbed. As he wept, I thought to myself 'if this is genuine, this guy could be the next leader in this facility'.

Another one of the guys started to reach out with a hand of comfort and I quietly said, 'let him cry, I think it is God's Perfect Will for us that we each weep over our broken lives'. At that, another guy started crying, and then another and then another, and Beth Rapha became a home of weeping for the whole morning.

In that dirty run-down building, where the windows and the walls had turned a dirty smelly yellow colour from the years of nicotine and drug smoke, and where the carpet was now black and stuck to the floor, where cockroaches came out at night to devour anything they could and the rats were of a frightening size, God's Holy Spirit met with men.

Later that day the scary guy sheepishly walked into my office and gave me his drug paraphernalia—syringes, spoons, the lot. He simply said, "I have to get serious with this Jesus" and walked out.

I sat and stared at the wall. God was moving where I had given up.

We had not been functioning a week yet and I had very gently been put in my place; this was The Lord's work, not mine.

As I relaxed one afternoon back at Dee's home, a guy in a white BMW turned up and started telling me that The Lord had called him into leadership at the Beth Rapha Ministry. I felt my heart sink. The overseeing Church of Beth Rapha had appointed two wealthy Afrikaans businessmen as the key players of the Beth Rapha Ministry board of directors, and it slowly and sadly went downhill from there. I had to check myself out a few times to see if my ego was under threat, because my immediate reaction was to recoil at the idea of a wealthy white Afrikaans leader who had no idea about the problems in and around the culture of addiction coming in and trying to govern.

Old resentments stirred within me around my release from prison and the feelings of being very subtly abused by well meaning Church members. My primary fear was that there would be unreasonable expectations placed on broken guys in my care. The last thing any of us needed—particularly the black and/or coloured guys—was anything even symbolic of superior talking to them from a pedestal. I was just starting a process of getting these guys to believe in me, to consider the possibility of believing in God and in getting them to a place of willingness to take on recovery. All it would take to sabotage that fragile progress would be the mere appearance of someone unqualified trying to look qualified, and someone would get hurt and/or severely ripped off.

The majority of what addicts see as the 'cultured society' simply cannot understand what needs to be done in order to reach the unreachable and to love the unlovable. Being 'nice and kind' and then going home in a big posh car is actually a right that has to be earned where the rubber hits the road first. Sitting in among the fleas and cockroaches and weeping with the men is far more Christ-like.

Fumigation

Each day when I returned to Dee's place, I stripped to my swimming costume whilst Dee fumigated me with a spray. I had seen scabies and fleas on practically all my friends and I suddenly became aware of every itch and bite.

Beth Rapha was a very dark place, but a morally moved leadership who visited twice a week with admirable ideals and grand plans only managed to disqualify themselves from running it by standing on the outside saying, 'this way, that way, do this, do that, don't do this, don't do that'. Some of the guys in our care were constitutionally incapable of being honest, so we needed to get in among them and walk alongside them before trying to suggest a suitable direction for them. We had to earn the right to tell them about The Innocent Nazarene who hanged on a tree, soaking up unto Himself the punishment of the sins of every lying, thieving, flea-bitten urchin within that Beth Rapha establishment.

Everyone tried their best to make Beth Rapha into something really special and my board of directors and I really put footwork into getting along. But nothing could stop the decay of mutual respect between us. I knew what it needed for Beth Rapha to turn into an addiction ministry, but because it went against what they wanted, we failed to connect.

Dee had no idea about my burdens; there was no need for her to know, until one day when we gratefully accepted an invitation to a meal at the chairman's home. As we arrived at his home, it hit me like a lightning bolt and I saw exactly why I was burdened. As we entered the house I noticed his son leaving the room, a guy in his early twenties, and as soon as I saw him, even from the back, I knew that he was a drug addict. I had no proof or reason for suspicion, but I just knew he was an addict, and I knew then that 'the call of God' into Beth Rapha by his dad was actually a desperate attempt, by a fear filled parent, at finding some form of sanity for himself and for his family. My heart went out to the whole family, but I could not allow compassion to overrule common sense; if they wanted my help I would give it, but I firmly believed that he was the wrong guy in the wrong position for the wrong reasons.

My five weeks' placement passed by very quickly, and before I knew it I was back at the airport heading home. I had started to graft into Deanna's family, and I had witnessed God start a work at Beth Rapha. As I settled back into my seat on the flight home several questions and concerns started to formulate, none more strongly than: "If we are not careful, we could kill this ministry". I had no idea whether or not I would play any further role at Beth Rapha, but I did know that the Church alone was unfortunately underqualified to make it work.

When I left, I knew that God had done enough already for it to grow, but only if it was allowed to. One of the more impressive residents had earned his way into a position of trainee leader and was working alongside my beloved friend and brother Malcolm, who himself had also come under some serious convictions and changes of heart and attitude during that five week period.

When that assignment came to an end it was a completely different looking program to the one we started with and we could always hear worship music in the background.

I returned to College on February 7th 2001, and as the dust settled and 'student normality' returned, I woke to a new knowledge about my future. I could not accept the position of head of Hope Now International Prison Ministry. I grew in zeal for what I now saw as a need for 'contextualized discipleship' within the drug culture.

In sending His disciples into 'all nations' to make disciples (Matthew 28:19-20), Jesus knew that cultural bridges would have to be built, accepted, and then crossed, but He also knew that these bridges would not only have to enter various cultures, but they would need to 'penetrate' the various contexts and mindsets within those cultures.

I had been formed and fashioned over many years, including that initial period of development which included the struggle and shame of an emotionally suppressed child in the lower working classes of North West England.

The other half of my preparation for ministry was rooted in 'my reaction' to my circumstances, which led me through the hell and the loneliness of a chronic heroin addiction. Running a prison ministry, where I would predominantly be preaching from a pulpit twice a week, telling guys how they should live when they get released into a culture where I'm not sure I could survive, had the potential to turn me into a hypocrite. I was always haunted by the question of what happens to the guys when they (a) make a profession of conversion and (b) when they leave prison. I only knew that I must not try to impress my western standards and expectations upon exiles and rejects of my hosting culture; they must learn to look after their own and I must stick to what I know best—addictions and making disciples.

Probably because I had survived a plague which had killed over twenty of my personal friends, my whole being yearned to make a difference within the despair of people's addictions. But there was also an insatiable love for God and for God's people within me which also needed to be nurtured. But the closer I got to the brethren, the more I believed that I was seeing characteristics of addictions sitting within the pews and, from time to time, even within pulpits of some of the churches I visited.

I kept having thoughts that I was seeing power-mongers harboring distorted motives for popularity and materialistic gain by means of finely tuned spiritually toned messages. Because it scared me I denied it; and because I denied it I drifted away from wanting to be in Church.

I had a startling preference to be among the lost and the destitute, and away from the lure of mass recognition and what I feared to be superficial falsehood. I love Church, and I love being with Christians and I get a sense of awe within me when I see Christians worshipping the true and living God, in spirit and in truth. But I was growing in dread that we not only had the unconverted infiltrating our ranks, but we also had new converts falling away from lack of authenticity.

It was going to be a big decision to turn down the Hope Now offer, because of all the security it offered me and because of the heartfelt gratitude of my heart toward Hope Now, but I had to be truthful and make way for a season away from them. I could only pray about it for a while and sit and listen to what God was saying.

I got on with my final term of studies with a sense of excitement growing in me about the Beth Rapha experience. I felt a very strong pull toward residential type discipleship, but not just for the marginalized. I kept meeting people who asked me the same question, and receiving letters from leaders and from Prison Fellowship members, and they all seemed to be saying the same thing: 'Most of the addicts we get in our Church, or the men from prison, soon feel under condemnation due to their past, and we lose them. What can we do?' From within me came an unthinkable solution: 'Stop trying to lead them to where you think they should be and help them work out where they are.'

I was given a 'need' for a discipleship environment wherein we all undergo the challenges of accountability, growth and change together. This would serve several purposes: it would create a sense of trust in the guy coming out of addiction and/or jail, who—up until conversion—had no concept of trust. It would create a sense of equality in the guy who is dying from the loneliness of being an outcast. It would create an application of Romans 3:23, 'for all have sinned and are falling short of God's glory', creating a sense of safety for converts, and produce authenticity of God's people and His Word. It would be like us all climbing into a sheep dip together, for sanctification and growth.

This way we could mature beyond just telling the outcasts that God loves from afar, and simply get on with the call of loving them.

Society's Wedding of the Year

Hope Now offered to pay for my dad's flight ticket out to Cape Town for my wedding. I had considered inviting Hayley, but my heart held a concern that it might be a little too much for her to handle on her own. I told my dad what Hope Now had offered, and he was just speechless. Slowly, over the last eight years, since he sat across the prison visiting table hearing me tell him I had become a Christian, he had witnessed a very obvious growth and maturity in me. I had previously made promise on top of promise about getting drug free, and time and time again I had let everyone down, right up to the heartbreaking moment for him when he disowned me as 'no longer his son'. His heart had been broken more than once too often, and he was left no alternative but to walk out of my life. He was strong enough and wise enough to see that I was hell-bent on destroying my life, but refused to allow my behaviour to destroy his life also. In his darkest hour as a dad, he let go of me, so deep was his love for me. And now, he was getting ready to fly to South Africa to watch me get married to a beautiful lady.

Then one day I phoned for a chat with my dad, and his wife Maureen very bravely expressed a concern about his health and his ability to fly so far. I asked my dad right out if he felt it would be wise. He conceded that it might not be beneficial to his health, and we therefore cancelled the idea. I said to him that I would rather see him at my anniversary than my wedding, and with that we agreed to cancel the idea. We ended that phone call with me reminding dad of his promise not to die before I graduated from College, and he once again promised.

On the 14th April 2001, just over one year after I gave my testimony at the very same altar and met Deanna, I stood at the altar of Meadowridge Baptist Church in Cape Town as Deanna appeared on her dad's arm, walking toward me to become my wife. I felt the way Adam must have felt when God presented Eve to him for the first time. I had never realised the symbolism of the father of the bride handing her over to him until that moment. It was heavenly. This totally proud father, the ex-chief of police was walking in my direction to give me his extremely beautiful daughter.

Andy Morris sat next to me as my best man. I had known God had a special place in my life for this man, but this exceeded everything I could have imagined.

Before flying back out for the wedding, Andy took me to purchase my wedding suit. It was actually said that we look like brothers. Alan and Linda could not make it to the wedding, which would have been first choice, but it felt so right to have Andy, my Christian mentor and friend, to see me through this awesome time. Almost the whole of the Hope Now Board of Directors and their families came out for the wedding and as I looked at each of them I kept repeating this verse: "You will know those who are truly converted by how they love the brethren" (1 John).

I had friends beyond measure. The outcast of the outcasts, once crushed by loneliness and a fear of the future now surrounded by true friends and to top it all off, Rev. Vic Jackopson M.B.E.—another ex-con—married Deanna and me, and when it was asked 'who gives this woman to this man', both of Deanna's parents stood, holding hands and tearfully said, "We do".

A fifty-strong black African choir from the Langa township church, built by Hope Now, then brought Africa into our midst as they boomed out like only Africans can, and in tribal colours too. It was awesome. And a far cry from injecting drugs in public toilets, or sitting on railway embankments weeping to myself in the middle of the night.

From the church we went to The Vineyard Hotel in Cape Town's lavish Claremont for the reception.

It was a perfect end to a perfect day. Vic pulled me to one side at the reception and asked me, 'How can a vagabond like you end up as the groom at society's wedding of the year?' He was so right. Deanna's parents pulled out all the stops to make their daughter's wedding something extra-special. Not only had they brought her into the world and brought her up to be the lady she is; they gave her away in the most wonderful fashion. Not only so, they then gave us flight tickets from Cape Town to Greece as a wedding gift.

Validation and Ordination

I had given my testimony at Ashley Baptist Church in the new Forest of Hampshire in my third year of College when straight after the service, a lovely husband and wife team, by the name of Chris and Ginney Balchin, approached me. Ginney did most of the talking and she told me of a flat they had in the attic of their home, and they were wondering if I would like to live in it for the final year of my studies. I seized this offer with both hands and moved in as soon as I could. On our return from honeymoon, Dee and I moved into the little flat at 14 Dilly Lane, and it became our first little nest together.

Chris and Ginney had given me a lovely warm, Christ-centred environment to come home to. And now The Lord had put the last missing piece in place—Deanna.

I had May and June to go to complete four years of study, and one more assignment to complete in order to qualify for a BA Degree in Applied Theology. I was almost there, and dad was still alive. I had had a prayer in my heart about dad being alive to enjoy this very exciting chapter of my life. I knew that The Lord was going to be performing many wondrous works through my life, as He had already done, but completing College was something I felt to be really special for my dad. He had a fantastic mind, but even he would not be able to make sense of this lot.

I settled in my little study at 14 Dilly Lane, and set about my final assignments. Many of my peers were striving for academic excellence, and I'm sure some of them got it. The problem with that desire, though, is that it is impossible to satisfy. At the start of my four years, I picked up on something one of the lecturers said. He simply said, 'just answer the question, and you will answer the question'. I could not believe it was that simple, but I tried it and four years later, there I was ready to graduate. I had no idea that the academic world placed such a vast amount of importance on the quality of a degree and I did not personally share that view. Simply being there was honour enough for me, so I relaxed quite early in my studies and was now reaching the end intact.

I was in the process of praying about the future and the wonderful ministry I had seen at Beth Rapha, when I got an email from the church in Cape Town offering me the job of heading up The Beth Rapha Ministry. I felt The Lord desired that I take it, and despite any problems that might occur among certain personalities, I accepted.

Quite soon afterwards, I received another email from the chairman of the board of Beth Rapha, telling where he wanted me to live and how he wanted me to answer to him. He even said that he felt The Lord had brought me into this ministry so that he could be a role model in my life. I thought he was having a laugh at first and expected the email to end with some humorous comments. I had never experienced such arrogance. I simply did not believe that he was 'called' of God to mentor me. I knew in my heart that his own son was an addict, and here he was, I felt, trying to compensate for his failings, by spiritually steam-rolling himself into a position of leadership in a drug and alcohol ministry and I knew that there were going to be major problems with this guy.

The future was slowly unfolding in front of me, and I woke one morning to the realization that I was extremely naive if I did not expect flies in the ointment. Christian ministry is warfare, and the enemy is more often than not in the one place we do not want to look—within our own ranks, even among the elect.

In my heart I wanted to be ordained under the hands of Vic Jackopson and Hope Now, and there was also a yearning to have my first ministers from Minchinhampton Christian Fellowship involved too. I loved these guys, and they had invested heavily in my growth. What no one knew, because he had requested that no one should know, was that one of my Elders, Doug Horton, and his lovely spirit-filled wife Dessie, had faithfully deposited £100 into my bank account every month for the four years of my studies. This couple, like many others in that area of my life, 'familied' me in every sense, and I know today that if ever I am within sixty miles of their home and do not visit, I will be in serious trouble.

I sent out invitations to Minchinhampton Christian Fellowship, inviting them to my Ordination on Saturday afternoon 30th June 2001. That morning was my year's Valedictory service. Not only had my brother, sister-in-law, sister, brother-in-law, and two nieces turned up; my dad was there, and my step-mum. Then to top it all off, Deanna's mum and dad flew in from South Africa to share this very special day with us. This went way beyond reconciliation. It was reconciliation, restitution and remuneration. God had reconciled, restored and added on to, everything that the dark years had sucked away from me. It went way beyond anything I would have asked for. I had attended previous years' valedictory and graduation services, and had to be honest that I found the valedictory service more meaningful. I thought the graduation service was more leaning toward an individual academic celebration, wearing what I thought were silly hats and cloaks. The valedictory service was more spiritual and a celebration of united completion. I felt extremely proud to be a part of that year's group.

I now think it was quite symbolic that, in order for me to get on the stage in order to collect 'The Charge' certificate, I would have had to do it all with my back to my family, facing the audience. I therefore went against the tide. I walked along the front of the stage in order to climb the steps at the opposite end to everyone else, yet facing my family. Cameras flashed and tears started to flow. This was very nearly the pinnacle of my family's joy at seeing their very own rebel without a clue—reborn and restored beyond measure—to a life of respectability and health. The best, though, was yet to come.

I left Moorlands College that day just as I had hoped four years earlier, with my dad, brother and sister tearfully celebrating what The Lord had done.

We were pushed for time, because the plan was to ordain me that same day, thirty miles away. At the church where I was to be ordained, a cheering Minchinhampton Christian Fellowship met us. It was awesome. I took a mortarboard hat and gown with me purely for a photo session. Vic asked me to don the hat and gown. I went off stage to do this, and as I returned to the stage, Dessie Horton could not contain herself. She leaped to her feet and started to clap and yell "Praise the Lord, Praise the Lord, Praise the Lord". It caught on, and within what seemed like seconds, the whole congregation was on their feet clapping and praising God for what He had done. It was so powerful. I was simply staring at my dad as he sat weeping in the front row. He looked old and tired physically, but a fire of joy burned from deep inside him. We had eye contact for a very long time wherein nothing was said, but everything was resolved. I think I knew what he was about to do before he did it, so I felt no surprise when he abandoned his walking stick and stood very tall once again, his old back straight for the first time in years, and he strode up onto the stage, and to hell with etiquette.

My Father Limped

Dad limped up to me on the stage, in the midst of all the cheering and he took my face in his big hands once again and said two things. He looked me right in my eyes and tearfully whispered, "That's my boy". He then said what I believe he had wanted to say more than anything else throughout all the years of sadness, and this was his moment: "You know your mum would be so proud of you, don't you son" to which I just said "I know" and at that point we just embraced.

The applause went from extremely loud to ridiculously loud. I heard the volume increase as dad and I hugged. I was also very aware that dad was just a frame of the man he once had been in a physical sense. Still every bit a giant, but a shrinking giant; and the thought of the grave taking him soon, crossed my mind. But now, it feared me less, because he had seen God's power first hand, and we were at one with each other.

The son had returned to the father and the father had returned to the son, and we hugged.

Gary Fitzpatrick was there also. I had visited him every time I went back up to Stockport, and I had seen his addiction slowly but surely eating him away. I had always made a point of calling in on him, just to let him know that there was a way out if ever he wanted it. It was a year earlier that I went to visit him and found him in a suicidal state. He had actually written his note of goodbye to his mum and daughter and was at death's gate when I walked into his dark little basement flat on Edgeley in Stockport. I saw deep sadness in his eyes. I said, "Fitz, pack a bag and come with me to the South Coast". Within twelve hours we were southbound, listening to worship music.

On the night of my Ordination, Fitz was twelve months clean, and is now doing well on the South Coast of England, drug free and working for a living. His daughter and her two sons have also moved to the South Coast now and Fitz regularly enjoys watching his grandchildren grow as he walks with them by the sea. He recently told me that he bought his two grandsons their first bikes for Christmas, with honest money.

When God turns a life around, He does so with such grace, kindness and long-suffering. Fitz does not frequent Church these days, because of what he has seen going on among the 'professing Christians', a fact which I find extremely unfortunate for all concerned. Gary experienced terrible gossip, lying and manipulation from within the ranks of a few professing converts who regularly went out of their way to tell Fitz of his need to be spirit filled, themselves claiming to be spirit filled, yet thought nothing of openly lying, causing division and pain. Why wouldn't he ask himself, 'is that what Christianity offers?' He got all that in the life he walked away from.

There is a picture in the Scripture that tells us there are people outside the Church who are going to heaven, whom the Church actually think are going to hell; and there are people inside the Church going to hell, whom the outsiders think are actually going to heaven (Matthew 22:1-13).

The Parable of the Wedding Feast

And again Jesus spoke to them in parables, saying, [2] "The kingdom of heaven may be compared to a king who gave a wedding feast for his son, [3] and sent his servants to call those who were invited to the wedding feast, but they would not come. [4] Again he sent other servants, saying, 'Tell those who are invited, See, I have prepared my dinner, my oxen and my fat calves have been slaughtered, and everything is ready. Come to the wedding feast.' [5] But they paid no attention and went off, one to his farm, another to his business, [6] while the rest seized his servants, treated them shamefully, and killed them. [7] The king was angry, and he sent his troops and destroyed those murderers and burned their city. [8] Then he said to his servants, 'The wedding feast is ready, but those invited were not worthy. [9] Go therefore to the main roads and invite to the wedding feast as many as you find.' [10] And those servants went out into the roads and gathered all whom they found, both bad and good. So the wedding hall was filled with guests.

[11] "But when the king came in to look at the guests, he saw there a man who had no wedding garment. [12] And he said to him, 'Friend, how did you get in here without a wedding garment?' And he was speechless. [13] Then the king said to the attendants, 'Bind him hand and foot and cast him into the outer darkness, in that place there will be weeping and gnashing of teeth.' [14] For many are called, but few are chosen."

Two interesting points, the first being that this poor wretch did not know he was incorrectly dressed; the other that those who should have challenged the king, said nothing.

Back to Beth Rapha

Deanna and I flew back to Cape Town one week later and I immediately started working on a 7-Step programme of recovery for drug addicts to follow for establishing a new set of principles to live by. I had told the chairman of the board that I did not want to live in the house he was offering for Deanna and me to rent, because I did not think it would work for my landlord also to be my 'colleague'. However, he could not hear my 'no', and made it his goal to have us live in one of his houses. He gave us a 50% rent subsidiary, but it still did not feel right. I have to stay vigilantly aware that my ego does not get in the way of receiving from men who threaten me in any way, and I conceded that this could well be the problem around this guy. After all, he had been invited to steer the committee of Beth Rapha by some extremely godly men from within the Church of a very large denomination. Who was I to question such high positioning?

The work at Beth Rapha went from miracle to miracle. Men were saved and started to count drug free days. I know from my own experience that recovery from long term drug addiction is a long term process, and I was reminded of something Charles Spurgeon once said about 'conversions': "Refuse to celebrate overnight something that is going to have to undergo years of testing'. I watched with a hint of scepticism as men started to confess Jesus as Lord. I could see that some had been converted, and often cried before God for His mercy; but somewhere along the line, false light was also 'shining'. I was actually waiting for activity from forces of darkness, because I knew it would come.

One young man kept sabotaging the group sessions we held, by threatening to kill himself and devouring group time. He had made this threat several times to Malcolm before I arrived for this second time. He was holding the whole house emotionally hostage with his threats. He said it once in my group and I pinned his ears to the wall for ten minutes. I told him that if he made that threat once more he would be back on the street before the next lunchtime. That night he left and went back to using heroin. He had made it look like my fault that he had left, and therefore had good reason to use. He was dead from a heroin overdose within a week. There was actually no evidence to suggest suicide, but the cruel reality of front-line ministry in the addiction field hit us all between the eyes. The day the news came through about this young guy having died, I asked two more guys to leave the house for attempted mutiny. They went straight back to full blown active addiction and I started getting questioned by the board members and by the residents under my charge; but I knew from my own experience that a drug addict whose soul still belongs to addiction will stoop to the most extreme depth in order to make his or her drug use seem logical—by making it look like someone else's fault.

Our line of uncompromised discipline, coinciding with the young man's death, gave the rest of the Beth Rapha occupants an opening to cause a split between their authority figures. The hard-core addicts went flat out to make the most of this, and manipulated their way into the hearts and minds of some well meaning, but extremely naïve members of the Church. I felt like I was standing alone, but I knew I had to stand firm and continue in the vein that I had set out: 'get in line with the programme or get out'. This was going to be the birth of a new ministry and we had to expect disruptions.

Truth, Grace and Mercy were going to be the engine room of this ministry, but it would be extremely naïve to expect a smooth transition from it being a full-blown house of horror to a testimony of God's Grace and a light in that dark place. I had witnessed PJ McCullough and Wynne Parry, in both treatment clinics of my past, standing firm in their knowledge of addiction against irate and frustrated family members, and I expected the same. It came. Mums and girlfriends were demanding answers as to why I had evicted the loved ones they had also rejected.

We pressed on.

Very slowly an attitude of change crept in. Day after day in the small group setting, the men would start to express how they felt about themselves, their childhood, their parents or the lack of, their hopelessness and their despair of being drug addicts. We started to get real about our condition, and The Holy Spirit started to help us get real about who God is. On the whole, we were dealing with heroin addicts. Addiction is addiction, and has its roots in sin, and the answer remains the same: surrender to the true and living God. But when it comes to ministering to heroin addicts, there seem to be more blocks to recovery than with addictive disorders involving other drugs. Heroin addicts have absolutely no pain threshold as they come off the drug. Heroin, in my opinion, could be referred to as the mother of hedonistic chemicals. It brings the ultimate in euphoric sensation. "It does not harm the body, but steals the soul". Information coming out of the Hazelden foundation states how heroin is the most pleasure-producing drug and long-term use is not physically harmful. Damage issues around heroin are mainly connected to misuse of the drug (overdose), and poor self-care (infection/malnutrition).

This ministry was extremely vulnerable. I met several more people from the church who claimed to be 'called by God' onto the steering committee of this ministry. Most were extremely wealthy businessmen from extremely lavish areas of Cape Town. I did not immediately believe that God had called them, because a ministry like this has to be run by foot-washing servants, equipped with empathy and understanding, and not by any other example. I knew God would produce fruit of confirmation from these, my potential 'bosses', because Jesus warned that people would come in His name, and there would have to be fruit from genuine disciples. Most of the committee had made a success of their lives by means of education and willpower, and, it has to be said, out of the old South Africa, where it had been white rule. Now we were ministering to all colours and creeds, without bias. To rule at this point by dominating would be nothing but counter-productive. We had to follow Jesus' example, very well portrayed by a Chinese proverb: "Go to the people, start with what they have'.

I went into Beth Rapha and gave the guys under my charge permission to forget finding work, forget their broken marriages, and not to worry about funding for their stay and counselling. When the chairman of the board approached me about this, he was quite adamant that 'these guys need discipline and routine; they need to feel good about themselves by earning honest money'. My worst fear was being realised: middle class standards and expectations were being placed on the classless. It was never going to work. The only way a person can truly 'feel good about himself or herself' is when they can look at themselves and see what God sees. That is the platform for salvation and it is the springboard into a healthy self-esteem. Not by working. In an unregenerate state, if a person looks at his or her state of alienation from God, it can only serve to strike up the required state of humility. Then in the new birth, that same person should be at wonderful peace with whom they are, knowing that they are so wonderfully loved from above.

Our line of discipleship went unheeded and the board members started employing guys from Beth Rapha before they had reached any level of spiritual maturity. Every one of them relapsed back into addiction. Our counsel was that the guys avoid major commitments for a two-year period, including romantic relationships, for the purpose of stabilising. Number one priority had to be the personal relationship with Jesus and learning how to live free from chemical dependency. A personal relationship with Jesus Christ does not mean the individual suddenly has the ability to live a chemical free life. It means the person is then able to 'start learning how to live in freedom'. Paul said to the Church at Corinth, 'But now I am fearful, lest that even as the serpent beguiled Eve by his cunning, so your minds may be corrupted and seduced from wholehearted and sincere and pure devotion to Christ" (2 Corinthians 11:3. Amplified).

Surrender to Christ is the end of the nightmare, but only the beginning of the war.

I was fortunate in that Jesus made Himself alive to me in prison where I did not have the seduction of romance to contend with, and in the six months leading to my release, I only had the one option: to sink in depth of intimacy with Him. The Beth Rapha guys were really up against it. We were surrounded by prostitutes and drug merchants, so it was essential that we eradicate as many other snares as we could, and too much responsibility too quickly was a major snare. And many fell.

I could see the frustrations of my superiors, but could not relay to them that addiction cannot be addressed by logic and common sense. Addictions function under emotional logic as opposed to intellectual logic, and none of it makes any sense. Therefore, the able and stable can, without knowing, actually get in the way. We went from obstacle to obstacle. One of the neighbours opened his door for our guys to use his weights gym and when I was told, my heart started to sink again.

We are dealing with addicts, masters of self-avoidance and approval seeking, if there is anything that will serve as avoidance to feeling any form of emotional pain, the addicted type will find it, and the gym was a common avoidance maneuver.

Our guys started to stand out in the Church environment and while most congregation members believed that they were starting to see 'miracles' I saw storm clouds gathering. I noticed that some of them, one in particular, would suddenly stand up just before the service was about to start, and walk to the other side of the Church. He had a big chest and bulging biceps from the gym and one of my family made the comment, "doesn't he look well", I said, "he does, but he is busy relapsing".

All the outward signs said that these young men were starting to feel good about who they were—but I saw broken men, full of bravado—getting their identities and esteem from any form of external stimuli.

It did not take too long before vulnerable (lonely) female members of the congregation fell under the persuasive 'charisma' of some of these 'miracles'. Consequently, and due to what appears to become an inability to listen to counsel, several 'spirit filled' Christians were run through an emotional battlefield where wrong was manipulated to sound right and anything or anyone who tried to stand up for what was right became the enemy. In one particular instance resulting from an incredible ability to deceive, one such lady, despite having many personal items stolen from her house, remained under the influence of her 'miracle mongrel' convinced that it was not him, right up to the day he flagged her down in the street and physically robbed her of her cell phone in her car.

The very needs which we each crave to meet too often seem to be the very areas wherein the most relational damages are caused. In the above scenario, it was not just a desire for a relationship that caused convenient deafness—it was the sincere belief that 'this was the relationship from God, because we pray together'.

Having worked his way into the hearts and minds of many unsuspecting congregation members, one of our 'good looking' mongrels actually put a R10 note in the collection plate as it passed him by, and then sat back and waited. Just before the ushers retired to the counting room, he then approached the guy in a very apologetic manner and said, 'Please forgive me, I only meant to put R10 in to the collection, but by accident I put my R100 note in instead. Can I please have R90 change; I need it for the train fare to visit my mum in hospital this afternoon?'

That's what you call grabbing someone by the emotional windpipe and robbing them in the aisles of a Church. This particular guy is dead now.

As the year unfolded, though, despite everything going against us, a great work was done in the hearts and minds of many who were close to death, in addiction and also in their families. We had reached many, and witnessed the development of a ministry of reconciliation which gave me the quiet assurance that I was equipped with the wherewithal to do what the successful secular treatment clinics did, yet from a Biblical foundation. I knew that if I fully exercised my gifts and corresponding talents under the government of discernment, grace, mercy, truth and discipline, we could produce an addiction treatment program as good as any of Europe's finest secular clinics.

I did however feel that it was possibly approaching the time for me to slowly start backing away from Beth Rapha. The guys we had worked with should soon be looking to run the facility for themselves. It was truly humbling to see how God was speaking into the lives of addicts in my charge, by the way their lives changed and how their attitudes gradually went from dark to light. The only heartbreak Deanna and I experienced was with a vagrant whom we adopted yet who I had to return to the street following several breeches of house discipline.

I loved him and saw much of myself in him, but I had to return him to the street during that early stage of Beth Rapha's development. He was busy relapsing and he knew that I was on to him and he slowly started to turn extremely threatening towards me. Then one Sunday he looked at me in such a hostile way that even Deanna wanted to run from him. That was enough for me, and he was gone.

I had worked at Beth Rapha five days a week for over twelve months and I slowly started feeling that some of the men were dependent upon me and that I was carrying up to fifteen men and their families. I was questioned day after day about Scripture and about living clean and paying one's way in life etc, etc. Wives would be knocking at the door wanting him to suddenly 'have it all together' and to 'start taking responsibility for the children'. It was non-stop. But we managed.

The committee had new plans and new visions for the future of Beth Rapha and with that I felt safe to move on. I explained that they would have to proceed without me because a conflict of visions had developed and I could not agree to the way they wanted to run the show, so it was best that we part company.

The men living at Beth Rapha and the new forming team of leaders sat me down and asked me to stick with them, or they would simply follow me. The love we felt for each other ran extremely deep and we all felt that trying to run a ministry—which held such a diversity of characters—under one specific denomination was not going to work. I responded by pointing out the dangers of wanting to follow personalities at the expense of principles and asked the guys to consider the possibility that they might be getting their security from me and that it might be time to make things work for themselves and to subject themselves to authority, even authority that they might not like that much. With much emotion, we agreed to part.

When separation was suggested at the final committee meeting the tension was tangible, but the change was made. The Beth Rapha Ministry went under an inter-denominational steering committee, and still is to this day; yet in all fairness, 10 years on it is still limping from crisis to crisis.

My fears were that the ministry was resting on my shoulders rather than on The Lord. I often suffered from self-righteousness and felt very important and very spiritual in that dark context. To add to this, it seemed that every time anyone came to me with questions, The Lord kept giving me the answers that brought depth of peace into many tormented souls. I knew it was God; it had to be, because many times I would sit and wonder how I was going to answer the next question, and very often I would hear answers coming out of me and I would think to myself, 'I did not know that I knew that'.

It was God. He was there every time.

My persistent struggle was in the area of pride and self-righteousness and I had to confess frequently the inner workings of my heart until that wonderful joy of God working through me remained steadfast. I find it amazing how negative feelings are just like negative photographs—they prosper in the dark, but simply die on exposure to the light.

The guys in positions of leadership were still quite vulnerable in their new lives, but strong enough, I felt, to carry on without me. This burden grew in me. Then one Friday morning, Malcolm and I sat in the office and prayed for another leader to come along. Until this point it was an all-white team, working in a multi-cultural setting. My fear was that we would fail to reach many if we did not bridge the cultural divide and that same afternoon, a coloured guy turned up with his holdall under his arm and simply said, 'I believe The Lord wants me in here'.

John Roberts, a coloured guy from the drug culture with twenty years clean time under his belt, joined the leadership of The Beth Rapha Ministry. I introduced John to the system and invited him to sit in on the group sessions for a month. John was blown away by the dynamic of the Beth Rapha group sessions as God showed up in wonderful ways each time we opened His Word.

One of the primary sections of Scriptures that we frequently explored can be found in 1 John 1:5-10:

Walking in the Light

5 This is the message we have heard from him and proclaim to you, that God is light, and in him is no darkness at all.
6 If we say we have fellowship with him while we walk in darkness, we lie and do not practice the truth. **7** But if we walk in the light, as he is in the light, we have fellowship with one another, and the blood of Jesus his Son cleanses us from all sin.
8 If we say we have no sin, we deceive ourselves, and the truth is not in us. **9** If we confess our sins, he is faithful and just to forgive us our sins and to cleanse us from all unrighteousness.
10 If we say we have not sinned, we make him a liar, and his word is not in us
(ESV)

During exegesis of these verses many of our clients would crumble and want to make confessions of some particularly shocking crimes.

My stability was shaken. I had placed intense emphasis on the need for confidentiality within The Beth Rapha Ministry, and now that confidentiality clause was about to start strangling me.

While I was silently pondering the dark corner in which I found myself, I was further horrified to hear of more atrocities like rape and incest and I saw a new depth of the depravity to which the heart of man can plunge and it was as if a plug had been removed and a fountain of stagnant sewerage water was now drowning me.

God was continually gracious to me and always met with me as I drove home after a day at 'the office'. By the time I got home in the evening I had usually sang and prayed myself back to the wonderful reality of my marriage.

At night, in our rented town house, Deanna and I would chat about the next leg of the journey. I started to express a desire for a pastoral position, even as an evangelist, because my entire ministry had been with gangsters and alcoholics. I longed for the little old lady who just lost her cat, or the husband in need of guidance, or the teenager whose body was coming alive. I wanted regular ministry. I needed to know that I could reach everyday folk with everyday issues.

I contacted Vic back in UK and this was also central to his heart for my next step in ministry. I left the employ of Beth Rapha and went back under Hope Now. Deanna and I put in an offer for a house in Fish Hoek, and within a week it had been accepted and we began to plan for the future. I approached King of Kings Baptist Church to ask if I could join their pastoral team, keeping the evangelist title, and they accepted us into fellowship with them with open arms. It felt really good to be in among 'relatively' level headed people. I set up my office in King of Kings, and started to pray about the exact direction The Lord would have me take next.

I became part of a team and found it extremely difficult. I'd gone from running the show, in among society's ragamuffins, to joining a team of middle class straight-heads. It was really weird, but really nice. At our induction I was introduced as being on the discipleship team, 'focusing mainly on the goats'. I now had an office to go to each day. I got what I asked for. People coming for counsel because of things like a death in the family, and for an alcoholic husband, son or daughter. Parents, who, in my opinion, had as many problems as the kids they were judging, brought wayward kids to me. I was amazed. I'd gone from young men who had committed killings in the gang world, and from men who had been systematically raped by family members as children, to what looked to me like mundane issues, and yet I saw the exact same depth of anguish from the sufferers. I was using all the same counselling techniques in a church pastoral seat as I had at drug rehab, and people were receiving some wonderful moments of healing. Men and women from 'Normal Street' were sobbing in my office, over what I might recently have seen as trivial.

I had so much to learn.

Discipleship Courses

During an early Morning Prayer time I sat in my study trying to seek definite direction for my talents. I began feeling a very strong pull towards the teachings of Doctors Henry Cloud and John Townsend. I had attended a Boundaries Course during the Beth Rapha period and I was amazed at how these guys had married psychology to theology. The treatment clinics I had attended in my days of havoc were psychology based, and had done an amazing job on and in me. They failed, however, to help me see the answer. They simply helped me secure what the problem was, therefore keeping it alive. Cloud Townsend tackled the psychology versus theology questions in me, and I suddenly found a teaching that scratched exactly where I itched. I could grasp that suffering and sickness is all rooted in sin, but could not find peace that suffering people simply had to repent for healing. I felt that was like asking a child to grow up. Not only is it impossible to turn growing up into an event, it is downright unfair and very damaging.

I found that Doctors Cloud and Townsend addressed my inner-most developmental needs and the tasks that I was required to undertake in order to grow in a maturation healing. I was ignorant enough to believe that God would perform miracles where personal responsibility was called for. I tapped into www.cloudtownsend.com and looked at their list of video discipleship courses. I felt very strongly that I had to follow this route:

1. Hiding From Love
2. Boundaries
3. Safe People
4. Changes That Heal

I knew that God desired my healing, but my tendency is to keep my broken parts hidden from the whole world, inwardly believing I can keep them hidden from God too. I was hiding from love. I had come out of that hiding place once in my life some years earlier—the day I wept over the loss of my mum in a room full of people—only to find that they wept with me.

I got vulnerable and love poured in. I, however, took that therapeutic touch of love to be my final answer and unknowingly went back into hiding on my return to my old culture where vulnerability was a weakness.

I came out of hiding, but had no means of standing stable in my new status, because I had no sense of boundaries to help me protect myself.

I came out of hiding, only to fail to recognise that the people with whom I surrounded myself were actually unsafe people for me in my new state of being.

I needed to come out of hiding, establish some boundaries and learn how to spot unsafe people. It was only then, in a place of spiritual, emotional and psychological safety, that I could look at my past relationships, and myself, and learn how to make changes that heal within me.

I knew that this was to be my next line of discipleship, for me as a child of God, and as a minister for God. I wrote to Hope Now and asked for a series of video discipleship courses. Within ten days, a parcel arrived from America containing all the above in the form of the Solution Group Discipleship Course, and an added one for Married Couples, 'Boundaries in Marriage'.

Once again, everything made sense. Every lonely minute of the addiction made sense. Every hour-long-minute of every prison sentence made sense. Every minute spent in every one of the self-analysis groups in every rehabilitation environment all suddenly made sense. It was all for just such a time as this. Every frustration I had felt with every brother and sister in Christ since my release from jail now also started to make sense. It was all for just such a time as this. Every doctrinally erroneous teaching I had encountered now suddenly made sense – I was growing.

God had not only allowed it all, He even guided me into and through them, for just such a time as this. I had brought a distorted view of what Christianity was all about from my old life, and then quite arrogantly transferred extremely high expectations on to the Church, from what my encounter with Jesus had been like.

I had set myself up for disappointment in the Church, by expecting every member of the Church to be Jesus all the time and for every sermon to be 'doctrinally accurate' according to my Biblical understanding. I left no room for the opinions or views of others and I realised that I expected perfection.

Accepting this expectation as being unreasonable allowed me a new level of personal freedom around the fact that each of us is equally flawed by virtue of our humanity. It was the enemy of my soul that stirred me to be dissatisfied with your soul. It was the critical eye of perfectionism and inevitable internal personal dissatisfaction that drove me to desire Biblical knowledge and wisdom. It was my finger of blame and resentment that stopped me looking at my own weaknesses and the inner longing for belonging that fuelled my desires to give testimony everywhere I went. I failed to notice that—even in the midst of what I thought was 'ministry'—the enemy was slowly gaining ground within me.

My motives shocked me.

I carried within me desires for:
- Perfection
- Beauty and Wisdom

And to be:
- Anointed and Ordained

So that I would have:
- Position, Power and Prestige

Walking in the light of the truth is such a difficult calling.

I began running the solution courses in the Church starting with Hiding from Love. I saw and personally experienced growth in a whole new way. I saw Christians opening up about a whole catalogue of personal issues like deep-seated hatred for spouses and buried resentments towards parents.

People started to talk and to heal, after years of believing that 'this is as good as it gets', a condition I have since heard to be known as 'saved but stuck'. These guys jumped at the opportunity of doing more of the courses, becoming hungry for growth, and it was the eagerness of my brothers and sisters in Christ to grow that re-energised me for God. Jesus said, "Blessed are those who hunger and thirst for righteousness, for they shall be filled" and I saw a new meaning to this text when His people started to weep over their sin and to release their secrets. I knew that I was at this place for another season for another reason, and as people wept in the small group discipleship environment, I felt God's peace around His desire for me.

I once again noticed that just like at Beth Rapha, people were hanging on my every word, and from time to time I again found myself feeling surprised by the insights I was seeing but this time I was nervous of climbing on to a pedestal for these guys. It felt as if they wanted to promote me from time to time, and my anxiety was that I might be blinded into stealing God's wonderful glory. For the sake of integrity, I decided to lead these courses in a threefold fashion. I made every effort to lead by example, I also lead by some pretty exciting Bible studies and I lead by limping with the wounded. I lead by example by testifying to The Lord's healing hand of mercy in my life; I lead by expository teaching; and I lead by limping in that I too underwent some exposure of personal flaws and needs for further development. At these moments of personal vulnerability I simply asked for and received help from the people around me and we gradually matured on to level ground as 'Bible based therapeutic community'. It was truly wonderful.

It became more and more apparent that God had placed quite a special anointing on my heart and on my mind. My problem was I was inclined to deny it through fear of being judged, until The Lord showed me that true humility is humbly accepting that we are who God says we are. Life seemed to be one life changing revelation after another since the day I met Jesus.

Still on the payroll of Hope Now in Southampton, and with the exchange rate of between 14 and 18 Rand to the pound, Deanna and I purchased a house in Fish Hoek, Cape Town. Our home sat upon a tiny hill, in the base of a valley, thereby giving us an all round view of the valley, with a sea and mountainous view to the front. God continually surpasses every desire and every dream. He is not just limited to grace and kindness, by nature He showers His children with grace upon grace, kindness upon kindness. Not only did that home consist of my wife and I which would have been more than enough for me. We also shared it with our daughter Georgia, two Jack Russell dogs and two cats.

Georgia Claire was born after Deanna had undergone a whole night of discomfort and then five hours of extreme labour pains. I was reduced to a humble observer. It would be spiritually and biologically impossible for me to love Georgia any more than I love Hayley, but to see Georgia arrive through the sufferings of her mum really touched me deep inside. I was in jail when Hayley was born, and my celebrations were immense but thwarted, so here again The Lord was restoring the blessings of a lost life redeemed.

I watched my wife transform into more of a woman right before my eyes, producing a new life that we had both planned and prayed for. The depth of love and respect that I felt for Dee intensified, and this new little life started to work her way into a new chamber of love within me.

Am I dreaming? Is this really happening to me? Was that junky guy really me? The 5½ years in 27 different prisons, the overdoses and rehabs, was it all real? It all seems as if it had happened to someone else, so radical was and is the change that took place within my heart. I have never experienced any desires to take up any form of drug since the day I entered into a personal relationship with God in and through Jesus Christ, and there we have the key to both the 'nightmare' and/or the 'dream'. Throughout this book there have been repeated references to the concept of 'relationship', and there is a valuable reason for this: it was in 'relationship' where all my pains and confusions were born and where they were fuelled, but the one relationship I did not have was with God.

Being in relationship with Him now teaches me how to be in relationship with you! He is author, creator and sustainer of the dynamic of relationship within the earth, so if I am disconnected from Him, all my relationships have to be 'self-centered' and 'unsafe'.

As I look at Georgia today and now also her younger brother Nathan James, I realize that when they look at me, and the way I relate to their mom and to them, they catch their first impressions of what a relationship model of life looks like. Without the foundational truths of God being implanted in them at this early stage of their development, they too would probably need to visit hell a few times before they realize their deepest need is to be in a personal relationship with Him as their Heavenly Father. As they walk by my side, stretching up to grasp my little finger for stability, and as they somehow know that they have my full approval, I see a delight in their eyes that the world will never offer them. I see the enormity of our parental responsibility in that Deanna and I are the primary role models in these God-given lives and we must continually seek closeness to God ourselves; because really, they are His.

During this Pastoral year I started to see that this was actually where God did NOT want me. We had experienced some beautiful times within the growth courses, but it became more than obvious to me that I was now misplaced, which was vital for me because I carried a sense of obligation to the Church. I felt that I had to be Church based because of what Christ had done for me, but I actually spent more time at my computer than I did in counseling or discipleship. It was time well spent though because I spent day after day looking at how and where we could have done things differently at Beth Rapha and I eventually knew that we had the potential for birthing an extremely influential ministry, if only we could achieve an undivided heart among the leadership.

Very slowly, a business plan was born and I decided to visit the top addiction treatment clinic in Cape Town, similar to the one I was sent to by the court and in which I had studied as a student, just to introduce myself. Following that visit I was extremely honored to be offered a job as a counselor with them and I immediately informed Hope Now of what I had in mind and I took the job on a three month trial basis.

During that 3 month trial basis I tried to absorb as much insight as I possibly could from the way they treated what they call 'the disease of addiction'. At the end of the three month trial period, I gratefully decline the offer of full-time employment. It was a trial period, but I was not the only one on trial—they were too—and I could not continue addressing addictions without offering the dying the message of eternal life. I declined on the grounds of having to take the final piece of the jigsaw home with me every night, because the preaching of The Gospel was forbidden.

During that term of employment I was devastated to see how many Christians were in there, pastors and children of pastors, paying ridiculous fees, to get help from the world. The Church of the living God, called to be the pillar and foundation of truth in society, turning to the world for help?

I fear we are losing the war.
I find that unacceptable.
I had to do something.

It was time to let go of the pull of the Pound, sell our home, and step out onto the water.

The Bethesda Recovery Homes

I spoke to Dee about a growing conviction in me that it might be time to resign from Hope Now and to set out in a ministry within our own calling. Rev. Vic Jackopson M.B.E. had been more than a role model for me in ministry for the best part of a decade; he had been, and remains a (very young) father figure, mentor and friend to me. He and his wife Sue had watched over me and guided me with purity of heart for many years and gracefully tolerated my many rough edges.

Deanna and I had bought our first house and made it a home; we were financially secure and to the outside world, settled and happy. However, in my heart, it haunted me that people were dying all around me from something that I had been set free from—addiction—so eventually in the October of 2004 I wrote to Hope Now and offered my resignation.

Vic was waiting for it.

It was agreed that I should leave Hope Now from March 1ˢᵗ 2005. Deanna and I both felt the shake of insecurity because in one way we had matured backwards into getting our security from third-party sources rather than directly from God, but now that was about to change because in a few months' time, it looked like I was going to be unemployed.

In the December of 2004 we agreed to take a holiday with Dee's family and get away from all the concerns of life for a few days. Because Georgia was still yet unable to climb stairs we wanted somewhere safe for her to crawl around freely too.

After some internet searching for vacant accommodation we eventually found what was described as an old hunting lodge in Storms River Village, in the Tsitsikamma Forest. It sounded great, and on December 27ᵗʰ, we drove the 7 hours to our holiday accommodation. I had several thoughts of relocating in order to start a rehab and 'The

Garden Route' sounded perfect. During one of my silent explorations of what we might call a rehab if we did move to this area, my brother in-law broke my thoughts with the question; 'how would you feel about relocating to the Garden Route'? My heart changed pace. I remember nervously feeling as if I had just been exposed in my secret planning.

We arrived in Storms River Village and pulled up outside what was known as the hunting lodge – an extremely beautiful 5 bedroom self catering B&B accommodation sitting at the foot of Formosa Peak. As soon as I saw it I knew 'This is where The Lord wants us'.

I kept my thoughts to myself for the whole day and silently prayed and waited for God to either confirm for me that this was going to be the venue for the next phase of our development, or make it clear that it was not. By the end of the day I was bursting with excitement and by supper time that night I could not contain it any longer. As we chatted and commented on the peace and beauty of the place I dropped the following bombshell: "I think this is where we are going to open a rehab".

There were a few nervous laughs at my comment and people flicked glances at me and at each other as they wondered if I was serious or not. Then there was a kind of uncomfortable silence for a few more minutes and then this eruption conversation exploded about the impossibility of it all as each person offered what I thought to be minor details like the place not actually being for sale, the extremely high cost of property in a place like the Garden Route and how it would mean selling our house in Cape Town. Naturally, everyone had very valid doubts, questions and fears to express, and we explored each of them, but then I could only respond with, "actually, none of that is my problem; those are all God's problems. I just know and I have to say that I believe that the Name of Christ is going over that front door".

The next day I phoned the owner of the property and the conversation went as follows:

Hi, I'm staying at your property in Storms River and I was wondering, how much you want for it?'

'It's not for sale.'

'That's not what I asked you, I asked you, how much you want for it.'

There was a long pause . . .

'It has been valued at R1.6 million.'

'I will give you R1.6 million.'

'What?'

'I will give you R1.6 million.'

There was another long silence, which I then broke by saying: "Let me rent the place from you for nine months, and then I will give you your asking price. If it is not a done deal by then, you get the place back and at the very least you will have rented the place out all year".

'Starting when?'

'March 1st 2005.'

'That sounds like a decent offer, let's talk some more.'

Feeling as if I might be on a roll I decided to push a few boundaries. 'I will rent it from you for nine months and then give you R1.6 million. However, if I can make a concrete offer to purchase within four months, you sell it to me for R1.4 million; if it takes me five months—R1.5 million; then anything between six and nine months R1.6 million. If it goes over the nine month period you can name your own price', and by the end of the next day, after he and his wife had chatted about it, we had a deal. It was as simple as that.

Dee frantically asked me, 'how can we be so sure that this is what The Lord wants'? I said, 'I'm not so sure yet. We need to ask for three, corresponding acts of providence. His name is Jehovah Provider. He will provide'.

In my business plan, I had allowed for R10, 000 per month for the rent of whatever property we found; I was expecting the rent for this Storms River plot to be R12, 000 per month.

The landlord rang back the next day and said R7, 000.

That was one.

We enquired about accommodation for us as a family, not wanting to bring Georgia up in a rehab. We were told, 'My husband does all the rentals in Storms River and there is nothing going. There is one possibility however. Go and ask the guy in the wooden cottage just down the lane'.

We knocked on the cottage door and I just said to the guy, who opened the door, 'We are Christians wanting to open a rehab in the village, but my wife, child and I need our own accommodation'. Slightly shocked, the guy invited us in and said, 'we are also Christians and we would really appreciate it if you guys rented from us. We only come here once a year, but we are not coming back now for a few years. How does R2, 000 per month sound?

That was two.

As we left this funny little cottage, we both started to feel nervously excited. I tried to close the door. I said to Dee, 'before we start getting carried away with this, I have to say I don't think there is any point in going any further; we cannot go anywhere without the help of a doctor who knows about addictions, and where are we going to find a doctor out here in The Tsitsikamma Forest?

As we drove back to the accommodation, I noticed a 'Village Surgery'.

I walked in and met the doctor.

'Hi, I'm Colin. My wife and I are just thinking of opening a rehab in the village".

"Oh wonderful, I used to work in rehab but had to stand down because I did not agree with what was taking place in there".

That was three and Amen.

Deanna, who will be the first to admit that she does not do change at all well, simply said, 'how can we NOT do this'?

The next morning I was up at 5, sitting in our car, listening to praise music and crying my eyes out before God. I sat there and sobbed. I just sobbed and sobbed. In a wonderful way I felt trapped and all alone with the breathtaking knowledge that God was liaising with me. Not only had He waited for and then met me in a trash-can, He was making His footsteps clear for me to see and He was now about to surpass my wildest dreams about catching souls from the enemy's backyard and presenting them with The Gospel.

Within a month, we had put our house in Cape Town on the market and sold it to the first person who came to view it for twice the amount we had paid for it. We then just ploughed everything back in, buying all the furniture, fixtures and fittings that a Christian rehab home would need. We were aware that we were stepping off the property ladder, and we both knew that this might not sound like a good idea for a young family to make, but we knew this much: The Lord gives, and The Lord takes away, all we need do is respond with an 'amen'. We had one focus: Kingdom work, knowing God to be faithful.

In mid February we loaded up and tearfully moved out of our little comfortable nest. I spent three or four days personally erecting the bunk beds in every room and it was with tears in my eyes that I prayed for every nut, every bolt, every mattress and every pillow in every room. On March 1st 2005, 12 beds were made with matching duvet and pillowcase sets and with corners folded back and the wait began.

It would be nice at this stage to bring this chapter of our journey to a happy ending with stories of hundreds of souls saved and baptised, which to a degree would be true. However, this is planet earth, and it is still deteriorating under the siege of human beings who themselves are under the destructive government of darkness. I'm not going to close with 'and we all lived happily ever after', I would rather keep it real and maybe even close with a reminder of how we are at war, from without and from within.

Attacks From Without

For the first 18 months of our ministry, we had to undergo extensive inspections and examinations by The Departments of Health and Social Development of South Africa. We were forced to jump through many loops by a developing system within the new South Africa. At times it seemed these guys were making rules up as they went along, even to the point of giving us the impression that they did not actually want us to succeed. We were regularly held back and strangled by miles of seemingly endless red-tape. The department then decided to send a team to our facility, and we then underwent weeks of stress whilst we waited and waited for them to arrive. It was all very taxing to our relationship and to our motivation levels. Eventually they arrived. We all sat in a large circle, Deanna and I, our nurse, our psychologist, and five members of the Department of Health and Social Development. It was all very tense. I was painfully aware of how Deanna had lost much sleep and had put in hours of meticulous effort into getting this right; and now, here we sat, at the moment of truth.

Once the meeting got underway, I suddenly felt my heart sink. Deanna and I were both expecting these guys to be impressed with our facility and the high quality of accommodation on offer. This was our baby. However, their opening line was to attack my integrity as a leader of this project. Their head of the department really threw cold water on the meeting as far as I was concerned. He failed to acknowledge anything about the facility and decided to challenge my motives and qualifications. He said, "What's in this for you and what happens to this place if you relapse on heroin". A lady off to my right then chipped in with, "I rang you 6 weeks ago to ask you about your social workers and you were rude and unprofessional to me telling me how I need to phone the social workers if I want to talk to the social workers".

My eyes stayed fixed on the head of the department and I thought he was finding it really disconcerting, he looked quite uncomfortable. As soon as the lady to my right sat back, apparently feeling very pleased with herself, I spoke to the department head: "excuse me sir", he looked at me. "Who gives you the right to come in here and bring up anything to do with my past? How dare you judge my future by my past? Not even God holds my past against me so who gives you the right?"

Out of the corner of my eye I saw Deanna's shoulders drop, and it was then that I thought, 'here we go, in for a penny in for a pound' and I then turned to the lady off to my right and said "madam, you have clearly been stewing for over six weeks on something that you have finally decided to be 'rude and unprofessional'. In my opinion, instead of stewing over the way I spoke to you, you should have spoken to me again rather than make your mind up what type of guy I am, and then come here and treat me with contempt. That, ma'am, in my opinion is rude and unprofessional".

At that point the meeting ended quite quickly.

As Deanna and I escorted the department members back to their vehicles I drifted away from them and was aware that the head of the department was following me. As we got out of earshot of the main group I said to him: 'Sir, please listen to me for one minute, I will return to England tomorrow morning if you tell me to, gladly. I am 6000 miles away from home, earning less money now than I was more than 25 years ago as an 18-old soldier in England. You need me more than I need you". He quietly whispered to me, "Colin, you'll be registered by the end of the week". And we were.

The Bethesda Recovery Homes started to function as a government registered Addictions Treatment Clinic.

Attacks From Within

Mongrels Mimicking Miracles

Spiritual Warfare

"I take no pleasure in the death of the wicked,
but rather that they turn from their ways and live."

Ezekiel 18:23

There are two primary errors when it comes to spiritual warfare—over-emphasis and under-emphasis. Some blame every sin, every conflict, and every problem and illness on demons that need to be cast out. Others completely ignore the spiritual realm and the fact that the Bible tells us our battle is against spiritual powers. I believe the key to successful spiritual warfare is finding the Biblical balance.

Jesus sometimes cast demons out of people and sometimes healed people with no mention of the demonic. The apostle Paul instructs Christians to wage war against the sin within them in Romans 6 and to wage war against the evil one.

I firmly believe that the only foolproof key to spiritual health is personal intimacy with the love of God 'that issue from a pure heart, a good conscience and a sincere faith' (1 Timothy 1:6).

Common sense tells me that it would be futile for the demonic to pick a fight with a heart of this condition and so close to God, but the righteous are promised persecutions and Biblical warnings must still stand steadfast and be regularly considered because we are all told:

Ephesians 6:10-12
"Finally, be strong in the Lord and in his mighty power.
Put on the full armor of God so that you can take your stand against the devil's schemes. For our struggle is not against flesh and blood, but against the rulers, against the authorities, against the powers of this dark world and against the spiritual forces of evil in the heavenly realms."

And:

Matthew 13:7
"Other seeds fell among thorns and *the thorns grew* up and strangled them"

With the blessing of hindsight I can now see how it was from that platform of God's love, a good conscience and a sincere faith that we personally and regularly witnessed miraculously corresponding acts of providence for the birth of Bethesda. Not only so, but Deanna and I now both know that during those early steps of faith we were each undergoing personal refinement and preparation for what turned out to be a ministry of threat and extreme disappointment. Had The Holy Spirit not been our divine bonding agent and guide from the outset, and if this ministry had not been built upon crystal clear miracles and grace, Deanna and I both know that we would not have survived the onslaughts of darkness and betrayal that lay ahead of us.

We saw, and see, many miracles of the lost coming to a saving knowledge of The Lord Jesus Christ in our rooms during our Bible studies. The feedback we get about how the Bible 'seems to come alive' in our midst is very common and many tears are shed under the watchful gaze of a Father who loves us.

However, we frequently stir up hornets' nests and that always means trouble.

We had two different women come to Bethesda on two separate occasions seeking counsel yet with frightening similarities: both came as victims of sexual abuse issues, both had eating disorders, both were sexual innuendos in their dress and in their speech, both tried to involve themselves in our ministry, both were very subtly manipulative and dominant around their weak husbands, both refused to recognise any form of male leadership. And both eventually tried to destroy me when they did not get their way.

As a Christian therapist I turned to two separate sources for guidance. As a Christian I turned to ministers of The Word with the following question:

"What is the Jezebel spirit?"

I got the following answer: There is a variety of opinions about what constitutes a *Jezebel spirit*, everything from a sexually loose woman to someone—man or woman—who teaches false doctrine. The Bible does not mention a Jezebel spirit, although it has plenty to say about Jezebel herself.

Jezebel's story is found in 1 and 2 Kings. She was the daughter of Ethbaal, king of Tyre/Sidon and priest of the cult of Baal, a cruel, sensuous and revolting false god whose worship involved sexual degradation and lewdness. Ahab, king of Israel, married Jezebel and led the nation into Baal worship (1 Kings 16:31).

Their reign over Israel is one of the saddest chapters in the history of God's people.

There are two incidents in the life of Jezebel which characterize her and may define what is meant by the Jezebel spirit. One trait is her obsessive passion for domineering and controlling others, especially in the spiritual realm. When she became queen, she began a relentless campaign to rid Israel of all evidences of Jehovah worship. She ordered the extermination of all the prophets of the Lord (1 Kings 18:4 and13) and replaced their altars with those of Baal.

Her strongest enemy was Elijah who demanded a contest on Mount Carmel between the powers of Israel's God and the powers of Jezebel and the priests of Baal (1 Kings 18). Of course there was no contest, but despite hearing of the miraculous powers of Jehovah, Jezebel refused to repent and swore on her gods that she would pursue Elijah relentlessly and take his life.

Her stubborn refusal to see and submit to the power of the living God would lead her to a hideous end (2 Kings 9:29-37).

The second incident involves a righteous man named Naboth who refused to sell to Ahab land adjoining the palace, rightly declaring that to sell his inheritance would be against the Lord's command (1 Kings 21:3; Leviticus 25:23).

While Ahab sulked and fumed on his bed, Jezebel taunted him and ridiculed him for his weakness, then proceeded to have the innocent Naboth framed and stoned to death. Naboth's sons were also stoned to death, so there would be no heirs and the land would revert to the possession of the king. Such a single-minded determination to have one's way, no matter who is destroyed in the process, is a characteristic of the Jezebel spirit.

So infamous was Jezebel's sexual immorality and idol worship that the Lord Jesus Himself refers to her in a warning to the church at Thyatira (Revelation 2:18-29). Most likely referring to a woman in the church who influenced it the same way Jezebel influenced Israel into idolatry and sexual immorality, Jesus declares to the Thyatirans that she is not to be tolerated.

Whoever this woman was, like Jezebel, she refused to repent of her immorality and her false teaching, and her fate was sealed. The Lord Jesus cast her onto a sick bed, along with those who committed idolatry with her. The end for those who succumb to a Jezebel spirit is always death and destruction, both in the physical and the spiritual sense.

Perhaps the best way to define the Jezebel spirit is to say it characterizes those who act in the same manner as Jezebel did, engaging in immorality, idolatry, false teaching and unrepentant sin.

To go beyond that is to invite conjecture and can possibly lead to false accusations and divisiveness within the body of Christ[10].

I know that we have to find and recognise a distinction between the *personalities* involved and the *principles* behind the attacks which were inflicted upon us. God's love was once extended to me, the filthiest of sinners, and I never lost sight of the fact that if He can reach and love me, He can reach and love anyone. So while we have open arms for true remorse and forgiveness comes quite easily, I knew that we were under the severest of attacks and that I had to seek as much help as was available to me.

As a therapist I sought advice addiction specialists and I was strongly warned against getting too close to any of the two women I was asking about, one of who had a particularly notorious reputation. One local doctor told me of how she would ring him at night while he was at home with his family and she would hound him for hours and hours until it reached a point where when he would hang up on her; eventually when he recognized her number on his phone he refused to answer.

Another of my key advisors pointed me to a section of 'Introduction to Psychology and Christian Counselling[11]' where I found the following personality description:

---

[10]   WWW.GOTQUESTIONS.ORG

[11]   PAUL D. MEIER, FRANK B. MINRITH, FRANK B WICHERN AND DONALD E. RATCLIFF, BAKER BOOKS, PAGE 291

'Histrionics may be seductive in order to prove that the counsellor is just like every other male. A female histrionic who entices a man sexually may then go on to tell everyone that *he seduced her* to try and ruin his reputation'.

The beginning of the end came very early one morning as our resident staff member was opening my office for the day. He was absolutely shocked to find one of these women standing all alone in my office, looking very guilty. She offered no reason for being there, or for how she had gotten in, but simply produced a hand written note in a fancy flowered envelope and passed it to him telling him she wanted me to have it. It read as follows, and I quote:

"You are the best Bible teacher I have ever heard and you bring God's Word alive to me, although your counsel is often very hard it is always very helpful and I want to thank you for helping me to find freedom".

At this point I expressed my fear to her that I believed she was trying to seduce me, maybe even to ruin me. There was always a distant hope in me that she might take ownership of her agendas and we could all pray about things and move on, but within a week of this incident, she had vanished again and teamed up with 'her best friend', the other 'victim'. Both of these ladies then set out, with weak husbands in tow, on a joint mission to destroy me personally and therefore quite foolishly, everything God was doing through us.

There were threats to have me kidnapped and killed; threats of sexual harassment allegations against me unless we paid R200 000. There was an international (YouTube) slander campaign launched where it was said that I was a male prostitute selling Jesus and selling sexual favours at our rehab. My watch was stolen and our accounts showed that we were R50 000 light. Our Church credibility was polluted within the minds of leadership, my friends were physically attacked, there was a horrible Church split and to top it all off, even a children's sports ministry was closed down.

Everything they did and said against me contained very sad and very ugly sexual connotations, yet both of these women had gone from professing to idolize me to wanting to have me killed.

Norman Shawchuck gives a pin-point accurate description of how and why these types of 'friendships' are always doomed to failure, in his 'How to Manage Church Conflict'.

In his section of the various Conflict Styles, he illustrates how:

> 'Accommodators' have one intension: to preserve a relationship
> which suits their cause at all costs. Accommodators who
> consistently employ this style of conflict will always present a false
> cooperation, false cheerfulness, and a false love
> for the other person.'[12].

Not many people know this these days, but I still consider myself to be in a recovery program from what psychiatrist and bestselling author Daniel Goleman calls 'Social Incompetence'. I suffered terribly from this for years, even into my walk with God. I would fear going to social events like cell groups for months until I got used to everyone. It is not something that plagues me today like it did in my early recovery years but I have to acknowledge that I can still find myself suddenly feeling quite vulnerable and nervous of people in social situations. I therefore always ensure that I allow limited intimacy with anyone outside of my family, let alone unstable members of the opposite sex.

The Lord himself brought me through the worst of it by bringing people into my life that came from a completely different social standing than anything I had ever experienced. I started to notice that I was having more and more interactions with ministers, and doctors and I even found myself with friends from the higher echelons of the British police force. One doctor who supported me through my

---

[12]   Norman Shawchuck, How To Manage Conflict in the Church, Spiritual Growth Resources 1983

early development and through my Theology studies was Dr. Andy Adam, a police coroner!

I was regularly invited to the homes of society's aristocratic circles, and these guys just welcomed me in and gave me another opinion of me. I will be forever grateful to God for these guys, but none more so than one particular family who welcomed me into their home, unconditionally, and just loved me—The Hill family: Derek and Jan, and their family of Doctors Lisa, Lorraine and Sally and James. These guys come from a completely different world to mine, but not only did they show me that 'I belong', it was this family who made the first financial contribution towards the start of what is now The Bethesda Recovery Homes.

They saw and believed in what God was doing in and through me and from their belief I took belief.

All of these guys, including our above mentioned accusers, have taught me how to love, and how to be loved, and that sometimes it is ok if I find myself having to strive to love some people. They, my friends and my accusers, have taught me the essential need to treat everyone equally, either because of who they are in Christ or because of how they are sadly dying without Him; and I do feel able to do that today.

Conclusion

I hope the thread of my story has steered many to expect or to hope for a 'happy ending' with songs of glory, resounding hallelujah's and Christian high fives all round, because, if you look closely enough, you'll see that it actually does.

As a direct result of the persistent onslaught of verbal and dishonest attacks upon our family name, challenging our integrity and our motives behind why we run Bethesda, my family and I actually drew so much closer to God and to each other.

I recently studied a book called 'Antagonists in The Church' where Kenneth C. Haugk makes the following observations:

> 'Be cautious of those who relate to you in an overly friendly fashion. They will make every effort to spend time with you; they will probe you along the way, actually taking copious notes whilst becoming intimately acquainted with you. Later, however, their inquisitiveness will turn to the proverbial cool contempt bred from familiarity'
> (Abbreviation mine: Augsburg Publishing. page 72).

I therefore feel obliged to add a warning to the close of my story, one which I feel I could have benefitted from had someone had the mettle to say it; it is this: the authentic Church of God in Jesus Christ is the most powerful institution ever known to man throughout history. In Christ we have communion with God in our midst and He speaks to us and comforts us by His Spirit and through contextualised teaching of The Bible. Christianity is an eternal life celebration of what God did for each of us and in each of us when He left the realms of Heaven to dwell among us, and when He died on a Cross for the punishment of our sins, and when He conquered the grave and rose again from the dead and ascended back in to heaven from where He sent us His Holy Spirit to give guilty but repentant sinners new life.

There is nothing else known to man that can compare to the Church and the wonder of being in fellowship with Bible based born again, believing Christians. There are no drugs throughout the whole earth that can compare to the peace and the joy and the personal significance of knowing Jesus personally.

However, it comes at a cost, because we also have the worst of enemies and the closer you get to a pro-active relationship with God, the more you will be hated and attacked by the very forces of hell itself. In fact, I would add: conversely, if you're not getting attacked, the devil must be pleased with you.

Blessings upon blessings have showered and continue to shower down upon our family and upon our ministry and that which was intended to be darkness and divisive has only served to drive my wife, our children and myself further into The Light and closer to each other. God is good, and all things work together for the good for those who love Him.

Today Deanna, our two children and I regularly and openly pray for each of the souls who set out to destroy us, and we ask that miracles will turn everything around for them and for their loved ones. While their venomous attacks took me to my darkest hour, it was there, in that old familiar dungeon of despair that God once again responded to my cry. While I was ashamed of my nightly anger fantasies within which I would 'get revenge' upon 'them', and in deep sorrow of finding myself reduced to such hostility, I prayed then following prayer:

"Lord, I am so sorry that I have allowed these behaviours
to bring the worst out of me"

And it was right there in that dark moment of my soul that God made His voice audible to me once again when He quietly whispered:

"Colin, my beloved son, that is My plan, I want the best of you to
surface, so first, the worst of you needs to be removed".

Thereafter, what I had been seeing as madness from mongrels, I now see as heaven sent gifts, sent to draw me to closer to my God.

We do not hate people for what they tried to do to us; that would mean we are being defined by the principles which sadly define them. We celebrate that we are still able to love, only because of what God has done for us in and through His only begotten Son, and that is something which even the darkest principles of hell itself will never be able to change.

I hope I've helped someone. You may have seen within my story extreme, mild or even distant similarities with yourself or of someone you know and love. It may be that you yourself rejected God during your childhood and very possibly for valid reasons. It could be that you did believe in God, but never actually acknowledged His existence nor your need of His input in your life. It could be that you are feeling as if you have fallen too far down the slippery pole of sin to be worthy of God's amazing forgiveness and that you have gradually taken on the belief of the devils favourite lie:

'God won't forgive you'

It could be that once upon a time you did turn to God in Christ, and that you did experience His love and the joy of knowing Him, but then it could be that people and events around you left you discouraged and feeling abandoned.

It could be that you are feeling ashamed of the way you have inwardly and publicly reacted to unsavoury circumstances and personalities in your life and you are therefore left feeling hopelessly lost and alone again.

In those circumstances, it would make absolute sense to me if you have even considered writing this Jesus off and throwing all your beliefs out with the garbage.

However, before you do, or even if you already have, please remember this truth: God is completely passionate about you my friend and He desires nothing more than to embrace you in and through The Lord Jesus Christ and to call you His child. Whatever your state or circumstances, whatever your frame of mind, if you will but turn to Him now, either for the first time or for the 1 000 000th time, and if you will honestly confess your remorse over your sinfulness and hopeless estate, if you will but trust Him now to forgive you, I know that He will welcome you and liberate you from the bondages of sin for the glories of His service.

My friend, if in your soul you are asking 'where is this God', please trust me, He is closer than you think, and you might even find—as was my case—He was right where I left Him, in the rubbish bin, waiting for me to return to Him.

It may also be that you find yourself out of passion for God due to what you perceive to be the failings of His people? I chuckle, because I know, and I want you to know that you're not alone my friend, but you will be if you don't work it out and take ownership of how God wants to expose and remove 'the worst out of you'.

I think it would be fitting to close with words from a favourite Hymn:

> The vilest offender who truly believes
> That moment, from Jesus, a pardon receives

www.bethesda4recovery.com